£14.95

AFRICAN WOMEN
AND DEVELOPMENT:
A HISTORY

The story of the African Training
and Research Centre for Women of
the United Nations
Economic Commission for Africa

Margaret C. Snyder
Mary Tadesse

UUP

Witwatersrand University Press
JOHANNESBURG

Zed Books
LONDON & NEW JERSEY

African Women and Development: A History was first published
by Zed Books Ltd, 7 Cynthia Street,
London N1 9JF and
165 First Avenue, Atlantic Highlands,
New Jersey 07716, USA in 1995.

Published in Southern Africa exclusively by
Witwatersrand University Press,
University of Witwatersrand,
Johannesburg, PO Wits, 2050, South Africa.

Cover design by Andrew Corbett.
Set in Monotype Garamond by Ewan Smith, London E8.

Printed and bound in the United Kingdom by
Redwood Books Ltd, Kennet House, Kennet Way,
Trowbridge, Wilts BA14 8RB.

A catalogue record for this book is available from
the British Library.

US CIP data available from the Library of Congress.

ISBN 1 85649 299 0 hb
ISBN 1 85649 300 8 pb
WUP ISBN 1 86814 281 7

CONTENTS

ACKNOWLEDGEMENTS

A year before leaving her post as Chief of the African Training and Research Centre for Women (ATRCW), Mary Tadesse proposed that we write this book together, so that African women could have access to that part of their history with which we were very familiar. Margaret Snyder quickly agreed: she was about to write a book on women, poverty and politics that would include some of the same source materials.

We have enjoyed an enriching collaboration, and have been well blessed with support from every side. Our colleagues at the United Nations Economic Commission for Africa (ECA) – especially Mebo Mwaniki and Nancy Hafkin – and the ECA's Executive Secretary, Layashi Yaker, gave of their time and interest. Molly Masai of the United Nations and Tadesse Alemu of the ATRCW provided valuable documentation. In the countries Margaret Snyder visited, the United Nations Development Progammes and UNIFEM offices organized efficient programmes and provided support services when they could. The many women and men we interviewed were patient, forthcoming, enthusiastic and full of ideas; they helped to shape our views. (Some interviews will appear in a second book.)

During the writing period, we had excellent research assistance from Kathy Larin, then a graduate student at Princeton, who continued to transcribe interviews after her graduation. Jenny Karumuna and Laurel Douglas helped with the Annexes. Caroline Pezzullo commented on selected chapters. Our very special thanks go to our editor, Nancy Murray, a talented and patient person who now knows a lot of that language called 'UNeze'. Mary thanks her son Alem Befakadu for his encouragement and technical help.

June Zeitlin at the Ford Foundation, Joyce Moock at the Rockefeller Foundation and their colleagues gave us financial support. At Princeton University Henry Bienen, John Waterbury, Gerry Horner and their colleagues provided institutional support. The person who opened all those doors is Ingrid Reed, now a Vice-President at the Rockefeller University.

A generous grant from the Swedish International Development Authority (SIDA) for the book's wide distribution to African libraries, universities and non-governmental organizations is deeply appreciated.

Finally, we both recognize that James Riby-Williams's skills and commitment were essential to the establishment of the ATRCW.

ACRONYMS

AAWC	All Africa Women's Conference (later renamed the PAWO)
AAWORD	Association of African Women for Research and Development
AFRIFEM	Women's Information Network for Africa
AMS	Administrative Management Service
APPER	African Priority Programme for Economic Recovery
ARCC	Africa Regional Co-ordinating Committee
ATRCW	African Training and Research Centre for Women
AWID	Association for Women and Development
CEDAW	United Nations Convention for the Elimination of Discrimination against Women
CSDHA	Centre for Social Development and Humanitarian Affairs
CSW	Commission on the Status of Women
DAWN	Development Alternatives with Women for a New Era
DIESA	Department of International Economic and Social Affairs
ECA (UNECA)	United Nations Economic Commission for Africa
ECOSOC	Economic and Social Council of the United Nations
ECOWAS	Economic Community of West African States
ESAMI	Eastern and Southern Africa Management Institute
FAO	Food and Agricultural Organization of the United Nations
FLS	The Nairobi Forward-looking Strategies for the Advancement of Women
GDP	gross domestic product
ICRC	International Committee on the Rights of the Child
ILO	International Labour Organization
IMF	International Monetary Fund
INSTRAW	International Research and Training Institute for the Advancement of Women
IPPF	International Planned Parenthood Federation
ITDG	Intermediate Technology Development Group
LOC	least developed country
LPA	Lagos Plan of Action
MCH	Maternal and Child Health Care

MSA	most seriously affected
MULPOCs	Multinational Programming and Operational Centres (of the ECA)
NATCAPS	National Technical Co-operation Assessments and Programmes
NGO	non-governmental organization
NIEO	New International Economic Order
OAU	Organization of African Unity
OECD	Organization for Economic Co-operation and Development
PADIS	Pan-African Development Information System
PAID	Pan-African Institute for Development
PAWO	Pan-African Women's Organization (formerly the AAWC)
PBFL	Programmes for Better Family Living
PPCO	Programme and Policy Co-ordination Office
PTA	Preferential Trade Area
SADCC	Southern African Development Co-ordinating Committee
SAP	structural adjustment programme
SIDA	Swedish International Development Authority
TAFWE	Task Force on Women in the ECA
TEPCOW	Technical Preparatory Committee Meetings of the Whole
UNDATs	United Nations Development Advisory Teams
UNDP	United Nations Development Programme
UNFPA	United Nations Fund for Population Activities
UNHCR	United Nations High Commissioner for Refugees
UNICEF	United Nations Children's Fund
UNIFEM	United Nations Development Fund for Women
UNPAAERD	United Nations Programme of Action for African Economic Recovery and Development
UNSO	United Nations Statistical Office
UNTFAD	United Nations Trust Fund for African Development
USAID	United States Agency for International Development
VFDW	Voluntary Fund for the UN Decade for Women (later UNIFEM)
WAWA	West African Women's Association
WWB	Women's World Banking
YWCA	Young Women's Christian Association

ABOUT THE AUTHORS

Margaret C. Snyder, the Founding Director of the United Nations Development Fund for Women (UNIFEM), has recently been a Visiting Fellow in International Studies at Princeton University. Her long association with development policies and women's issues in Africa has also involved work as a Regional Adviser for the United Nations Economic Commission for Africa, where she initiated the Women's Programme, headed the Voluntary Agencies Bureau and was co-founder of the African Training and Research Centre for Women. She received her PhD from the University of Dar es Salaam and was honoured at Makerere University in 1993 for her 'distinguished contribution to the advancement of women in agriculture and education'. A co-founder of Women's World Banking, Dr Snyder is a frequent lecturer on international affairs. Her varied publications include *Farmers and Merchants: Some Observations on Women and the State in Africa*; *Politics, Poverty and Participation: a History of Women's Leadership in Development*; and *Women: the Key to Ending Hunger*.

Mary Tadesse has until recently been the head of the African Training and Research Centre for Women at the United Nations Economic Commission for Africa. A former Vice-Minister for Education and Culture and Assistant Minister of Education in Addis Ababa, Ethiopia, she has been extensively involved with developing and advancing policies and strategies for the advancement of women in developing countries on both a regional and global level through such organizations as the Council of African Advisers to the World Bank, the Board of Trustees of the International Research and Training Institute for the Advancement of Women (INSTRAW), the Africa Regional Co-ordinating Committee for the Integration of Women in Development, and the Federation of African Women Entrepreneurs. Ms Tadesse has given numerous papers at academic and governmental conferences, including 'The Role of African Women in the Informal Sector: Problems and Prospects' and 'Women and Development Planning: an Issue Paper'. She has promoted a string of publications designed to stimulate action on behalf of women and development in Africa.

PREFACE

I welcome the invitation to write this preface. If there has been a momentous period in the history of African women, it is in the last thirty years covered by this book. For the first time, the spotlight has shone on the ordinary woman of the continent, highlighting the crucial roles she plays in her community and nation. In this book the authentic voices of women are heard, and their aspirations and their struggles for survival are described.

The African woman has always worked outside her home, in the fields, in marketplaces and in community action. This book tells how a United Nations entity participated in bringing her rich experience to centre-stage, to the national, regional and global forums.

Peace, stability and development – or their absence – in Africa have a strong bearing on women's conditions and the well-being of Africa's people; at the same time, women are the very instruments to achieve those goals. I fully subscribe to this view of the authors.

This is the first comprehensive book on women and development in Africa. I believe it can act as a springboard for the continent's 'platform of action' for the future.

Gertrude Mongella
Secretary-General of the
Fourth World Conference on Women,
Beijing

To African women past and present:
for their tenacity, wisdom and survival

The authors and publisher would like to express their deep gratitude to the Swedish International Development Authority (SIDA) for its generosity in making it possible for this book to be donated to selected libraries, universities and other organizations in Africa

INTRODUCTION

This book is a testament to the women of Africa, and to their determination to achieve justice and well-being for present and for future generations. It also bears witness to the pioneering work of the African Training and Research Centre for Women (ATRCW, newly named the African Centre for Women – ACW), which emerged from the United Nations Economic Commission for Africa (ECA) to become a model in this field and for translating vision into actions. The authors' intention is to provide the international community, economic planners, foundations and especially African women themselves with a history of the centre, not just for research purposes but for what it has to say about the human spirit and about improving the quality of people's lives.

We take an historical approach. An initial overview of women's contributions in the Africa of the past, and of their experiences under colonialism, will show that the seeds for women's activities during the decades of independence were planted long ago by others like themselves. The ongoing need in the latter half of the twentieth century has been to devise new and ingenious ways to nourish their historic roots in order to claim a fair share of the harvest and to ensure a plentiful harvest for tomorrow's men and women.

With the advent of the ECA in 1958 came the long-awaited opportunity for women to institutionalize their issues and concerns at regional and national levels. The ECA found women already acting upon their conviction that they must be partners with men in building their newly independent nations. In the early 1960s, African women formed an Africa-regional organization and held national and sub-regional seminars to adopt strategies for their participation in their new nations, side by side with men. They created the concept of women's centrality to development that would later inspire a transnational movement. It is of historic interest to note that they acted well before Western women renewed their own women's movement towards the end of that same decade.

The late 1960s was a propitious time for women as concern for the development of the new countries reached a high point in the halls of the United Nations. The First United Nations (UN) Decade for Development had brought with it policies and programmes that appeared to offer economic security to the newly independent countries of the world. But the grand designs for that decade failed. Very few of the expected benefits were realized, or 'trickled down' to communities and individuals in Africa or elsewhere. Instead, old legacies and new factors kept impinging on the development efforts of the nations that were attempting to move towards true systemic and social change.

By the end of the First Decade for Development, there was a growing impetus to formulate new policies that would impact directly on the people – the people are the heart and foundation of African society. All during that decade, under the aegis of the ECA and of the United Nations itself, governments and women's groups had been consulted and data were collected and analysed. What added strength to the discussions and arguments on behalf of a change in direction was the lack of positive results during the First Decade for Development, together with the hard proof that had been amassed of the importance of women to economic life.

More and more evidence built up to indicate that women played central roles in the economy and that their participation at all levels was essential if development was to succeed. The information assembled by the ECA had been carefully documented, and it proved beyond doubt that, when the real-life situations of women were not factored into policies and programmes, the reality for Africa's people grew worse instead of better.

The point was that not just women, but both men and women must be lifted from poverty; both must contribute to and benefit from development efforts. Those were to be the essential and planned results of women's advancement. The movement was in no sense a battle against men, although it highlighted the disparate effects of development on men and women.

Such a holistic vision anticipated and helped to shape the mature international women's movement of the 1990s that fuses the more individualist, human rights approach of the dominant stream of Northern feminism with the community, social justice and economic self-reliance priorities of Southern women.

Whilst several persons played key roles in setting up the ATRCW, above all it was African women themselves who gave impetus to its creation. As the following pages show, women set their priorities and the strategies that became the ECA Five-year Women's Programme in 1971, and later the ATRCW programme. Their new insights on development led to the building of institutions that would guarantee the long life of the movement that had begun.

The pressures from women during training courses in countries of the region in 1973 inspired plans for the creation of the ATRCW. At the 1975 International Women's Year Conference in Mexico City, this new centre – the only regional centre of its kind anywhere – would come to be seen as the prized prototype for institutions concerned with women and development.

Never perceived as a 'bricks and mortar' training and research centre, the ATRCW was part institution and part network. It was, first and foremost, a partnership programme, given life by a coalition of organizations of the United Nations, governments and non-governmental organizations (NGOs). The centre trained women and leveraged resources for them to undertake research, create institutions and form networks of mutual interest. It became a resource centre for the women of the region. There was no model for the ECA to follow: the ATRCW was a pioneering institution in the United Nations system.

The centre was initially guided by the decisions of regional meetings of women, and later by an executive group of representatives of African countries. History thus makes clear that donors did not dictate the ATRCW's programme. On the contrary, having heard of the programme, and been urged on by women leaders and women's non-governmental organizations in their home countries as International Women's Year (IWY) approached, donors came to Addis Ababa with offers to finance the planned activities.

After the unique global celebration that was IWY, the ATRCW's work with women in the region expanded. There were national women's commissions and bureaux to assist, a volunteer corps (the Task Force) to organize, appropriate technologies to demonstrate and disseminate, training courses to plan, and information to distribute.

There was also the need to bring women's presence into every ECA activity, through its specialized divisions: for example, agriculture, technology, statistics and economic planning. And there were bureaucratic obstacles to remove, potential donors to attract, staff to be selected and regional conferences to plan. Most important was the ongoing dialogue with women of the region, their governments, and the centre's institutional partners. The centre was, in the words of one staff member, the only genuinely inter-agency partnership programme within the UN system.

The momentum of the ATRCW, and of the UN Decade for Women, reached both men and women. By the late 1970s, with a firm operational base, the ATRCW could pursue two particular strategies: policy formation and outreach. It could respond to a far higher level of awareness about the African situation than had existed before.

For policy purposes, the next step was to create an advisory body, the Africa Regional Co-ordinating Committee (ARCC), that would guide the centre's work, effect co-ordination among national commissions on women and development, and, most important, link women's concerns directly into the ECA's governing body, its Conference of Ministers. Then there was the long-postponed outreach, the stationing of women staff at ECA offices in the African sub-regions, which afforded more women opportunities for direct contact and involvement with the ATRCW. Some of the centre's seventeen staff were deployed to the Multinational Programming and Operational Centres (MULPOCs) that had been set up by the ECA.

The work was decentralized at ECA headquarters as well. New concepts arose within what was now a global women and development movement. One of these concepts, gender, influenced the ECA to formalize existing practices by issuing directives to its substantive divisions that staff be assigned to incorporate gender concerns in their programme activities. The ATRCW itself was relocated within the ECA as its headquarters role was revised and its sub-regional offices were reinforced. It had been transformed from being primarily a direct operational organization with its major focus on human resource, policy and institutional development, to serving as a catalyst and resource centre. Its main focus, however, remained on ensuring the inclusion of women's economic contributions, counting among them their entrepreneurial potential, in the strategies for regional development.

In the context of the global and African political, economic and social environments, and following the tradition of consensus and institution-building that had inspired the conferences at Rabat, Addis Ababa and Nouakchott in the 1970s (see Annexe 15), African women adopted new, comprehensive strategies in Arusha and Abuja in the 1980s. Those latter regional conferences proposed measures to expedite the attainment of equality and participatory development.

All through the years, the main strategy of the centre as a United Nations organization has been to interface women's reality with overall African development realities and concerns through practical programmes.

Now, as the democratic movement sweeps across Africa, there is hope for profound change. African women are on the move. The legacy of their mothers and grandmothers, the experience of colonialism and in-dependence, chances for education and training, the communications revolution, and the global women's movement have all contributed to women's vision for the future. Young women are becoming impatient activists. This book is intended to help them to have pride in their heritage. The roots of the women and development movement lay in the independ-ence movement. The fruits may come with the democracy movement.

At the end of each chapter, we add to the experiences of the centre the views of women who were involved with its work in the region. We look towards the future.

CHAPTER I

DEVELOPMENT MODELS AND WOMEN'S MOVEMENTS: THEORIES AND APPROACHES

To understand fully the story of the African Training and Research Centre for Women (ATRCW), it must be placed within the context both of the larger history of development and of the women's movement in Africa. The centre stands at the meeting place between those two significant trends.

We speak of global and Africa-regional events and trends throughout this book. While many of these influences are most visibly political or economic, they have a variety of dimensions. These influences are largely outside women's own control, and yet they impact strongly on women's possibilities for contributing to their own progress, and to the well-being of their families and their nations. For example, apartheid and other despotic systems put serious and often unbearable constraints on women and their families; so too do some economic structural reform measures; and so too do famine, war and civil strife. Opportunities for education, gainful employment and access to technologies can have the opposite effect.

As we write this book, a new democratic era is arising that promises to make governments in Africa more accountable to the people and allow everyone far greater freedom of expression. Women's, as well as men's, voices will be heard whenever they choose to speak. The flip side of that coin is less optimistic. The international economic environment is highly volatile and unfavourable, the prices of African countries' exports continue to plummet, the costs of debt servicing weigh more heavily day by day, and flows of external financing are drying up. The result is increasing poverty and malnutrition, and declining health and education conditions.

These factors must and do eat away at the quality of life of every citizen excepting a few elites, and they affect women most seriously. A few devastating facts tell the story: financial flows to Africa declined by 14% in 1991 and by an almost unbelievable 43% in 1992 – while in the same years they rose by 11% and 21% respectively to developing countries overall. Africa's indebtedness in 1992 equalled 93% of its gross domestic product (GDP), and debt servicing cost about a third of foreign exchange earned.[1]

Our point is that women exist amidst external environments, and those environments must be perceived as integral to the 'women and development' concept and movement. They, too, are women's issues. Neglecting development issues when speaking of women is just as bad as neglecting women when speaking of development. Yet some development and some sex/gender approaches persist in doing both.

The external influences on women, and on their nations, cannot be treated comprehensively in this brief book, whose primary concern is to record the history of the United Nations' Africa-regional work with women. It is the hope of the authors that readers will seek out other complementary sources of information on the macro influences. As an introduction, however, we will first explore the major development theories that prevailed during the three decades that frame the ATRCW's history. Then, an overview will set out the dominant and varied approaches to 'women and development' that have affected that movement in Africa as elsewhere, especially since the United Nations Decade for Women, 1976–85.

'Women and development' is an inclusive term used throughout this book to signify a concept and a movement whose long-range goal is the well-being of society – the community of men, women and children. Its formulation is based on the following suppositions:

— 'Development', in accordance with the International Development Strategy for the Second Development Decade, means 'to bring about sustained improvement in the well-being of the individual and to bestow benefits on all'.[2]
— Because women comprise more than half of the world's human resources and are central to the economic as well as to the social well-being of societies, development goals cannot be fully reached without their participation.
— 'Women and development' is thus a holistic concept wherein the goal of one cannot be achieved without the success of the other.
— Women, therefore, must have 'both the legal right and access to existing means for the improvement of oneself and of society'.[3]

Development theories

Development theories subscribed to by the international community and popularized in the United Nations have had powerful influences on the economies, societies and politics of new nations in the past half-century. Those theories have shifted several times since the end of World War Two. The earliest theory was 'modernization'. It contrasted 'traditional' with 'modern' societies, and consequently was called the 'dual economy' theory. It made Western industrialization its prototype. 'Trade not aid' was the favoured approach and economic growth that would 'trickle down' to the poor was the promised outcome for developing countries after a certain 'take-off point' was reached.

The ECA adopted the modernization approach in its early years, namely the end of the 1950s. The theory was then modified in the early 1960s, when the ECA's executive put a new emphasis on internal markets, farm-to-market roads and small-scale industries – all of which were aimed at self-reliant development that would bring broad benefits to people. It became increasingly clear, however, that the effects of modernization were of little if any help to the poor.

In the mid-1960s, modernization theory began to be challenged by 'underdevelopment' or 'neo-Marxist' concepts. The most important of these was the 'dependency' theory, whose major thesis was that global capitalism operated to 'underdevelop the Third World'. Developing countries called for a new international economic order that would release them from dependency. The ECA sought that goal, while championing national self-reliance and increased interdependence among developing countries.

Rather than work towards a new global economic order, however, the reaction of the donor community to the negative impacts of modernization on the poorest people of the world was to stress basic needs. Minimum family requirements for consumption and essential community services were the elements of the 'basic needs' approach. Thus, water supplies, transport, food security and overcoming 'absolute and relative poverty' through the generation of incomes for the poorest people, together with population control, became the chief internationally promulgated strategies for development co-operation in the 1970s.

The economic crisis of the 1980s gradually fostered a new consensus, that the crisis came from giving governments too much power and from constraining market mechanisms. Privatization, deregulation and retrenchment of the public sector became popular prescriptions for developing countries. These policies were packaged in economic 'structural adjustment programmes' (SAPs), and they constituted conditions for loans and debt restructuring by the International Monetary Fund (IMF) and World Bank. The conventional wisdom had returned to pre-World War Two values – the survival of the fittest. The plight of the less fit became an international issue with the publication of *Adjustment with a Human Face*, which documented the frightening effects of adjustment programmes on the most vulnerable members of societies.[4] The ill effects on women, who bore the brunt of education and health cutbacks, began to be discussed in this book.

These beliefs fed 'dependency reversal' theories, which held that the reasons for underdevelopment lie within developing countries, and that capitalism is 'the only reliable path to development and eventually to socialist revolution in the Third World'.[5] They dealt a heavy blow to dependency theory through their belief that the dynamics of development 'are being molded by third-world states themselves rather than by international economic factors only'.[6] With responsibility for development laid at the doorstep of developing countries, their participation in the highly competitive 'free markets' of the global economy became the new popular prescription for progress.[7]

The strategies that were set out in three international plans for African recovery and development between 1986 and 1991 called for increasingly democratic and market-oriented approaches on the part of African countries, coupled with expanded capital flows to Africa from the soft-loan affiliates of multilateral agencies and from Organization for Economic Co-operation and Developemnt (OECD) members.[8] Dependency-reversal theories and a global economic downturn stood in the way of implementing those strategies. The flow of external stimuli – the donor part of the agreement – receded drastically, even though many African countries took the prescribed steps and progressed towards democratic participation.

Meanwhile, the international community took up new development themes. Dominant among them were the environment, and the goal of 'sustainable development' that does not use up resources that future generations will need. In the 1990s, 'human development' has also returned to prominence.

The gravity of the impacts of many of the theories discussed above on women's work, incomes and family responsibilities is evident, for example, in the now plentiful literature on the impact of structural adjustment programmes (SAPs) on women.[9] That information strengthens the point that 'women and development' concepts and programmes cannot ignore broad development theories and practices, and still remain realistic and relevant theoretical constructs.[10] Yet, as the review that follows shows, not all 'women and development' theories take account of macro trends and strategies.

Women and development: concepts and approaches

Concepts relating to women and development originated within the independence movements of the 1950s and 1960s. They have been influenced by development theory itself and, starting in the mid-1970s, by feminist theory. As they evolved, the concepts in turn had their own impact on feminist theory.

There is now widespread agreement about the fact that women are all but excluded from access to and control over national and international resources, and about the harm to human well-being that results. There is less agreement among theorists about the approaches that should be taken to resolve that problem. We will identify and examine six of those approaches: one of them, human resource development, describes the ECA's early activities on behalf of women.[11]

The reader should be aware, however, that the terminology relating to women and development is subject to differing interpretations because the movement has existed for less than twenty years and definitions are still evolving. Also, some of the conceptual categories overlap.

The welfare approach

As the oldest approach to women and development, the 'welfare' approach is founded on the theory that women are solely passive recipients of development benefits because their major roles are reproductive ones – motherhood and childrearing – whereas men's work is identified as productive. This approach follows the Western social welfare model, and was common in colonial times. It dominated United Nations assistance through the 1960s, going hand in hand with modernization theory. In the 1970s it was an aspect of the basic needs activities described above. The United Nations Children's Fund (UNICEF) has consistently and effectively employed the welfare approach, as has the UN High Commission for Refugees (UNHCR).

Writers on women and development usually identify population programmes with the welfare approach. An awareness of the world's exploding population and of its limited natural resources occasions a massive flow of monies to family planning programmes. Some countries resisted these in the 1960s and 1970s, but over time the programmes were widely accepted by governments in Africa as elsewhere.

Initially, the population approach emphasized the goal of reducing the world's population and showed little understanding of or consideration for women's health and family responsibilities. Gradually, as in the ECA Women's Programme, that strategy was revised so that family size and its relation to women's health and family well-being became integral to a variety of training programmes,

Because of the work of women like Nafis Sadik, MD (who guides the United Nations Fund for Population Activities – UNFPA) women's health, education, and employment are now recognized as critical factors relating to fertility and population issues. Some major funding organizations, however, still speak about these issues in terms of numbers rather than of the human beings involved. Given that population programmes tend to proliferate and seem to command more resources than other approaches to women and development (welfare excepted), it is unclear why scholars have not isolated population control as an approach of its own.

On the plus side, the welfare approach promotes the availability of much-needed maternal and child health care (MCH), with a consequent reduction in infant and to some extent maternal mortality rates. It has saved millions of refugees, displaced persons, and victims of drought and natural disaster from starvation and given them shelter. The major weaknesses in the welfare approach can none the less be devastating because it lacks a developmental perspective. First, it fails to consider women's productive activities and their economic responsibilities. Second – and this is implied in the term 'welfare' – it tends to foster dependency rather than self-reliance. UNICEF and the UNHCR have begun to take these facts into account.

The human resource development approach

The human resource development approach takes an opposite stance. It leads to profound and lasting changes for women by recognizing not just their reproductive roles but also their productive roles, that is, their active participation in the economy. Using a contextual framework, it argues that:

> Women's needs are intricately bound up with the priority needs and aspirations of the nation, and must necessarily be viewed as features of overall national development and the advancement of the total society.[12]

This approach underscores the point that development, at the highest level, cannot be achieved without women. This perspective, called 'efficiency', was later identified as an approach in its own right (see below). The goal of human resource development is identical to the goal of development itself, namely 'creating better lives, with greater freedom and well-being, for members of the family, the local community and the society as a whole'.[13]

The strong development component of this approach rose out of women's engagement in the liberation of their countries and their subsequent readiness to participate in shaping their new nations. (That process in Africa is described in Chapter 2). Further, the human development emphasis was possible because, by the 1970s, modernization theory was in decline and the goal of the people's well-being was ascendent (see Chapter 3).

The ECA pioneered the human resource development approach as early as 1971 by identifying women as economic producers and community managers. Its initial policy premises flowed from recommendations made by African women in the 1960s (see Chapter 4). That recognition of women's centrality to development justified the creation of the ECA Women's Programme in 1972 and later, in 1975, the ATRCW.

This approach challenged modernization theory's premise that the benefits of development would 'trickle down' to women and others. It made women's access to productive resources a development issue, bringing with it self-reliance and a voice in setting priorities. At the same time, the strategy reduced the likelihood of resistance on the part of member states to programmes for women. It avoided being identified with extremist elements within the Western women's movements for equality, liberation and status, elements that carried with them a connotation of being against men.

Relying on the fact that women comprise more than half of the productive human resources of a country, the approach sets conditions for their full participation in development. These include ways to lessen women's burdens and to increase their productivity by providing access to resources such as education, technology and income, often through women's own solidarity groups. An important condition calls for women's active participation in planning and policy-setting.

The human resource development approach has been given little attention by feminist scholars, who began their analysis of women and development in the second half of the 1970s when other theories and approaches dominated the donor community and the UN.

Equity and human rights

The main thrust of the 'equity' approach, an offshoot of the concern for equality between the sexes, relies on legal methods. Gaining equality for women was in fact the primary approach of the UN Commission on the Status of Women (CSW) through the 1960s, and it is the strategy of the Convention on the Elimination of Discrimination against Women (CEDAW) today. Equity entered the women and development field when Western women exerted pressure on their international development agencies in the 1970s. This occurred after the human resource development approach had gained momentum, so 'equity' was not 'the original women and development approach'.[14]

The ECA resisted adopting the equity approach because it lacked development emphasis and because, at that time, legislation appeared to have a limited potential to impact on the vast majority of women, those who were illiterate and rural-based. Further, the equity movement's priorities and strategies generated an 'understandable reluctance to confront sexism' within the women and development movement.[15] For example, women preferred to spend their energies on increasing their incomes rather than on confronting their menfolk, because their highest priority was providing for their children's well-being. Some analysts also considered equity theory's central theme of patriarchy as, in reality, only one among a number of 'sex–gender systems'.[16]

Under the theme 'women's rights are human rights' an aspect of the equity approach that has gained worldwide recognition in the 1990s recalls the UN Commission on the Status of Women's Origins in the Commission on Human Rights. In Africa, human rights activities are often led by the growing number of women in the professions, notably lawyers. Priority is given to reforming inheritance law for widows and children, and to land ownership. Movements to eliminate violence against women are also growing.

Equity theory's major concern with inequality between men and women contrasts with the concern of the human resource development approach with the quality of life for all.

The anti-poverty approach

The shift to an 'anti-poverty' approach to women and development corresponded with the shift to the basic needs and absolute poverty theories of the 1970s that were promulgated by the International Labour Organization (ILO) and the World Bank respectively. Women became the central focus in strategies to overcome the hunger and malnutrition that accompany poverty because they and their dependent children dominate the poorest groups. Organizations such as the World Bank targeted women from the perspective of population control, which was key to their anti-poverty mechanism.

Among the anti-poverty activities put in place by women and development programmes were income-generating and entrepreneurship projects. These have been criticized for the most part because of their small scale. (Ironically, small-scale projects of non-governmental organizations have now become very popular indeed with major funding agencies.) Despite their limits, these enterprise projects made a major contribution to fostering the spread of community revolving loan funds, thus opening the question of women's access to formal financial institutions such as banks and co-operatives. Some of the projects grew in scale; others were replicated; and still others went out of existence.

The ECA Women's Programme combined the human resource development and the anti-poverty approaches in its first training programmes for trainers of rural women, who constituted more than 80% of all women in Africa.

The efficiency approach

'Efficiency' is another approach to women and development. Its meaning has undergone sweeping change over time. As an element of the human resource development approach discussed above, the efficiency approach was development-oriented and sought to increase productivity in order to enhance the quality of people's lives, rather than solely to achieve economic growth.

Women's involvement in the design and operation of development activities was expected to expedite overall development because women constitute half of the available labour force and bear heavy economic responsibilities; increasing women's productivity would logically lead to economic growth. Agricultural economist Ester Boserup warned, however, that women's productivity would be jeopardized as technologies advanced unless women had access to technological innovations.[17]

Over time, efficiency theories became almost exclusively market-oriented. The turning point came in the second half of the 1970s, when the global economy went into crisis and structural adjustment programmes (SAPs) were introduced.

Today's efficiency approach is closely tied to dependency reversal theory (see above), which places responsibility for development solely with developing countries themselves, giving scant recognition to the influence of global political, technological and economic factors. It is on this ground that the efficiency approach is criticized: it is seen as the premiss underlying the least desirable elements of economic adjustment, whose prescriptions include severe cutbacks in government personnel and operations, reliance on the private sector for growth, and participation in the 'free markets' of the global economy.[18] Among the immediate effects of the shrinkage of national budgets in the name of effcency are unemployment and sharp declines in health and education systems.[19]

The efficiency approach in terms of the marketplace, that is, economic growth alone, led to serious setbacks in the gains made by women. Responsibility for health and education shifted to the voluntary sector, mainly to women; women lost income for family support when formal sector employment was retrenched (women are often the first to be released); and female sexuality became commoditized as girls and women looked for incomes to support themselves and their children.

The empowerment approach

The 'empowerment' approach came into its own in the mid-1980s. Its champion was Development Alternatives with Women for a New Era, the Third World women's group that calls itself DAWN. Its African founding members included Fatima Mernissi (Morocco), Achola Pala Okeyo (Kenya) and Marie-Angelique Savane (Senegal).[20] DAWN saw women's experiences as varying with their race, class, colonial history and position in the economy. It challenged some prevailing development paradigms by questioning whether women wanted to be integrated in societal systems that oppress both women and men.

DAWN's view of society was from the vantage point of poor and oppressed women, and it was with that perspective that it regarded all of the poor. DAWN emphasized mobilization and consciousness raising, with women's organizations, especially grassroots groups, as the source of empowerment. Women's access to productive resources such as land, credit, education, and training was stressed. DAWN also addressed macro-systemic issues including the debt crisis and military expenditures. Population programmes were questioned when they assumed that poverty could be controlled by limiting fertility.

DAWN selected key elements of earlier approaches to women and development in forming its empowerment concept and strategy. For example, its approach reflected and refined strands of the ECA's early approach in its concern for both women and men:

> we cannot propose a social/political/economic programme for women alone … we need to develop one for society from women's perspectives.[21]

Within the process of achieving empowerment, DAWN speaks of personal autonomy.[22] Autonomy for women, for the poor, and for nations of the developing world, means that they are able to make their own choices in the realms of politics, economics and society. The approach calls for participation and seeks to create self-reliance, ensuring that targeted measures reach women through autonomous women's organizations.

From women and development to gender

The term 'gender' became popular in the later 1980s as a replacement for 'women and development'. It is of Western origins and is in several respects a second-generation concept of equity.[23] Gender is a social construct that asserts that the expectations and responsibilities of men and women are not always biologically determined. Whilst not denying that data have for decades been presented by gender (as demonstrated in the division-of-labour data in the ECA's documents at the beginning of the 1970s), advocates of this approach prefer the term 'gender' over 'women and development', claiming that gender more easily accommodates race, class, ethnicity, and male–female power relationships. Gender theory is applicable from the household to the international economy, advocates say, and there are patriarchal influences all along that continuum. None the less, the most frequent applications of the theory are to the household and to employment.

Gender analysis and gender training became common parlance and practice in national and international development agencies in the early 1990s. In this book we use both terms – 'women and development' and 'gender' – as and when we consider them appropriate to history and meaning.[24]

The pioneering contributions of the ECA
and the ATRCW

The theories of development and of women and development that we have reviewed create the context for understanding where and how the ECA and its African Training and Research Centre for Women made path-breaking and unique contributions to the theory and practice of development itself and of women's participation in it. For example, the ECA Women's Programme and the ATRCW pioneered the human resource development approach, which contained elements of the equity, efficiency (in its original sense), welfare, anti-poverty and empowerment approaches, and both bodies practised gender analysis before such methods were labelled by scholars. The ECA, as will be seen, considered women in the context of history and made women's grassroots solidarity groups one of its own key policy concerns. It also emphasized that women-specific organizations and institutions are critical to an effective women and development concept and movement – a point few analysts stress today.

In general, the ATRCW and its predecessor, the Women's Programme, saw development as many-faceted and complex. Their approaches were more community-based and institutional than individualistic. The centre took an empirical rather than a theoretical approach to its work, following the lead of the women of the region.

The history of the ECA's work with women casts a new light on the history of the transnational women and development movement in four ways. First of all, it places the origins of women and development concepts squarely in developing countries, and associates those origins with the rise of the independence movement. Women embraced the goals of that movement, the freedom and well-being of all citizens, regardless of sex. These facts rule out the claim of some scholars that the women and development approach is an offshoot of Western feminism. The ATRCW's history thus questions the perception of some that the transnational women and development movement was 'weaker for turning its back on its theoretical roots' – which are identified solely as feminism.[25] Such a view overlooks the roots of the concept in independence struggles.

Second, the history of the ECA and ATRCW demonstrates a distinctly African approach to women and development. Women were seen as central to their countries' progress, particularly in agriculture and food security as well as in the family. The point was not to confront men, but rather to bring everyone – all available human resources – to the task of creating a better society for all. Gender-separatist stances and anti-male movements were rejected.

Third, despite women's important contributions, the history illumines the overriding reality that the greatest obstacles to their advancement and the consequent advancement of their countries are almost invariably beyond women's reach, and not infrequently beyond the control of their nations. The most visible and well-known obstacles are civil strife, war and famine. Less documented are those that come from the national and global political economy, a sphere in which hardly any women are as yet present or even have a say. Women are not present in critical numbers in governments; neither are they in control of technology or business. The results of their absence are often devastating.

Finally, the history illumines the role of the UN as the major vehicle for promoting the international women and development movement. The ECA's pioneering leadership was fundamental, soundly based and an early catalyst. The United Nations headquarters took global leadership, meanwhile. Thus, institutional leadership arose both in Addis Ababa and in New York.

Notes

1. See 'Update on New Agenda for Africa', *Africa Recovery*, United Nations, New York, December 1993. Other current views are more sanguine but also highly speculative. 'Investors who Discovered Africa', *New York Times*, 3 April 1994, calls Africa 'a hot new target for international investing' in recent years. It states also that the ten-year low on commodity prices is changing.

2. A/RES/2626/XXV, 1969.

3. Snyder to Aiyegbusi, 1974.

4. Giovanni Andrea Cornia, Richard Jolly and Frances Stewart (eds.) *Adjustment with a Human Face*, Oxford University Press, New York, 1987. Of interest is that seven years earlier, M. de Vries of the IMF had warned of the negative impacts of adjustment programme on women. See *IMF Survey: Supplement to the Fund*, IMF, Washington, September 1979.

5. Such theory located the source of poverty in the faulty vision and low energy levels of the poor, and of the poorest countries. See Jan Pronk, *Solidarity Against Poverty*, Evert Vermeer Foundation, Amsterdam, 1990, Chapter 2.

6. Atul Kohli (ed.), *The State and Development in the Third World*, Princeton University Press, 1986, p. 15. Dominant among dependency reversal theories is the 'modes of production' theory whose proponents identify themselves as Marxist, yet reject dependency theory.

7. Leslie Sklair, *Sociology of the Global System*, London, Harvester Wheatsheaf, 1991, p. 35.

8. The three strategies were the Organization of African Unity's African Priority Programme for Economic Recovery (APPER), which formed the basis for the UN Programme of Action for African Economic Recovery and Development 1986–90 (UNPAAERD); and the UN's New Agenda for the Development of Africa in the 1990s. The latter was adopted by the UN General Assembly in December 1991, following its five-year review of UNPAAERD.

9. Jean Vickers, *Women and the World Economic Crisis*, Zed Books, London, 1994. See also Raj Bardouille, *Research on Zambian Women in Retrospect and Prospect: an Annotated Bibliography*, SIDA, Lusaka, 1992.

10. The question of 'women's issues' versus 'development issues' is addressed in this book. Our position as stated differs widely from those of some writers. For example, see Kathleen Newland, 'From Transnational Relationships to International Relations', in Rebecca Grant and Kathleen Newland, *Gender and International Relations*, Open University Press, Buckingham, 1991, p. 128. Newland states: 'A number of First World delegations, which were always at a disadvantage in General Assembly debates, tried for a while to keep the focus on women's issues. But they too succumbed to cynicism and entered the political fray.' From that perspective, 'political issues' and 'women's issues' appear to be diverse and unrelated.

11. From our study of the women and development movement, and our years of experience in the Africa region, we identify an additional approach to women and development. Human resource development was the ECA's overriding policy; it interfaced the women's and the development movements. For more detailed but different discussion of the approaches, see Caroline Moser, 'Gender Planning in the Third World: Meeting Practical and Strategic Needs', in Grant and Newland, p. 83. See also Mayra Buvenic, 'Women's Issues in Third World Poverty: a Policy Analysis', in Mayra Buvenic, Margaret Lycette and Silliam McGreavey (eds.), *Women and Poverty in the Third World*, Baltimore, Johns Hopkins Press, 1983, pp. 14–31. See also Jane Jaquette, 'Gender and Justice in Economic Development', in Irene Tinker, *Persistent Inequalities: Women and World Development*, Oxford University Press, New York, 1990. Note that we differ profoundly with Tinker on the question of the origins of the women and development movement; that author places it with 'the UN Commission on the Status of Women and the US Womens Movement' (p. 28), whereas we see it arising mainly from the independence movement, but with support from the United Nations, including the CSW.

12. Opening Address by J. Riby-Williams, Chief of the ECA Human Resources Development Division, Rabat, 1971.

13. ECA, *Factors Affecting Education, Training and Work Opportunities for Girls and Women within the Context of Development*, Addis Ababa, 1971.

14. See Moser, p. 99.

15. Newland, p. 130.

16. Claire Robertson and Iris Berger, *Women and Class in Africa*, Africana Publishing Company, New York, 1986, p. 31.

17. See Ester Boserup, *Woman's Role in Economic Development*, St Martin's Press, New York, 1970; Jaquette; Tinker; and Myra Buvenic et al. See also Moser.

18. See Moser, pp. 103–6.

19. See Cornia et al. See also Bardouille.

20. Gita Sen and Caren Grown, *Development, Crises and Alternative Visions*, New York, Monthly Review Press, 1987.

21. Ibid., p. 96.

22. Ibid., p. 22.

23. For a good explanation of gender, see Eva Rathberger, *Operationalizing Gender and Development*, Association on Women and Development (AWID), Washington, DC, 20–24 November 1991.

24. Critics of the use of gender fully support viewing the division of labour from gender perspectives and considering men's roles in changing societies. Their concern is that measures targeted specifically to women to overcome discrimination and poverty not be jeopardized. They call for strength through mobilization of

women and for support of women-specific institutions as a strategy to reach long-range development goals. In this regard, they wish to guarantee that the gender approach should not exacerbate the flight of attention and capital from women-specific activities; that flight began with the integration and mainstreaming theories of the 1970s and 1980s. They also question whether the current practice of conducting one or two brief training sessions in gender as a means of transforming attitudes and practices can effect long-term transformation of societies.

25. Newland, p. 131.

A conversation with Justice Annie Jiaggie

Q: How did the women and development movement arise in Ghana?

AJ: We've had women's movements at various times – church movements, market women's movements – but they were not political. When Ghana began fighting for independence, the women became politically active. A new breed of woman came out of that, then went on to the new sphere of development.

I was hit with the problems of women when I was on the UN Commission on the Status of Women. My first shock was the confidential reports on women's lives in various countries. For example, when heads were counted, women were not counted. A brother had a lawful right to kill a sister found in adultery, but the other way – no. I was incensed from then on.

The Ghana National Council was one of the first in Africa. What is its history?

We voted the idea when I was on the Commission on the Status of Women. Ghana dragged its feet until just before the Mexico International Women's Year conference in 1975. Government wanted to show something for Mexico, and they asked for my help. A group of us decided that the words 'status of women' frightened the men, who thought women wanted to be the ones to wear trousers. So we decided to call it the National Council on Women and Development (NCWD). After rejecting two drafts from the Ministry of Foreign Affairs, we wrote the instrument ourselves so that women who were working full-time could sit on the council and participate fully. The council was made up of women workers, women who were housewives, and several men.

How did the council start its work?

We had a number of committees, constituted of persons with special expertise. At first, we thought the most important thing was to help women become literate, so we could contact them through the written word. Then we decided to ask the women themselves. We invited women's groups from all over the country to send two representatives to a conference in Accra. What the majority wanted was not literacy but increased incomes. So we made that our main focus, and our technical team went to research institutions to find out how they could help. They found quite a lot, for example the chorker fish smoker, and charcoal made from waste cocoa pods. We introduced those technologies to women's groups, and they started making money.

Technology became a major focus?

Yes. We visited village markets. After the men finished talking, women asked questions relevant to their occupations. That was what we wanted to hear. The women were selling gari, made from cassava, and wanted to mechanize the processes of grating, squeezing out the excess starch, and seeding. They did the roasting themselves, because that process greatly influenced the quality of the product. We found a technician to produce a machine that could easily be repaired by women themselves. Our idea was that women would produce the gari together. That did not work out. After the mechanical processing they each went back home for the final step – roasting. They wanted to be at home with the children.

Did men understand the purpose of this work ?

The men wanted to take over, and this would not do. As we progressed, the village women took up courage and were adamant that it was their factory. Then they were ready to get a tractor, so that they could grow more cassava.

When eventually men see the point, they support the work, and support it so well that you begin to wonder: was it just ignorance, or was it that they thought women couldn't think well enough – had no ability? Or was it just that they were so filled with themselves that they couldn't see women's needs? I wondered.

What is women's main concept of development?

When women think of development, they think of meeting the needs of their children and their families. That's number one. Then they think of access roads to their farms, of water, light, and habitat – where to live. As they themselves say, money generates activities. I'm talking about women who have no schooling. The imagination is there, and once you have the enabling factor of the income to deal with it, they go into areas that were not women's lines in the past.

Accra
December 1993

CHAPTER 2

THE AFRICAN CONTEXT: WOMEN
IN THE POLITICAL ECONOMY

The African women who witnessed the independence of their countries possessed rich traditions as leaders, as participants in women's movements and, along with men, in liberation struggles. They had tangible records of economic activity, largely in peasant societies but also in monetized 'modern' cultures. None the less, the introduction of cash crops and technologies, of education and wage employment opportunities, had usually bypassed them. As men had been drawn into the modern sectors, women's productivity was eroded during the pre-independence era, the colonial perception of women as home-makers eclipsing women's substantial political and economic activity.

This imported view would persist even after independence, when it was sometimes justified by references to 'elements in traditional societies' that gave men preferential access to resources. Happily, the newly created United Nations Economic Commission for Africa (ECA) found such a view misleading.

The United Nations recognizes Africa

During the years immediately following World War Two, the United Nations had taken the lead in designing a variety of institutional components to meet the needs of the global community. In that same period, African nations, claiming their independence from colonial rule, joined the United Nations and looked to it for support as they reconstituted their governments. The UN responded by creating the Economic Commission for Africa (ECA) in 1958. As the African arm of the United Nations, the ECA, with its own advisory Conference of Ministers, reported to the Economic and Social Council (ECOSOC) of the UN, and then to the General Assembly.

Dag Hammarskjöld, who was then Secretary-General of the UN, in creating the ECA proclaimed that its establishment marked 'the point at which Africa began to play its full role in world affairs'.[1] With its mission of facilitating development, the ECA provided the thirty-six new nations on the African continent with an instrument for raising the level of economic activity and levels of living, and for strengthening the economic relations between African countries and with other countries of the world.[2] Implicit in that mission were the economic and social contributions of both men and women.

African women's legacy

Among the women leaders of the nineteenth and early twentieth centuries in Africa were warrior queen Yaa Asantewa of Ghana (about 1840–1921) who was outstanding among Asante queen mothers because she led her people in battle against the British colonizers in the Anglo-Ashanti War. Queen Ranavalona III of Madagascar reigned between 1883 and 1897; she successfully faced foreign threats and domestic tensions. Empress Taitu made crucial contributions in the period 1883–1910 to the domestic and foreign policies of Ethiopia as consort to Emperor Menelik II; she was described as the 'most powerful woman on the continent of Africa in her time'.[3] Queen Amina of Zazzau became famous in Nigeria, and Chief Martha Yoko of the Kpa Mende gained fame in Sierra Leone. The latter used diplomacy and even went to war to bring fourteen chiefdoms under her rule.[4] In Egypt, Hoda Sharawi followed the example of the female pharoahs such as Hatshepsut when she launched the Feminist Union in 1922, which counted among its accomplishments the raising of the marriage age for girls to 16 and for boys to 18. In due time the Feminist Union helped to end the wearing of veils by Egyption women.[5]

Historical evidence indicates that African women's participation in economic life was deeply rooted everywhere on the continent. While generalizations are risky in a region so vast and so varied as Africa, we can state that in a large number of early African societies the gender division of labour allocated responsibility for cultivation to women, who could barter or sell their excess produce, while men engaged in hunting. The division of labour was different in other societies; for example, in Ethiopia men ploughed the fields and women weeded and harvested along with them. In parts of West Africa too, women and men farmed side by side.

The burden of food production generally fell to women, despite exceptions like the cocoa-growing areas of Nigeria. 'In most of Africa, women were the backbone of rural farming,' said Achola Pala-Okeyo of Kenya.[6] They usually cultivated community-owned land allocated to them by male political or lineage heads, to whom they in turn paid over some of their produce.

Besides agriculture, women engaged in commercial activity locally and with European merchants, as recorded as early as the eighteenth century in West Africa. Whilst the merchant princesses of West Africa remain legendary for their wealth and overseas trade, it is true that almost all the women in that area engaged in some kind of trade. Women in other parts of the continent also traded or bartered in the local markets. Thus, for most women on the continent, petty trade or agriculture was the source of livelihood.

Clearly, in traditional African societies, whilst it cannot be said that all women had equality with men, despite class differences, a balance of economic responsibility did prevail between women and men, and the work of both was valued in a largely non-competitive division of labour. Parallel gender-based institutions were common in such an environment, and men's and women's groups each managed their own affairs. In south-western Nigeria, for example, there were women's courts to impose fines and women were the market authorities who fixed prices and settled quarrels. In Cameroun, the best of the Bemileke female farmers belonged to a special women's society. Both men and women participated in some functions of overall government and women at times reached positions of high authority.[7]

The colonial period

Profound changes came with colonialism and its attendant technologies, cash cropping and a wage economy. Colonial officials tended to visualize women in terms of a Victorian image of what a woman ('a lady') should be, instead of observing women's actual functions. From that perspective they envisioned women's responsibilities as largely limited to nurturing and conserving society, while men engaged in political and economic activities. Colonials equated 'male' with 'breadwinner' and, as a result, introduced technologies to men and recruited men for paying jobs which often took them off the farm. Anthropologists and other researchers did little to rectify that one-sided view; they themselves were inclined to underestimate women's productivity.[8]

As the international market economy encroached more rapidly on Africa, major setbacks to women arose from male migration to mines, plantations and towns. Whether men left by choice, by necessity, or by force, their migration left women on the farm doing both men's and women's work. Those women often had many dependants – children, elders and the ill to care for – without enough adult workers. In the colonial system, as in many other systems at the time, men were favoured with opportunities for education, employment and access to resources.

But perhaps the most serious setback for women came when land consolidation and settlement schemes gave title deeds to men as 'heads of household' even when they were absent from the farm. This was often in direct contradiction to the use-rights that were customary and that en-couraged women's productivity.[9] With the titles came men's right to the proceeds of the land, including the products of women's labour that women had previously contributed to family maintenance. The prestige accorded to women's work in the parallel-society system of earlier eras was consequently downgraded, even though women often worked continuously and for many more hours than the men.

The confrontations that arose were rooted in women's traditional and central position in economic life. It should have come as no surprise to the colonial administrators that African women's farm and merchant groups mobilized to protest against those colonial policies which appeared to jeopardize their economic activity. Recognizing the reality of the encroaching capitalist economy, women organized to preserve their chances to meet their responsibilities for the well-being of their families. The colonial officials held firm, regarding these women's efforts to preserve subsistence crops as reactionary and detrimental to the development of a market economy.

In the 1940s and 1950s, for example, women in Cameroun, Côte d'Ivoire, Sierra Leone and Uganda resisted the introduction of cash crops such as coffee, sisal and tea, to which the most fertile lands were being allocated and which added weeding and other tedious tasks to their already heavy workloads. The 'Women's War' was an anti-tax rebellion against the colonial powers by women in southern Igboland in Nigeria.[10] Kenyan women protested against unjust labour regulations as early as 1902.[11]

Women continued to persist in their economic activities during colonial times, despite the formidable odds they faced. One example is the way they mobilized to form corn mill societies in western Cameroun in the 1950s. Over time 200 such societies were formed with a total membership of 18,000. They used grinding mills that were owned in common, fenced their fields, and constructed water storage units and co-operative stores.[12] In some countries, when the introduction of cash crops could not be prevented, women devised alternative strategies for meeting their family responsibilities, such as requesting wages for their labour or threatening to leave their husbands.[13]

In other words, 'for generations women established some form of collective actions to increase group productivity, to fill-in socio-economic gaps wherever the colonial administration failed, or to protest policies that deprived them of the resources to provide for their families'.[14]

But despite such well-organized efforts, colonialism and its market economy continued to revolutionize the family division of labour, and the family itself. Pala-Okeyo identifies the colonial period as the beginning of the deterioration of food production in Africa.[15] That observation and the need to feed growing populations would underlie the selection of rural development and food production as the initial emphases of ECA programmes directed to women in the early 1970s.

Independence movements

Women's historic protests against economic policies laid the groundwork for them to join with men in the struggle for independence from colonialism and became the foundation of the women and development movement. More than eleven thousand women were jailed during the MauMau Emergency of the 1950s.[16] Women fought side by side with men in Algeria, Angola, Zambia, Mozambique and Guinea-Bissau. The heroism of Mbuya Niyanda of Zimbabwe and Mama Chikamoneka of Zambia is legendary in their countries. Women constituted over 25% of the cadres of the Zimbabwe African National Union Liberation Army (ZANLA) and a full one-third of some of the opposition fighting forces in the 1980s in Ethiopia.

The independence movements of the 1950s and 1960s allowed the roots of the women and development concept and movement to take hold. After the experience of struggle, women were determined to be fully participating citizens of their new nations. Though this wish is not yet fully realized, the solidarity groups and organizations they evolved from their work still 'rank among the most important components of African civil society'.[17]

It was against this background of women's history of leadership, of their strength in adversity, and of their economic activities and community participation that the United Nations Economic Commission for Africa invited women to be advisers and participants in development activities just after it was founded in 1958.

Notes

1. 'ECA: Its Role; Its Organization', United Nations Economic Commission for Africa, Addis Ababa. Mimeo, undated, M78-510.

2. 'Terms of Reference and Rules of Procedure of the ECA', United Nations, New York. E/CN.14/111 Rev. 8.

3. See Chris Prouty, *Empress Taitu and Menelik II: Ethiopia 1883–1910*, Red Sea Press, Trenton, 1986. Much of the information in this chapter is expanded in Margaret Snyder, 'Farmers and Merchants: Some Observations on Gender and the State in Africa', published in *Africa Contemporary Record*, Vol. XXII, forthcoming, Africana Publishing Company, Holmes and Meier, NY.

4. Carol P. Hoffer, 'Mende and Sherbro Women in High Office', *Canadian Journal of African Studies (CJAS)*, Ottawa, Vol. 6, No. 2, 1972, p. 153.

5. For these and other historic citations, see Adebayo Adedeji, 'Statement at the Fourth Regional Conference on the Integration of Women in Development in Africa', UNECA, Addis Ababa, 1989. See also Agnes Aidoo, 'Asante Queen Mothers in Government and Politics in the Nineteenth Century', *The Black Woman Cross-culturally*, Cambridge, Mass., 1981; Margaret Jean Hay, 'Queens, Prostitutes and Peasants: Historical Perspectives on African Women', and Audrey Wipper,

'Reflections on the Past Sixteen Years, 1972–1988, and Future Challenges', (*CJAS*), Vol. 22, No. 3, 1988, pp. 409–21 and 431–47.

6. Achola Pala-Okeyo, *Towards Strategies for Strengthening the Position of Women in Food Production: an Overview and Proposals on Africa*, INSTRAW, Santo Domingo, 1985. See also Kathleen Staudt, 'Women Farmers in Africa: Research and Institutional Action 1972–1987', *CJAS*, Vol. 22; No. 3, 1988, pp. 567–82, Ester Boserup, *Woman's Role in Economic Development*, St Martin's Press, New York, 1970.

7. Philomena Chioma Steady, 'African Feminism: a Worldwide Perspective', in Rosalyn Terborg-Penn (ed.), *Women in Africa*, Howard University Press, Washington DC, 1989, pp. 3–21.

8. Nearly all research during the colonial period was undertaken by expatriates and thus inclined to be influenced by the European perspective on women at the time.

9. Pala-Okeyo. See also Jane Parpart and Kathleen Staudt, *Women and the State in Africa*, Lynne Reiner, Boulder, 1990, pp. 12–13. On the question of forced labour see Steady, p. 11.

10. Judith Van Allen, '"Sitting on a Man": Colonialism and the Lost Political Institutions of Igbo Women', *CJAS*, Vol. 6, No. 2, p. 172.

11. Cora Ann Presley, 'The Mau Mau Rebellion, Kikuyu Women and Social Change', *CJAS* Vol. 22, No. 3, p. 502.

12. Margaret Snyder, 'Gender and the Food Regime: Some Transnational and Human Issues', in *Transnational Law and Contemporary Problems*, University of Iowa, 1991.

13. Ester Boserup, p. 64.

14. Snyder.

15. Pala-Okeyo, p. 11.

16. Presley.

17. Snyder.

The origins of 'Women and Development': a conversation with Margaret Kenyatta

Q: Why did you organize the first Kenya Women's Seminar?
MK: It happened in the early 1960s, when our country was about to attain independence from colonial rule. Kenya women were involved in non-governmental organizations and other groups. Many of the women who were leaders decided to mobilize themselves as a group, so they could mobilize women all over the country to do something for themselves as women, for their children, and for the country as a whole.

That is why we organized the Kenya Women's Seminar, to make women realize that they had roles to play in their independent country, and that they could organize themselves to seek ways and means of training and educating themselves to become useful citizens for the development of their young, free nation of Kenya.

You organized in Kenya in 1962 and 1963, then in East Africa in 1964?

We organized the East African Women's Seminar, for Tanzania, Uganda and Kenya. It also met in Nairobi. We had a lot of contributions from women, a lot of resolutions on their future and their participation in the development of their countries.

This was the beginning. Women in East Africa started thinking that we had a part in leadership in our own countries, and that we could do something to assist development. From then, women in our countries have been doing a lot.

We were also part of the All Africa Women's Conference, which met for the first time in Bamako, Mali, and later met for a full meeting in Dar es Salaam in 1962. Kenyan women participated. We felt good that we were there in those days when African women met, and we were meeting in East Africa at the same time.

You give the credit to women all over Africa?

Everywhere, women of Africa were meeting by themselves. Before that, we had no contact because we were under colonial rule, and we had no right to meet as African women. But from 1962 onwards, we knew what other African women were doing in their own countries.

Our Kenyan, East African and African women played a major part in the UN Conference for women in Nairobi in 1985. We were in Mexico City when the Decade for Women was declared in 1975, and we went to Copenhagen in 1980. So we were together. We were looking at what women can do for themselves.

Now we are not only women of Africa, of Kenya, of West Africa or what; we have joined other women of the world to build up more participation for women. To look for more education for women, training, so that they can be more useful citizens in their own countries than before.

You were Chairman of the 1985 Women's Conference in Nairobi. What is your wish for women of the world today?

The one thing I could wish is peace for the women of the world. Then, after that, if there is peace which will enable us to do other things, we want development.

And, especially in the developing world, we need more education and training for our women, so that they can get better opportunities to work, to be economically independent, to bring up better families, and to be of some use to their countries.

Nairobi
November 1993

CHAPTER 3

THE 1960s: DEVELOPMENT STRATEGIES, WOMEN'S INITIATIVES AND GLOBAL INFLUENCES

The late 1950s and the 1960s were a time of hope and expectation in Africa. Self-government was perceived as a basic human right, and the winds of change carried colonialism into history as nation after nation gained independence. The initial stimulus of independence turned into a long-term and sometimes discouraging development effort, because nation building was a complex task. In addition, colonial systems tended to be retained and even to grow in influence, and as a result, economic dependence persisted long after political independence was achieved.

Prevailing development prescriptions

At first, everything rested on the anticipation of rapid economic take-off and on the social progress that was expected to occur when the long-colonized African nations became independent. In hopes of ensuring economic take-off, modernization theories of industrialization and 'trickle-down' economics were globally promoted and then translated into development strategies during the First United Nations Development Decade of the 1960s.

Aspirations for the 'new Africa' were described by the ECA's Bax Nomvete:

> to create economic, social and political conditions which will ... release the energies of our people, and our resource potential [from colonial influence] so that through co-operative effort we can speed up our economic development and raise the standards of living of our people.

Nomvete none the less warned that, because Africa was a poor continent whose net output per head was $200, as compared to $1,200 in industrial countries, it would be necessary to mobilize all natural, human and economic resources for 'productive investment in both the rural and urban sectors of our economies'.[1]

The underlying tenet of that widely held view was that growth of gross national product (GNP) would yield benefits for the poorest peoples.[2]

Thus the prevailing prescription of the First Development Decade was applied to large-scale, market-oriented agriculture and both heavy and light industry.[3] The stress was on industrial development, many new countries spent large portions of their financial reserves on industries. They were also on the receiving end of a flow of aid – both concessional and tied – from Western countries. One result was an accumulation of debts that would soon accrue formidable interest payments.

Institutionalizing women's concerns

Meanwhile, in that post-independence environment so filled with promise, and several years before the 1968 revitalization of the Western women's movement, African women laid the foundations for the women and development movement by institutionalizing their concerns. Women of the then socialist-oriented countries – among them Egypt, Ghana, Guinea, and Tanganyika – led meetings in Bamako, then in Dar es Salaam in 1962 to establish the All Africa Women's Conference (AAWC) that was later renamed the Pan-African Women's Organization (PAWO). The delegates selected Jean Martin Cisse of Guinea as Chairperson.

Women also started to insist on participating in decision making in individual nations. In Ghana, for example, the First Republic (1960–66) gave seats in Parliament to twelve women, and a ministerial post to a woman as well.[4] In Kenya, Margaret Kenyatta, whose father would be her country's first president, led women to hold their first national Women's Seminar on 'The Roles of African Women: Past, Present and Future' in 1962, and their second, called 'The African Woman Builds the Nation', in 1963. Asked nearly three decades later why she was moved to organize those seminars, Kenyatta replied unhesitatingly:

> Independence was coming and we wanted women to participate fully in our new nations. We wanted women to realize that they had roles to play in their independent country, and they could organize themselves to seek ways and means of training and educating themselves more to become useful citizens for the development of their young, free nation of Kenya.[5]

Kenyan women collaborated with women from neighbouring Uganda and Tanganyika to sponsor East African Women's Seminars in subsequent years.

South Africa's Pumla Kissosonkole, who then lived in Uganda, set the tone at the first of those seminars:

> These days the cry of the 'role of women' is being heard in Africa from East to West, and from North to South. What is the answer for East Africa? It is this: times have changed and are changing very fast, and the woman must change with them in order that she does not become the 'forgotten factor' ... and [she]

will be ready and willing to play the fullest part in shaping the destinies of her country.[6]

Kissosonkole's note of realism – that women themselves had to seize opportunities because independence would not automatically bring benefits to them – was echoed at the second seminar, held in 1963. A.L. Adu, Secretary-General of the East African Common Services Organization, reminded the participants of the example set by Yaa Asantewa in his own country, Ghana. She galvanized the attention of some chiefs who were on the verge of compromise with the British colonists, by telling them that she and other women would take up battle themselves if the men continued to be so weak. It took little time thereafter for women and men together to lay siege to the colonists.[7]

Partly as a result of Adu's presentation, seminar delegates petitioned the colonial governor with a request that at least four women be nominated to fill national seats in the new legislature and that at least one be appointed as representative at the UN. They also called for new legislation on women's right to inherit property.[8]

The seminar series exemplifies the spirit that infused the women and development concept. What was new was the fresh insight on women as full partners with men in shaping their new nations. Such thinking also stimulated a transformation within some of the seminars' sponsors, the existing women's organizations that were national, like Maendeleo ya Wanawake (Progress of Women), and offshoots of international women's organizations such as the Associated Country Women of the World and the International Council of Women.

Africa's human resources

All during the First Development Decade forces were at work at the ECA that changed its focus from reliance on capital-intensive industry to the productivity and well-being of Africa's most abundant resource, her people. The expected economic growth had not been achieved. The ECA took on the work of promoting community and social development programmes and of organizing conferences at the Africa-wide level. Training and research projects were also instituted by the ECA to allow women's voices to be heard. All those early initiatives laid the foundations for what would eventually become the African Training and Research Centre for Women (ATRCW), located with the ECA in Addis Ababa.

As early as 1960, the second session of the ECA Conference of Ministers agreed that a training course for women on methods for their participation in community development should be an element of the ECA's overall community development programme.[9] That training, however, was amalgamated with a United Nations headquarters, Department of Economic and Social Affairs, workshop, and unfortunately took on the then dominant and largely Western, Victorian image of the African woman that was inherited from colonialism.[10] The perception of women as primarily and almost exclusively mothers was evident in the workshop title: 'The Extension of Child and Family Welfare Services within Community Development Programmes'.[11] Women's issues were still confined to home and family.

A seminar was organized by United Nations headquarters in the same year; it took place in Addis Ababa. One of its recommendations is worth quoting in its entirety, for it reveals how far away those involved were from an adequate understanding of how the introduction of advanced farming technology would affect women's work.

> That mechanization of agriculture should be encouraged because it would decrease the workload of women ... and free them for other roles. [It would] tend to eliminate polygamy since wives would no longer be needed as a cheap source of farm labour and increase school attendance since children, particularly girls, would no longer be needed for work on the farms.[12]

Even though the expected impacts of 'modernization' that were described in that recommendation would prove to be the exact opposite of the reality, these workshops none the less provided the seeds of the ECA strategy to engage and benefit the continent's people that would be designed by Robert Gardiner of Ghana after he was appointed the ECA's Executive Secretary in 1962. While not entirely discarding the prevailing industrial approach that characterized the modernization model, Gardiner called for 'multiple small-scale investments ... projects of a labour-intensive type ... small or medium-scale industries geared to national consumption patterns, and transportation and communications links between the farmer and the consumer'.[13] Each of these measures had the potential to transform both women's and men's lives.

In 1963, while this interest in the farmer and the local community was building, and while women's post-independence voices were beginning to be heard at national and regional levels, the ECA added social affairs to its community development concerns.[14] Expert advice was sought on ways to integrate social planning with overall development planning, both urban and rural. By 1964 the ECA was able to report to its Conference of Ministers about the results of its first regional conference ('Workshop on Urban Probems: the Role of Women in Urban Development') which had been held in Lagos and had been committed solely to women and development:[15]

> Although it was not until the following year that population growth became a subject of worldwide concern, the ECA had already opened itself to considering population issues. The 1964 conference requested a study on 'population growth

and the role of women in development', and the United Nations secretariat assured it that the role of women in economic and social development 'was not being ignored'.[16]

The subsequent ECA-sponsored publication *Status and Role of Women in East Africa*[17] gave evidence of the commission's intention to listen to women in accordance with requests from both the 1964 workshop on urban problems and UN General Assembly Resolutions.[18] Reviewing the situations in Ethiopia, Kenya, Malawi, Tanganyika, Uganda and Zambia, the study found that

> women often carried a major portion of the economic burden ... at the same time, they occupied an honoured position and exerted much power and influence in society.

It went on to credit women's groups with playing a great part in national independence movements, citing the strong women's sections in liberation movements. The study also commented curtly that 'few developing countries have involved women in the early years of community development programmes'.[19]

By the mid to late 1960s, disparate research findings began to become available that verified women's centrality not only to social but also to economic progress in their countries. The following are some of the facts that were discovered:[20]

— In Lesotho, 90% of road building under the food-for-work programme was done by women.

— In Gabon, women worked 200 days a year in the fields, while men spent few if any days there.

— In Tanzania, men worked 1,800 hours as compared with women's 2,600 hours annually in agriculture; President Nyerere stated that women in the rural areas of Tanzania worked harder than anyone else in the country.

— In Cameroun, women's land holdings for food production were becoming so fragmented as to necessitate hand cultivation.

— In Kenya, when cash crops were introduced no innovations were offered to the woman farmer beyond her own additional labour – which was not reduced but multiplied with mechanization.

— In Uganda, the Faculty of Agriculture at Makerere University was established in the late 1930s, but it was only in 1967 that the first two women were enrolled.[21]

— Women represented 60% of the sellers in urban markets in Dakar in 1959; 66% in Brazzaville Bacongo in 1962; 83% in Lagos in 1960; 85% in Accra in 1959.[22]

— In Kenya, by 1962, rural women had established 5,000 nursery centres, to get an early start on enhancing their children's chances in school and in life in the new Africa.

Such information would gradually help to transform the leftover colonial images of women into realistic ones.

Popular participation: women and development

1969 proved to be a very significant year. First, in response to the mounting information on the situation of women, 'the role and participation of women in national development' was listed for the first time, under the theme 'Popular Participation in Development', in the ECA Human Resource Development Division's Programme of Work that was presented for consideration to the Conference of Ministers and later to ECOSOC.[23] Programme sections included a regional meeting to be co-sponsored with the German Foundation for Developing Countries, as well as studies on the role of women in economic and social development in West, North and Central Africa.

At about the same time, the Swedish International Development Authority (SIDA) offered to finance two posts at the ECA in order to enable a follow-up on resolutions generated at regional meetings of women. That offer was prompted by Ambassador Inga Thorsson, who had been inspired by her own journey through Africa to persuade the Swedish Parliament to mandate government support for women through its foreign assistance programmes; such legislation was passed in 1964. Thorsson later became Director of the Social Development Division at UN headquarters.

The Regional Meeting on the Role of Women in National Development took place in 1969, in Addis Ababa. The recommendations of the participants included two that would later be seen as the historical beginnings of pressures on the ECA to institute operational programmes for women. The first called for the establishment of an Africa regional training institute, and the second, the creation of a regional standing committee on women. Comparative country studies on womanpower resources and a study on the role of African women in trade, business, industry and agriculture were called for, as was a workshop on crafts.[24] As a follow-up to that Addis Ababa meeting, a planning committee was convened in Berlin. It proposed that a 'Conference on Education, Vocational Training and Work Opportunities for Girls and Women' be held in 1971. Along with the 1969 decisions, that conference would galvanize the ECA's commitment to an Africa-wide programme.

Few if any historians and analysts of the women and development movement acknowledge or perhaps even recognize that theoretical roots for the movement were being put down in Africa in the early 1960s, as the independence movement sparked women's conviction that they must be part of their nations' development in order to bring benefits to all. The Africa region, assisted by the ECA, was to take a lead in giving birth to the women and development concept and movement. As that movement later became transnational and even global, largely by using the United Nations as its vehicle, the African position in time became influenced by exposure to external development concepts and experiences, women's visions of development, and feminist analysis.

International factors

While the ECA's planning was in process at the turn of the decade, four international factors interfaced with it to underscore the importance of the ECA's evolving programme for women and to propel it into a pioneering position in the UN system.

The first factor arose from the independence movements of the 1950s and 1960s noted earlier, and the subsequent rapid increase in UN membership as fifty new Third World nations sent delegates, including women. The UN Commission on the Status of Women (CSW), for example, stimulated by members from Africa and other developing regions, in 1970 produced the long-awaited Programme of Concerted International Action for the Advancement of Women, which the General Assembly approved. It spoke to women's 'contribution to the country's overall development plans and programmes', and to the need to study 'the positive and negative effects of scientific and technological change on the status of women'.[25] The programme thus overturned the general consensus reported by governments to the CSW in 1962, that there were 'sufficient facilities and programmes available to provide the assistance needed to further advance the status of women'.[26]

Instead of concentrating heavily on legal matters as was its early practice, the CSW began to develop a more holistic perception of the centrality of women to the economic and social development of their countries: a development perspective. Women delegates from developing and some industrial countries in the UN collaborated with women staff in the international civil service and with representatives of women's non-governmental organizations to form coalitions that were strong enough to make the UN the major vehicle for promoting the international women's movement.

The second international factor was, as we have seen, that the prevailing international development theories of the 1960s failed to stimulate an end to poverty, and so alternative development models were sought. At UN headquarters, Secretary-General U Thant led the criticism of the industrialization strategies of the First Development Decade. He found fault with the assumption that adequate external investment in developing countries would lead to economic development by raising the GNP, and thereby would broadly benefit the people.

In its own review of the decade, the ECA also found that the 1960s emphasis on capital-intensive industry and cash crop agriculture led to the perpetuation of structural imbalance in African economies. Those GNP-based modernization theories not only did not work, but they also appeared to worsen the situation of the poorest peoples. Trickle-down economic theories were both sterile and ineffectual.[27]

U Thant called for 'integrated social and economic goals' in the Second Development Decade, the 1970s. In response, the UN General Assembly – by this time a body with wide representation from developing countries that had gained independence in the 1950s and 1960s – identified the ultimate purpose of development: 'to bring about sustained improvement in the well-being of the individual and to bestow benefits on all'.[28] That emphasis on human betterment enabled women as well as men to be seen as essential to the development process.

A third international factor would revolutionize prevailing perceptions of the position of women. It was the mounting evidence of the centrality of women to economic life and thus to national as well as family progress. There were clear indications that women's access to resources such as education and technologies was severely limited; consequently, brakes were put on the whole process of development. To prove that point, the landmark volume *Woman's Role in Economic Development*, brought together data culled from censuses, other official statistics, research studies and many special surveys – mainly from Africa and Asia.[29] The ECA's study *The Role and Status of Women in East Africa* was among the evidence provided.

The author of *Woman's Role in Economic Development*, economist Ester Boserup of Denmark, summed up her own findings by commenting that together the modernization of agriculture and male migration to the towns had caused a new gender pattern in productive work 'for better or worse'. The danger, she said, was that 'in the course of this transition, women will be deprived of their productive functions, and the whole process of growth will thereby be retarded'. Because Boserup was widely respected for her earlier agriculture study,[30] her new volume added legitimacy to the ECA's evolving positions and programmes. Together, they effected an early transformation of development strategies from a welfare orientation to that of human resource development and efficiency.

The fourth and final factor that underlined the importance of the ECA programme was the re-emergence of the women's movement in industrial countries, in about 1968. That phenomenon opened up the possibility that Western women would press their governments to guarantee that women as well as men in developing countries should benefit from Western 'foreign aid'. Progress towards that stance had already been evident in the Swedish legislation directing that country's development assistance to women, and in the UN Declaration on the Elimination of Discrimination Against Women of 1967.[31] The feminist revival also prepared Western women to contribute to the women and development concept and movement.

All those international factors combined to increase the momentum that had been building up in Africa as a result of both the regional conferences and the studies on women that had been conducted. (This history of African women and development, in addition to demonstrating that the concept and movement were offshoots of the independence movement, also indicates that Western women's actions, such as the 1973 Percy Amendment to the United States Foreign Assistance Act, were in fact responses to the concerns of women in developing countries.)

The impetus for change was further strengthened by the new patterns of thought which were prompting the ECA and the UN itself to direct their assistance programmes towards economic activites rather than only to projects that were mainly welfare-driven, such as the maternal and child health programmes of UNICEF.

Besides effecting a significant change in the evolution of its overall development strategies, the ECA adopted more technical and professional approaches to the concerns of women. Experts in education, health, industry, economic planning and social work were brought in to design strategies that would give women access to the tools of development.

African women themselves had begun to engage in self-education to determine the kind of development they wanted after independence. The ECA asked women to speak, and then responded by preparing to move forward rapidly in the seventies to support the strategies that women had articulated.

Notes

1. Bax Nomvete, 'The Hopes and Aspirations of New Africa'. Keynote address to The Kenya We Want Convention, Nairobi, 12–17 August 1962, p. 34.

2. W.W. Rostow, 'The Take-off into Self-sustained Growth', *Economic Journal* 66, March 1956, pp. 25–48.

3. UNECA, *The New International Economic Order: What Roles for Women*, Addis Ababa, 1977.

4. The Second Republic of Ghana reduced the number of parliamentary seats to two.

5. Margaret Kenyatta interviewed by Margaret Snyder, Nairobi, October 1993.

6. Report of the Kenya Women's Seminar, Nairobi 1962, pp. 18–19.

7. Ibid., p. 14.

8. Ibid.

9. *Annual Report of ECA, 7 January 1959–6 February 1960*. E/CN.14/54. *Programme of Work and Priorities for 1960–61: IV. Community Development and Related Activities in*

Social Fields, a training course for women on women's participation in community development, ECA, 1960.

10. The Department of Economic and Social Affairs, United Nations, New York. The Human Resources Division of the ECA also interacted with the UN's Commission on Social Development and with its Commission on the Status of Women.

11. The seminar was held in Accra in November–December 1960. That same December, a seminar on Participation of Women in Public Life was organized by the United Nations HQ in Addis Ababa under its programme of Advisory Services in the Field of Human Rights. See also Note 12 and Annexe 13, which contains a complete list of regional conferences.

12. *Recommendations of Regional Meetings for Africa on the Role of Women in Development,* UNECA, Addis Ababa, 1975, p. 7. See also: Annexe 15.

13. *Annual Report of the ECA, 1965–1966.* E/CN.14/393 p. 3.

14. *Annual Report of the ECA, 1961–62,* 4th session 1963. E/CN.14/168.

15. Lagos, 1964, document E/CN.14/241. The United Nations sponsored an Africa regional seminar on the Status of Women in Family Law in Lomé, Togo, later in the same year.

16. *Annual Report of the ECA, 1964–1965.* E/CN.14/343 Rev. 1, paras. 166, 168.

17. ECA, *Status and Role of Women in East Africa,* Addis Ababa, 1967. E/CN.14/SWSA/6. The document was the work of the ECA Social Development Section.

18. The resolutions included: 'UN Assistance for the Advancement of Women in Developing Countries', Res. 1509 (XV); 'Participation of Women in National, Social and Economic Development', Res. 1920 (XVIII); and 'The Elimination of Discrimination Against Women', Res. 1921 (XVIII).

19. ECA, *Status and Role of Women in East Africa,* pp. l, 53, 57. Appropriately, in the following year, 1968, the UN (HQ) organized a seminar on the civic and political education of women, in Accra.

20. All the citations are from ECA, 'Women: the Neglected Human Resources for African Development', *Canadian Journal of African Studies,* Vol. 6, No. 2, 1972, pp. 359–70, unless otherwise noted.

21. Jane Wills, Faculty of Agriculture, Makerere University, RDR 44, 1967.

22. ECA Human Resources Development Division, 'The Impact of Modern Life and Technology on Women's Economic Role: Implications for Planning', Addis Ababa, 1972. The document was presented to the FAO/ECA/SIDA Seminar on Home Economics Development Planning for English-speaking Countries in Africa. ESN: THEP/A/72/9-A.

23. ECA, *Annual Report of the 9th session of the Commission, 1969.* Work Programme, ECA E/CN.14/453 Vol. II.

24. The requested studies were incorporated in the ECA 'Programme of Work and Priorities for 1971–73', together with an evaluative study of unemployment among school leavers, and of secondary school enrolment in relation to middle-level manpower requirements.

25. A/RES/2716 XXV, 15 December 1970. The programme had been initiated in 1962. The importance of the new presence of Third World women was emphasized in an interview with Helvi Sipila, a member of the CSW and later the ASG, by Margaret Snyder in 1993.

26. E/CN.6/403 Rev. 1, para. 116.

27. 'Note on Preparations for the Second Development Decade with Special

Reference to the Social Aspects'. E/CN.5/438 14 January 1969, paras. 11, 16, 18; and E/CN.5/441 17 February–3 March 1969.

28. A/RES/2626 XXV in: *Official Records of the 25th Session*, Supplement Number 28; and Provisional Summary Record CSW 21st Session. E/CN.6/SR 535, 542, 7 February 1969.

29. Esther Boserup, *Women's Role in Economic Development*, St Martin's Press, New York, 1970.

30, Boserup had worked with Gunnar Myrdal on *Asian Dilemma*. Her earlier path-breaking work was *Conditions of Agricultural Growth: the Economics of Agrarian Change under Population Pressure*, George Allen and Unwin, London, 1965.

31. See Karin Himmelstrand, 'Can an Aid Bureaucracy Empower Women?', in Kathleen Staudt, *Women, International Development and Politics: the Bureaucratic Mire*, Temple University Press, Philadelphia, 1990, p. 104. The Declaration on the Elimination of Discrimination Against Women: A/RES/1921, XVIII, 7 November 1967.

Women in the Sahel:
a conversation with Jaqueline Ki-Zerbo

Q: When were you first involved with the ECA?

JK: I represented my government at a regional conference in 1960 in Addis Ababa, and at several others thereafter. The ECA was a very good entry point for African women to development. At that time, the ECA was a strong point of communication and co-ordination of ministries of planning and it was very important to have women's issues discussed there.

Did the ATRCW influence national policies?

Yes, I'm sure. The ATRCW brought together African women leaders, to discuss their problems and to learn from each other. By setting up the sub-regional committees and the ARCC, women leaders could think through and discuss problems and make recommendations to governments. Those regular meetings were important for us to see from one point to another what were the priorities, what had been done, and what was left to do.

What is the ordinary woman's idea of development in your region?

I think that, for African women, development is the reverse of how they live every day. Development is seen as a positive answer to the needs for food, water, health, education and employment. It would change the lives of African women.

These days people are talking about getting away from having special resources for women. What is your view from thirty years' experience?

We need to keep a double stream, to have specific support for women while at the same time trying to involve them in the mainstream of decisions and actions. You can't take just the main-streaming approach when you are doing experimental work that is meant to show the constraints and the particular needs of women. You cannot mainstream from scratch. Ideally, in the long term, at some point, specific projects for women won't be needed. For now they are essential.

You have worked with and for women from the grassroots, and also with women at a policy-making level. How does one innovate effectively?

The first thing is to work with people on their own needs and priorities. Listen to them, learn what they know and try to build on that. Consider them a source of information and knowledge. Also, take economic capacity into account; there is no use introducing a technology when there is no money to buy it.

Making women a source of knowledge is also a way of empower-ing them. For example, we had stove technicians and researchers interviewing village women, taking as a basis for their improved stoves the traditional techniques of building houses. And once new fuel-saving stove designs were completed, women were filmed cook-ing on them. All that had a positive effect on women's self-esteem and the respect others give them.

What should be the major concern of the ATRCW?

The situation in Africa has changed a lot. The first days of the centre were a time when we had the one-party political system in nearly all African countries. Now that is different. The centre should reflect that reality. Now, intergovernmental meetings take place on development and peace, like the Kampala meeting. The centre should focus on the outcomes of those meetings. And at the same time, we have a new generation of young women. The centre must be re-sponsive to them.

Ouagadougou
December 1994

CHAPTER 4

THE DEVELOPMENT OF POLICY CONCEPTS: THE CENTRALITY OF WOMEN

As the 1970s began, the exhilaration of independence subsided and harsh realities once again emerged. Millions of people relied on a subsistence type of agriculture that was itself dependent on the often punishing vicissitudes of nature. Complicating the people's lives even further was the legacy of severe deficiency in their nations' infrastructures, for example in roads and water supplies, and in the capacity of young governments to plan and implement policies.

Just one indicator of the impact of those impediments on the thirty-six newly independent states of Africa was the problem of illiteracy, which continued to burden the people and to impede their progress. In the age group 15–24, for example, 70% of the women and 35% of the men in Algeria were illiterate. The respective figures in Botswana were 36% and 46%; in Ethiopia 99.6% and 88.4%; in Togo 83.1% and 51.5%.[1] Illiteracy and poverty continued to exist hand in hand, with one feeding into or upon the other.

The Western model of development through industrialization and GNP growth had failed, but the acknowledgement of that failure brought with it an opportunity to search for more efficacious development paradigms. As the ECA moved into the 1970s, however, it still had to cope with many dilemmas. For example, the search for more effective models had to take into consideration that ineffective models in the hands of in-experienced and/or opportunist leaders had already caused many countries to be vulnerable to military coups. (Needless to say, women were seldom a part of military decision-making groups.) New strategies had to obviate that type of outcome.

Another dilemma was found in the realization that so-called modern-ization policies and programmes hit women and their dependent children most harshly. And yet all the evidence showed that without women's active participation, there was little hope for successful development. The move to resolve that quandary by involving women in every aspect of develop-ment was unconditionally supported by two senior Ghanaian officials at the ECA, James Riby-Williams and Robert Gardiner. They were both men

39

who understood intellectually and from personal experience that women were central to Africa's economic and societal well-being.

The ECA position

As Chief of the ECA Human Resource Development Division, James Riby-Williams often expressed his hope and confidence in Africa's greatest resource – her people. Delivering an opening address at the Africa Regional Conference on Education, Vocational Training and Work Opportunities for Girls and Women in African Countries in Rabat, Morocco, in May 1971, Riby-Williams made a critical connection that later became a fundamental tenet in the ECA's work with women:

> Women's needs are intricately bound up with the priority needs and aspirations of the nation, and must necessarily be viewed as features of overall national development and the advancement of the total society.[2]

Re-emphasizing that involving women in development activities would benefit not just women but the 'nation as a whole', Riby-Williams went on to insist that conference discussions should not be abstractions but should deal head-on with the vulnerabilities of newly independent Africa. He gave as an example the lack in African governments of an adequate way to measure manpower and training requirements. That deficiency was especially evident in the rural sectors, which engaged between 80 and 95% of the female labour force. Those sectors were the chief source of raw material for existing and planned industries, and they provided the main source of foreign currency for procuring capital goods for development activities.

'Not a single African government has evolved a system for assessing the strength and characteristics of its rural labour force,' Riby-Williams stated. At the same time, he challenged women to 'aspire to practical leadership and form intelligent and forceful pressure groups to cater for their special needs', adding, 'we cannot wait for ... sophisticated statistical data to be obtained and perfected before we act'.[3]

Turning to practical matters, Riby-Williams confirmed the ECA's commitment to the creation of an operational programme for women by announcing that a senior officer had already been appointed to that task, and another would soon be identified at the ECA in Addis Ababa. Their assignment was clear: through a series of studies, meetings and advisory services, to transform the resolutions of regional women's conferences into a programme that the ECA would carry out.[4]

The main working document prepared by the ECA for the Rabat conference, 'Factors Affecting Education, Training and Work Opportunities for Girls and Women Within the Context of Development', provided the initial effort towards programming, and towards strengthening resolutions

Table 4.1 Percentages of girls in total enrolments in technical and vocational education in Africa

0–10		10–20		20–30		30–40	
Upper Volta	3	Ghana	10	Zaire	21	Côte	
Nigeria	4	Somalia	14			d'Ivoire	33
		Mali	15	Malawi	24.5	Dahomey	37.5
Congo	7.5	CAR	17	Cameroun	28.5		
(Brazzaville)							
		Guinea	19.5				

Source: The Data Base for Discussion on the Interrelations Between the Integration of Women in Development, Their Situation and Population Factors in Africa, ECA, Addis Ababa 1974.

with relevant research.[5] The document stressed the point made by Riby-Williams that the final objective of development was 'creating better lives, with greater freedom and well-being for members of the family, the local community and the nation as a whole'. It was later recognized as historic and path-breaking: the first in a series of seven documents written for widely varied audiences, ranging from government representatives to scholars, and from foundations to women with minimal levels of formal education. The titles of the other six documents provide an indication of the development of policy concepts:[6]

'Women: the Neglected Human Resources for African Development', *Canadian Journal of African Studies*, Vol. 6, No. 2, 1972.

The Impact of Modern Life and Technology on Women's Economic Role: Implications for Planning, ECA/FAO/SIDA, 1972.

Women and Rural Institutions, ECA/FAO/SIDA, 1972.

'Women and National Development in African Countries: Some Profound Contradictions', document prepared for the Ford Foundation, 1973.

The Data Base for Discussion on the Interrelations Between the Integration of Women in Development, Their Situation and Population Factors in Africa, Addis Ababa, 1974.

Women of Africa: Today and Tomorrow, Addis Ababa, 1975 (the popular version of *The Data Base*).

The knowledge and policy base in these documents evolved in a period of time in which there was an almost incredibly small amount of data and research about women in African countries. Traditionally, few scholars or government offices disaggregated data by gender, and what little information existed was often hidden in musty anthropological volumes or simply in university mimeographs.[7] Despite those obstacles, valuable information was uncovered.

For example, Table 4.1, on the percentages of girls in technical and vocational education in Africa, illustrates the great gaps, even in the most elementary data. It also shows why the collection and analysis of credible data and research gave the ECA Women's Programme strong arguments to present to diverse publications and to meetings of governments and others. *The Data Base* also rallied the confidence of potential donors in the programme.

Five key policy premisses

Examination of the core documentation reveals that five key premisses for policy were advanced by the ECA as its data and research base was expanded between 1971 and 1974. These premisses formed the conceptual basis for the Women's Programme and later for the establishment of the ATRCW; the unique genius of the early Women's Programme and the centre was their capacity to translate policy decisions derived from women's advice into action programmes. They reveal an African regional interpretation of the concept and objectives of 'women and development' as these were understood in Africa – the first of the world's developing regions to involve women extensively in its UN programme.

1. *Participation*

The most serious problems of development defy solution without the active participation of women.[8]

'Whether one holds a pragmatic or a humanistic view of development, the participation of women is necessary, and their involvement will hasten the development of the whole society,' the Rabat document stated.[9] The logic of this position was straightforward.

> If all of the persons who are involved in the human tasks of survival and creation of a better life are allowed to share the opportunities available to apply scientific knowledge and technological advances, development will be achieved at the most rapid rate possible.[10]

Within those overarching arguments there were detailed, gender-specific reasons for involving women. The analysis of women's traditional and prevailing responsibilities demonstrated that they filled significant roles in the economy and in society, such as cultivation, food processing, animal husbandry and marketing, in addition to caring for their homes and families. Women were thus identified by the ECA as 'the neglected human resources for African development'.[11]

Robert Gardiner, the ECA Executive Secretary who later established the ATRCW, underscored that appraisal by posing critical questions:

Can we overcome hunger and malnutrition without involving the women who cultivate, process and cook our food? Can we overcome ignorance without the women who are the first teachers of our children?'[12]

Gardiner also pointed out that the enormous actual and potential contributions of women to the development of the African continent and its people were too often taken for granted.

This first policy premiss, based on an African concept of women and development, offered a unique Third World perspective. It recognized that, by planning for women's advancement, the end – and desired – result would be to lift both women and men out of poverty. With inclusive strategies in place, both women and men would be enabled to contribute to development as well as benefit from it.

2. *Grassroots solidarity*

Women's grassroots initiatives – their solidarity groups and organizations – are uniquely functional and supportive to communities and nations, but they are endangered.

Women's capacities for co-operative action were a large part of the reason for identifying them as the 'backbone of rural development'. They organized themselves for wide-ranging purposes: mutual savings and loan systems, house construction and improvement, co-operative farming and marketing, collecting money for scholarships, starting nursery centres and installing water supplies.[13]

In rural areas, reciprocal service was the common basis of solidarity groups. In market-trading regions, such as West Africa, women joined to provide cash when needed, to regulate trading practices, and to stabilize prices among themselves with systems for penalties built in. They also provided child care and maternity services for members. Whilst both women and men undertook community voluntary work, such work – including the construction of farm-to-market roads, schools, health clinics, and latrines – remained largely dependent on women's labour. In other words, it continued to be women who most often performed the allotted family service and the food-for-work labour.

'The associations of market women in West Africa are outstanding for wielding political clout from an economic base,' said the ECA. Yet, 'women's participation with men, and in their own organizations, does not on the whole carry the strength of that of men'. This was because women lagged behind men in formal and non-formal education and training, and in access to resources. Women were also 'so heavily taxed physically and psychologically that they [had] little time or energy to put to changing their situations'.[14]

The reality was that, despite the very substantial accomplishments of women's groups, and their potential as vehicles for meaningful change, their initiatives were endangered because the women lacked specialized skills. New government policies, technical resources, involvement of younger (educated) women, and a rising national consciousness of women's work for development were among the changes required to increase the returns on the efforts made by solidarity groups and organizations.

3. Transformed attitudes

Attitudes of both men and women towards women often blocked the progress of women as a whole and the progress of the nation.

Attitudes that impacted on 'women's self-image and men's perception of the role and status of women' were seen as the fundamental obstacle that resulted in women being overlooked or ignored by developers.[15] Those ingrown attitudes continually reinforced the conservative mentality that many women and girls shared in common. The result was a passive acceptance of the limitations of their traditional roles and a hesitancy to try new fields.

Among the underlying causes of such outlooks, which seemed to grow more inflexible over time, were 'the economic realities of the subsistence economy, cultural and religious traditions, and the beliefs and practices of early European traders, colonial administrators and missionaries'.[16]

Figure 4.1 depicts the most prevalent attitudes that were seen to build barriers to women's progress. The ECA's hope was that, by publishing and disseminating such a diagram, change in or modification of attitudes would occur, especially 'if sufficiently compelling alternatives were presented and appropriate measures adopted'.[17] The ECA highlighted these specific attitudinal roadblocks:

— that productive tasks in subsistence sectors – for example, provision of water and fuel, food production and processing and distribution of foods and goods – could not be valued in the GNP[18]
— that the active labour force for employment was predominantly male[19]
— that the employment of women would take jobs away from the men who were responsible for family support[20]
— that African women's work was traditionally limited to the home
— that relieving the burdens of women would leave them idle.

All the evidence available to the ECA at that time showed that each of those entrenched attitudes had no basis in reality. It was already widely recognized that women were responsible for most of the processes relating to domestic food availability in a large percentage of countries, and that they frequently shared in the field work for cash crop production as well. Despite that common understanding, however, women were still identified as 'unpaid family labourers'.

As far as taking jobs away from men was concerned, it was an already established fact that employment in Africa depended far more heavily 'on

TIME TO GIVE EARLY EDUCATION TO THEIR CHILDREN

LEISURE

PARTICIPATION IN SOCIAL AND COMMUNITY ACTIVITIES

ACCESS TO LOANS AND CREDIT

PARTICIPATION IN NATIONAL PLANNING

LITERACY

FORMAL AND NON-FORMAL EDUCATION

VOCATIONAL AND TECHNICAL TRAINING

WAGE EMPLOYMENT AND MONEY-EARNING OPPORTUNITIES

DECISION-MAKING IN FAMILY AND COMMUNITY

TIME AND LABOUR-SAVING TECHNOLOGY

TRADITIONAL VALUES AND PRACTICES

IMPORTED VALUES AND PRACTICES

Figure 4.1 Barriers to progress for women: traditional and imported values and practices create attitudes which confine women within their traditional roles and deprive many of wider opportunities.
Source: Women of Africa; Today and Tomorrow, ECA, Addis Ababa, 1975, p. 22.

the creation of ... possibilities for new jobs through teaching new skills than on the existence of "jobs"'. Those skills were particularly needed by the many women who were solely responsible for the support of their extended households.

So long as women's work continued to be seen through the Victorian lens as limited to the home – an attitude that the ECA found 'absurdly unrealistic' – the ECA and others realized that development would be held back. Women would continue to be taught only such things as sewing rather than also acquiring the new skills they needed for successful farming. And rather than being left idle if they were relieved of such burdens as water portage, women could instead turn their energy and labour to more productive use. In fact, the ECA observed, efficient and easily available water supplies would enhance crop production, small animal husbandry and human health.

4. Productivity and social progress

The failure to acknowledge women's economic activity put brakes on the development process.

Women's traditional roles in economic activities were 'neither evident nor even acknowledged in the modern sectors of agriculture, industry, commerce and government', and their representation in areas influenced by science and technologies and the money economy ranged in most countries 'from token participation to invisibility'.[21] Not only was the efficiency of production affected by that oversight, but the whole fabric of life was weakened – from families to the labour force to society as a whole. Opportunities that might have brought change were allowed to slip away.

a. Economic productivity was depressed. The ECA Women's Programme contained the following assertion:

> Few persons would argue against the estimate that women were responsible for 60–80% of the agricultural labour supplied on the continent; that women formed the majority of the commercial sector in many African towns and cities, and that they contributed much to the self-help projects of rural development programmes.[22]

Based on these realities, and using Kenya as an example, the ECA illustrated how productivity was depressed. Kenya's Million Acre Settlement Scheme of the mid-1960s had provided only men with the opportunity to become landholders and to join co-operatives. In reality, women were the ones who grew and marketed pyrethrum in that region and their profits paid their families' expenses. As a result of the settlement scheme, however, the co-operatives took a share of the women's profits and gave the rest to the husbands because they were the landholders and co-operative members. Pyrethrum production fell, which affected the Kenyan economy, and fingers were pointed at 'those peasant farmers'. More careful examination showed, however, that the women growers went on strike to protest the fallacy of the Scheme.[23]

The problem was not confined to Kenya. The Women's Programme determined that wherever women suffered from inappropriately planned development programmes or from being deprived of modern skills to increase productivity and profits – whether in family production, in wage employment, in self-employment or as unskilled school leavers – the whole economy was adversely affected. Inefficiency resulted.[24]

b. The needs of the younger generation were neglected. Women by and large were responsible for the support of their families and used their income to meet their children's needs. When this income was inadequate, children experienced deprivation. Money was not the only factor, however. Because women had to work many hours a day, and because they were frequently pregnant, they had neither the time nor the strength to care for or to educate toddlers during the formative years.[25]

The ECA Women's Programme identified the root of the problem: it rested on the age-old division of labour by gender. Young girls were often not enrolled in school or were forced to leave because they were needed at home. Whilst they carried water for the family in smaller pots, walking behind their mothers, and worked beside their mothers on the farm, the boys were excused from such chores so that they could study and do homework.[26] Generations of young girls continued to grow up without an adequate education or marketable skills. In their search for economic security, some turned to prostitution, and unwanted pregnancies often resulted.[27]

Such realities led the only woman delegate to the Food and Agriculture Organization's Seventh Regional Conference to issue this challenge to the men who were present:

> We want nurseries; we want child care centres. When we work in the fields, we have to work with babies on our backs. It is harmful for both mother and child.[28]

Since the conference as a whole had already acknowledged that women did in fact produce most of Africa's food, she knew her demands were legitimate.

c. Half of the available labour force might be driven out of economic production. Existing information suggested that 'except for the few who were privileged with secondary or higher education, the situation of women and girls was improving only slightly, stagnating or deteriorating as modern life and modern technology created their impact on Africa'.[29]

Table 4.2 Participation in marketing according to sex

Area	Male (%)	Female (%)
Copperbelt (Zambia) (late 1950s)	59	41
Rhodesia (late 1950s)	majority in larger markets	majority in smaller markets
N. Somalia (late 1950s)	—	women dominate the open markets
Hausa (Nigeria) (late 1950s)	men dominate the public markets	women trade from their homes
Dakar (Senegal) (1959)	40	60
Brazzaville (Congo) (1963)	34	66
Nigeria (1963)	30	70 (of petty traders)
Ghana (1960)	16	84
Dahomey (1967)	11	89

Source: The Data Base for Discussion on the Interrelations Between the Integration of Women in Development, Their Situation and Population Factors in Africa, ECA, Addis Ababa 1974.

For example, women depended heavily on petty trade for their incomes, as shown in Table 4.2, because very few of them were privileged to have a secondary or higher level of education. And yet, as modern life and technology impacted on African society, women traders and the market women were 'in danger of being squeezed out of business by big commercial undertakings'.[30]

Between 1950 and 1963, the percentage of women in commerce decreased from 84% to 70% in Nigeria alone.[31] The Young Women's Christian Association (YWCA) of West Africa noted that trading was an undesirable option for women but there were no others; there were 'no noticeable new openings for women's employment'.[32] It was also observed that economies that were pulling themselves up by their bootstraps and families that were living in sub-standard conditions simply could not afford to let productive members of the labour force be withdrawn or forced out. 'It is small profit for a developing economy if the gains made in male productivity are neutralized by losses in the productivity of females.'[33]

d. Opportunities for development were missed. What had become evident to the ECA was that, if women had received training and other assistance, they would have been able to cut their labour in half while doubling their productivity at the same time. The potential for rural development and transformation had not been realized because women lacked appropriate resources. The fragmentation of women's land holdings had begun when land consolidation and settlement schemes were instituted; the best lands were consigned to cash cropping, and men obtained title deeds. In densely populated areas, women's plots were often miles apart and were usually so small that they had to be cultivated by hand.[34]

Other opportunities for development were missed because women were offered courses in European-style home economics but not skills for farming, small animal husbandry and trading. Poorly planned schemes were introduced that succeeded only in adding more burdens to already over-worked women.[35] For example, poultry raising was introduced to a rural community without plans for an adequate water supply, despite the fact that many extra litres of water were needed for the chickens each day. The task of fetching that supply fell to the women and significantly reduced their productivity.[36]

e. The social goals of development were not achieved. As men were forced to migrate to towns or plantations in search of wage labour, women increasingly became the sole support of the family at home. Divorce and separation became much more common. Even when the husbands did not leave, rural women were under a great deal of strain. There was no underutilized labour; quite the contrary. 'Excessive claims press upon their time ... leading to low incomes,' the ECA noted, and it added: 'There is the ever-present risk of the calamity which may make it no longer possible to cope.'[37]

A great deal of tension was also created by the divison of labour in cash crop economies. The income from cocoa, for example, was monopolized by men even though the women contributed to its production. The ECA described how that arrangement created tension in the family, because it 'led to the woman being permanently in the supplicant situation of dependence on the husband'.[38] Women were no better off in the towns. As noted above, many of them turned to prostitution, which further weakened the traditional family unit.

f. The rural–urban imbalance was exacerbated. This was a final, unforeseen negative impact resulting from the neglect of women's interests. With male off-farm migration, women became heads of household and farm managers. The result was that agricultural production was left to one, ...her than two adults in as many as one-third of rural families. Ironically, this was occurring at a time when agricultural production had become the primary emphasis of African governments, due to the near-disastrous years of favouring export crops to the neglect of food production. It was also the time when resources such as fertilizers and seeds went mostly to men, the land owners. As the Women's Programme noted, no planner would have chosen such consequences.

5. Institution building

The spheres of participation, grassroots solidarity, transforming attitudes and augmenting productivity needed sustained, long-term institutional support at national and regional levels.[39]

After listening to African women, the ECA judged that a combination of institutional approaches was needed: first, special institutions directed solely to women and, second, putting pressure on existing institutions of governments and United Nations organizations that were supposed to be, but were not, catering to both men and women.

In regard to new institutions with specific concern for women, the Women's Programme gave priority to two. First, a regional training and research centre for women was proposed. It would be the focal point for the mobilization of African women, to broaden their horizons and to strengthen their skills. As such it would serve as a corrective to the neglect of women's interests by development programmes. That centre's long-range general objective would be to enable member states of the region to make full use of their human resources for development ... by offering women more education and training, and by involving them in the planning and execution of development activities.[40]

The second type of institution proposed was at national level. Governments should establish national commissions that would examine and evaluate women's contributions to development and would study areas where their participation could be strengthened. Such commissions would develop and promote programmes 'to integrate women in all sectors of national development' and take legislative and other measures against taboos and customs that discriminated against women.[41] There would also be technical women's bureaux within government structures, to serve as the secretariats of the commissions.

From policy premises to programmes

The early development schemes, for the most part based on international theories, had had little effect on the endemic conditions of poverty, underemployment, illiteracy. As the schema for new programmes, ECA made use of the five policy premises it had identified from its study of the recommendations of African women and from the evidence it had accumulated. New premises would be added to keep step with the

continent's increasing realization that political independence was not automatically accompanied by economic independence. It also became clearer
over time that processes external to societies and nations impacted heavily
upon gender relations and upon the effectiveness of development initiatives
in economic, political and family spheres. Those issues would begin to get
comprehensive consideration in the second half of the decade in the
ATRCW's policy document *The New International Economic Order: What Roles
for Women?*[42]

Notes

1. UN Statistical Office, *The World's Women: 1970–1990*, United Nations, New
York, 1991, pp. 50–51.

2. J. Riby-Williams, 'Opening Address by Chief, Human Resources Development
Division, on behalf of the ECA', Rabat, 1971.

3. Ibid. pp. 6 and 7. Thirty-six new African countries joined the United Nations
in the 1950s and 1960s.

4. The posts were financed by SIDA; the co-author of this volume, Dr Margaret
Snyder, was appointed in 1971 as ECA Regional Aviser and was the senior responsible officer for the Women's Programme/ATRCW until Mary Tadesse
(Ethiopia) was appointed as ATRCW Chief in 1976. The second SIDA post was
filled by Daria Tesha, former Tanzanian secondary-school headmistress, in 1972.

5. ECA, 'Factors Affecting Education, Training and Work Opportunities for
Girls and Women Within the Context of Development', ECA, Addis Ababa, 1971.

6. See Annexe 14 for a complete list of documents of the ECA Women's
Programme and the ATRCW.

7. Few former colonies had census data, and scant research about women had
been done at the time: hence the dearth of data for planning purposes.

8. ECA, 'Women and National Development in African Countries: Some Profound Contradictions', ECA, Addis Ababa, 1976, p. 1. The document was prepared
for the Ford Foundation.

9. 'Factors Affecting Education, Training and Work Opportunities … ', note 5,
p. 20.

10. Ibid., note 8, para. 2.

11. 'Women: the Neglected Human Resources for African Development', *Canadian Journal of African Studies (CJAS)*, Vol. 6, No. 2, 1972. See also Rebecca Grant
and Kathleen Newland, *Gender and International Relations*, Open University Press,
Buckingham, 1991. See also Fred Harbison, 'A Human Resource Approach to the
Development of African Nations'. Preliminary draft, Princeton University, January
1971. Human resource development was a priority at the turn of the decade.

12. ECA, *Women of Africa: Today and Tomorrow*, ECA, Addis Ababa, 1975.

13. ECA/FAO/SIDA, *Women and Rural Institutions*, ECA, Addis Ababa, 1972. It
is interesting to note that some scholars who support and value women's solidarity
groups also adopt the apparently contradictory position of being against 'separate
women's projects' and women-specific institutions. See Anne Marie Goetz, 'Feminism and the Claim to Know', in Grant and Newland, p. 139.

14. *Women and Rural Institutions*.

15. 'Factors Affecting Education, Training and Work Opportunities', p. 3.
16. *CJAS*, Vol. 6, No. 2, p. 360.
17. 'Factors Affecting Education, Training and Work Opportunities'.
18. Some progress has been made in this area of valuing women's work, but much work remains.
19. See Annexe 3: 'Economic Participation', for data on the active labour force for selected years.
20. ECA/FAO/SIDA, *The Impact of Modern Life and Technology on Women's Economic Role: Implications for Planning*, ECA, Addis Ababa, 1972.
21. Ibid.
22. *CJAS*, Vol. 6, No. 2, 1972, pp. 359–70.
23. ECA, 'Women and National Development', p. 37.
24. ECA/FAO/SIDA, *Impact of Modern Life and Technology*, p. 9.
25. See ECA, 'Women and National Development', p. 23. Over 73% of wage-employed women took care of children and supported their parents, parents-in-law and other relatives.
26. Ibid., p. 29.
27. Ibid., p. 37.
28. Ibid., p. 11.
29. Ibid., p. 8, Table 3.
30. Recommendation 24, Rabat Conference, 1971.
31. *CJAS*, Vol. 6, No. 2, 1972.
32. Ibid.
33. ECA, 'Women and National Development', p. 30.
34. Addis Ababa 1969; and Rabat 1971.
35. *CJAS*, Vol. 6, No. 2, 1972, p. 5.
36. Ibid., p. 9.
37. ECA, 'Women and National Development', p. 40.
38. Ibid., p. 14.
39. Addis Ababa 1969; and Rabat 1971.
40. ECA, 'Comprehensive Project Description: Pan-African Training and Research Centre for Women and African Women's Development Task Force', ECA, Addis Ababa. M75–629, 1975.
41. ECA, *Recommendations of Regional Meetings for Africa on the Role of Women in Development*, Addis Ababa, 075-183, 1975.
42. ECA, *The New International Economic Order: What Roles for Women?*, Addis Ababa, 1977.

Economic roles of women: conversations in Swaziland

Q: Swaziland's rural development project for women started in 1975 with assistance from the ATRCW, the UN, the UNDP and the Netherlands Government. It began small, but has grown and trained 3,000 women at five centres countrywide. When the revolving loan fund was introduced with UNIFEM grants, 96% of Swazi women could not get credit. What are your views on the project?

Christabel Motsa, Ministry of Agriculture: The reason the Economic Roles of Women project at Nfonjeni got started was the conscientization, the workshopping that preceded it. So by the time the project came in 1975, society was almost ready to accept it. And it was accepted because it started with traditional skills. The things that were really significant, like the revolving loan fund, the brick making, welding and shoe making were added on gradually as time went on. The project went forward because we had a dynamic project manager, Linda Vilakati, who was willing to talk about women and development anywhere.

We had been doing a lot of training in different skills, in a variety of agencies. But the women and development project, with its revolving loan fund component, was such a breakthrough for Swazi women! I have seen that since that project, financial institutions have been more willing to provide loans to women.

Mphaya Simelane, Agriculture Manager, Swaziland Development and Savings Bank: The bank had been lending to small growers, but the majority of them were men. In the past, women had to get their husband's consent and go through a lot of red tape before they could get a loan. But under the Economic Roles of Women project they could borrow, they had the training they needed.

The bank has learned from those experiences that peer pressure works. Now we are encouraging people to borrow as groups. Not just women – it started with women – but also men. We no longer rely on cattle as security, we rely on group pressure.

Women borrow to get mortar machines for making bricks, and use the bricks to build houses. Their own houses. Quite a number of them are involved in building schools, because women want their children in school. If it wasn't for my mother, for example, I would not have gone to school.

We now have shown people that women can be involved; we can lend to women. What is essential now is to take them a step further, to produce for a specific market.

Tars Makama, Under-secretary, Ministry of Home Affairs: The

project has been very, very effective. It has influenced policy. In Swaziland we feel that because of various factors which are beyond our control in the developing world, if our women are strong enough, then certain things in the economy will be uplifted, and the social aspect of life will be enhanced.

Isabella Katamzi, Under-secretary, Ministry of Economic Planning and Development: In Swaziland, you have to look at two levels when you ask how women define development. In the Swazi national land, the subsistence sector in particular, what is important is to have your house and have your family taken care of with all its needs. Education is a priority. In the formal sector, the working class, most women are looking for security – securing a place within their profession, because they have got their basic needs.

As long as we have revolving funds like the one set up in the Economic Roles of Women project, opportunities will be there for the women to actually be emancipated and to be more part of development.

Senator Mary Mdziniso, first Swazi woman senator: Women today should do as much as they can to help their fellow women. If they are self-sufficient, they should not sit still and say everything is okay. They should think of their sisters, and see what can be done for women in the rural areas. If you develop alone, you say: 'I am all right.' That is not development.

Mbabane
November 1993

CHAPTER 5

PATH-BREAKING YEARS: FROM A FIVE-YEAR PROGRAMME TO A WOMEN'S CENTRE, 1971–1975

For the United Nations Second Development Decade, the 1970s, the purpose of development was 'to bring about sustained improvement in the well-being of the individual and bestow benefits on all'. That goal led to both micro and macro concerns. At the micro level, there was a new emphasis on people's basic needs and the elimination of poverty at the grassroots, where the vast majority of Africans found their livelihood. At the macro level there was a heightened awareness that the economic legacies of colonialism were not easily shaken off; attention then turned towards the international economic system. The regional women's conferences in Addis Ababa (1969) and Rabat (1971) set out initial guidelines for the ECA's work with women during the 1970s.

In 1971 the first of the two new staff positions relating solely to women and development was filled by Margaret Snyder. The second would be filled a year later by Daria Tesha of Tanzania. The design of a five-year programme which would correspond with the five-year plans of member states was given top priority. The programme would have to mesh the needs of African women with the abilities and the limited numbers of ECA staff, and be within the parameters of the ECA's function as a regional UN institution. The central purpose of the programme would be to effect 'the participation of women as human resources for national development', as the Rabat conference had insisted.[1]

The final plan evolved and was designated 'The Five Year Programme for Pre-Vocational and Vocational Training of Girls and Women Towards Their Full Participation in Development (1972–1976)'. Using the discussions held with governments and women's organizations as a basis, and combining them with the policy recommendations of regional meetings, the programme focused on efforts to address the issues facing African women. To that end, research and training projects were identified in sectors in which women were already active. Five major areas were targeted:

1. modernization and its impact on rural women
2. women in wage employment

3. self-employed women in marketing, industry and the services
4. pre-vocational and vocational training of school-leaver girls
5. national planning with women as resources for development.

Each project would involve workshops and conferences, and in those
areas where data and information were scarce, studies would be commissioned. Training courses would also be provided, and pilot projects
would be established.

The Five Year Programme became the foundation for the ECA
Women's Programme that was formally established within the Human
Resources Division of the ECA in 1972. It later served as the rationale for
the ECA once again to incorporate women's concerns into its overall
Programme of Work and Priorities for 1974–76. That decision was first
approved of in 1973 by the ECA's Conference of Ministers and later by
ECOSOC at UN headquarters, which then invited all the UN economic
commissions to follow suit.[2]

Because it was at the cutting edge of the international women and
development movement, the Five Year Programme was perceived to be the
model for other developing regions. It was appended to the working
document for the UN Expert Group Meeting on Women in Economic
Development that the ECA's regional adviser attended in 1972. That historic
gathering was organized by Aida Gindy (Egypt) of the social development
staff at UN headquarters who had previously served at the ECA in Addis
Ababa. Its chief adviser was Ester Boserup (Denmark), whose landmark
book *Woman's Role in Economic Development* was noted above as a major
impetus to the women and development concept and movement. The
Chairman, globally recognized economist Sir Arthur Lewis, was then
President of the Caribbean Development Bank. Both Boserup and Lewis
had served on UN development planning bodies, and their fame added
prestige and importance to this first global women and development meeting
ever to be convened by the United Nations or any other organization.[3]

Closing the information gap: national studies on employment and womenpower

Planning for the full participation of women in national development
called for a solid base which had to include research findings, government
statistics, and the exact number of women and men who comprised the
active labour force. That women in rural areas were seldom counted as
active labourers was a constant annoyance to ECA staff.

> If both quantitative and qualitative factors were taken into consideration, for
> example, if actual hours and types of agricultural labour were measured, if
> seasonal labour were considered, and if women's dual role as housewife and
> farmer were accepted, the active labour force data would be different.[4]

Table 5.1 The division of rural labour by gender (% of total labour in hours)

	Men	Women
Cuts down the forest; stakes out the fields	95	5
Turns the soil	70	30
Plants the seeds and cuttings	50	50
Hoes and weeds	30	70
Harvests	40	60
Transports crops home from the fields	20	80
Stores the crops	20	80
Processes the food crops	10	90
Markets the excess (including transport to market)	40	60
Trims the tree crops	90	10
Carries the water and fuel	10	90
Cares for domestic animals and cleans the stables	50	50
Hunts	90	10
Feeds and cares for the young, the men and the aged	5	95

Note: From numerous studies carried out by anthropologists, sociologists and extension workers in rural areas of Africa, we can roughly estimate the division of rural labour into tasks for men and for women as above. This division of labour shows that men are almost universally responsible for the initial clearing of the new fields. But from that time, women share or more often take over the work of sowing, weeding, harvesting, storage, processing and marketing.
Source: *Women of Africa: Today and Tomorrow*, ECA, Addis Ababa, 1975, p. 6.

In other words, the staff maintained that it would no longer be possible to say that 55% of men and only 25% of women in Africa were economically active if the female labour force in the rural areas was counted. When the non-market labour of women is valued, the difference between men's and women's economic activity shrinks. Table 5.1 on the division of rural labour by gender and Table 5.2 on economic activity and work by gender in Côte d'Ivoire illustrate that fact. The ECA provided data in the format now titled 'gender and development', a method of quantification that became a vital tool for the programme.

Whenever and wherever there were gaps in the research on women that related to the Five Year Programme, they were identified and listed. That system encouraged further research on women's changing roles in the economy and society and formed the foundation for national planning action. One such list from 1972 illustrates some of the subject areas needing additional data:

— hours and types of agricultural and household labour, by gender
— decision making in the family on fertilizers, seeds, hired labour; family activities like school fees and transport; household improvements like technologies for milling, lighting, cooking

Table 5.2 Time spent in work by gender in rural Côte d'Ivoire (hours per week)

| | Market work | | Non-market economic activity | Total | Unpaid housework | Total work |
	Wages work	Own account and family				
Women	–	11.9	10.3	22.2	25.4	47.6
Men	–	20.3	3.0	23.3	4.2	27.5

Notes: Includes unpaid work in family enterprises and subsistence agriculture and other unremunerated economic activity in households such as water carrying, fuel gathering and own construction.
Source: Statistical Office of the United Nations Secretariat, *The World's Women: 1970–1990*, United Nations, New York, 1991.

— land use and consolidation of holdings
— traditional and modern co-operative and savings associations; reasons for their success or failure; and their potential further economic uses
— markets for small-scale rural industries; availability of credit, of expertise for design, management, and marketing
— types of labour-saving technologies for agriculture, milling, water portage, storage, food preservation, transport to markets
— the situation of the school-leaver girl: her migration, residence, means of support, opportunities for continuing education
— the situation of the market woman: use of co-operatives and loan societies; access to credit; bookkeeping methods; assessment of market fluctuations
— relevance of training in home economic to the most pressing needs of women
— wage-employed women: data on absenteeism, maternity leave, levels of responsibility, promotion, equal pay for equal work; attitudes of employers, superiors, fellow workers and women themselves; responsibility of working women for support of self, children, other dependants.

The indispensible foundation for the Five Year Programme was a series of Country Womanpower Studies that was requested at Rabat and approved by the Conference of Ministers.[5] The studies detailed the work of African girls and women in trade, business, industry and agriculture, and the pre-vocational and vocational training opportunities that were available to them. Research assistant Classina Kidane Mariam compiled the series of forty reports; research assistant Nellie Okello analysed them. The resources that were used for the womanpower studies included government annuals, ECA mission reports, and fugitive university studies. The training opportunities detailed ranged from small-scale self-help projects to university degree programmes.

The documents went beyond isolated statistics on programmes, however, to provide background on the many factors that impact on the types of training available for women in any given country. Some of the factors resulted from the attitudes discussed in an earlier chapter, such as traditional and cultural barriers to women's education, training and employment. Other factors were: national demographic characteristics; school enrolment statistics; economic conditions; and, importantly, national development programmes and policies.

The studies were primarily intended as the knowledge base for the Five Year Programme, but they also served for vocational guidance purposes and were used by agencies interested in initiating programmes to analyse the training situation in Africa. They provided the formerly absent and much-needed data and knowledge base behind the series of technical and advocacy documents that set out the ECA's policy on women in Africa between 1971 and 1974.

A brief look at some of the forty studies reveals considerable variations in the numbers and types of vocational training programmes available at the time they were written. There were trends in most countries, however, toward expanding opportunities, and a growing awareness of the importance of training women as well as men. The compilation and circulation of the reports about different countries generated further interest in providing vocational training to women.

An important breakthrough in establishing a knowledge base on women in Africa occurred in the employment sector with the co-operation of the International Labour Organization (ILO). At that time, the concept of including unpaid women workers in labour force data and in employment studies was still very new. But in 1972, the ILO turned to the ECA Women's Programme Unit for assistance in gathering information on the actual and potential economic activity of women in Ethiopia, as a component of their 'Report to the Imperial Ethiopian Government of the Exploratory Employment Policy Mission'. It was the first time women were to be included from the outset in a labour force study in Africa.[6]

In response to the ILO request, a report – Towards Full Employment of Women in Ethiopia – was prepared by the Regional Adviser and Daria Tesha, the Social Affairs Officer and deputy officer for the Women's Programme.[7] Information on women was extremely scarce in Ethiopia, and data on their economic activity was even more rare.

Drawing on a wide range of sources, the staff pulled together facts about the division of labour by gender in the diverse rural zones of Ethiopia, the sociological factors affecting women's employment, the wage employment of women, and education and training statistics. In doing so, they provided awareness of the importance of including women in 'labour and employment' studies.

The report highlighted the vast amount of economic activity performed by women and refuted the misconception that women competed with men in the labour market by demonstrating that the work performed by women complemented that done by men. Consonant with the Women's Programme policy, to seek the well-being of the whole society while directing its operations to women, the report also pointed out the importance of developing strategies that would raise the income of all adults.[8]

The Full Employment Mission in Ethiopia was followed by a similar mission in the Sudan. There, the Women's Programme's researcher and lawyer, Nellie Okello (Kenya), was assisted by a Sudanese team. They drafted 'Employment of Women in the Sudan' for the ILO Comprehensive Employment Strategy Mission of 1974.[9]

Consultations with member states

With the Five Year Programme in place, and with the country studies that comprised its knowledge base almost completed, the next step was to fulfil the research and training provisions. A mission to Kenya, Zambia, Lesotho, Botswana and Swaziland sought the advice of government officials and NGOs on training needs in that sub-region. In addition, the mission responded to the request of the Chair of the Kenya National Council of Women for assistance in establishing a women's bureau.

What the mission discovered was exciting. Training programmes were expanding and expectations of a greater role for women in the economy were embodied in ambitious training plans in most of the countries visited. In Lesotho, the only country in Africa where women were on average better educated than men, women were found to be the most enthusiastic and motivated students on courses such as horticulture and poultry raising. A course on rural economy designed specifically for women included extension methods, home industry, statistics, agricultural economics and community development, in addition to the more traditional home economics subjects.

In Swaziland, women were only just beginning to recognize their own entrepreneurial potential but observers had high hopes, stating that 'handicrafts are the kindergarten of economic development' because they can lead to micro and small-scale enterprise. Kozi Noge made such a transition with her fashion business Swazi Flame. In general, however, all countries, especially Botswana and Zambia, began to recognize that their efforts to train women were constrained by the poor levels of education attained by girls, and by the inadequate national infrastructure. The mission, by compiling information on the visions and priorities of people in the field, and on the constraints that they faced, was later instrumental in the development of the ECA's training and seminar programmes.

Access to scientific and technological resources

Increased access to available scientific and technological resources was necessary on the one hand to lessen women's burdens and on the other to augment the productivity of their labours. The ECA noted that women did work for development but the existing situation indicated that, while they had to function in a technical and monetary economy, 'few of them had access either to the skills or to the resources to do so most effectively, most usefully for themselves, their families and their countries'.[10]

It was clear that if those skills and resources were made available to women the burdens of their labour would be lifted and productivity would increase. Concomitantly, women would be able to spend more time and resources on their families, thus improving the social aspect of national development. Without that access, women's labour would remain unproductive and exhausting. During the busy agricultural seasons, rural women's sixteen-hour working day would continue to be filled by such tedious tasks as walking to the fields, collecting firewood and water, grinding grains, cooking and other domestic chores, in addition to the tasks of ploughing, hoeing or weeding. The ECA recognized that an improvement in the input:output ratio of women's labour called for education and training, employment, scientific and technological innovations, access to capital, plus health and family planning services. This broad scope of possible training areas was prioritized by reference to existing programmes.

The particular issue of access to education and training had been a high priority at the Rabat conference, which called for radical reform in the content of training courses. 'While stressing the importance of training girls and women for better home and family life, there is a parallel necessity for vocational training for engagement in gainful economic activities,' delegates said.[11] Such training was especially important for women who had to depend on petty commerce for the entire family income, and others like them who also lacked literacy and economic skills, and consequently feared to risk modern commercial practices.

Agricultural production was the paramount concern of the region overall, and over 90% of the female labour force lived and worked in rural areas. As the ECA noted: 'if rural areas are to be transformed, the women who are cultivating them need assistance'.[12] As male migration continued, women's dependency ratios rose on the farms where they remained to care for their dependants and to produce the family food. Ironically, ownership of the land they tilled eluded them since acreages were awarded to male 'heads of household', as noted earlier.

Even when both spouses worked on the farm, the pressures on women were enormous. 'The less agriculture is mechanized, the more women are employed in it'; and yet when agriculture is mechanized, the 'toilsome

Table 5.3 Women in many developing regions must spend hours each week drawing and carrying water

	Hours per week
Botswana, rural areas	5.5
Burkina Faso, Zimtenga region	4.4
Côte d'Ivoire, rural farmers	4.4
Ghana, northern farms	4.5
Kenya villages: dry season	4.2
wet season	2.2
Mozambique, villages: dry season	15.3
wet season	2.9
Senegal, farming village(s)	17.5

Source: The World's Women 1970–1990

handwork is relegated to women'.[13] For every gain, there seemed to be a setback. Evidence showed that the increase of acreage under cultivation when crop rotation was introduced obliged women to spend more time in the fields throughout the year. As a result it became more difficult for them to attend literacy classes and meetings on nutrition, child care, improved gardening and handicrafts.[14]

Data were also becoming available on the hours women and girls spent each week carrying water, which varied seasonally but ranged from 2.2 to

Table 5.4 Percentages and numbers of rural populations served with water

Country	% of population served with water	Population (1,000s)	
		served with water	not served with water
Cameroun	20	1.170	4.191
Dahomey	4	0.095	2.271
Ghana	11	0.820	6.631
Kenya	15	1.500	8.538
Lesotho	10.4	0.105	0.913
Liberia	5	0.050	0.906
Madagascar	3	0.180	6.022
Nigeria	10	5.605	50.444
Sierra Leone	10	0.229	2.065

Source: WHO, Community Water Supply: Report of a Seminar, Brazzaville 21–27 April 1971, AFR/EH/113–July 1971/WHO.

17.5 hours a week in some countries, as shown in Table 5.3.[15] The ECA charted the small percentages and numbers of rural populations that were served with water, as seen in Table 5.4.[16] Because of the magnitude of the water problem, women identified the types of technology that would relieve the burdens associated with portage, such as equipment for bore holes and wells. Their needs list also included maize mills, charcoal or kerosene stoves, better tools and methods of farming, as well as fertilizers, pesticides and good-quality seeds.[17]

With those issues and needs under consideration, and with nine out of ten women working in the countryside, training for rural life skills began to assume the highest priority for the ECA. The decision was clinched by Executive Secretary Gardiner's pungent and very practical illustration: 'There is no point in teaching our women to embroider pillows with "sweet dreams",' he said, 'when the malaria mosquitoes won't let our people sleep.'[18]

Training to improve the quality of rural life

The emphasis on rural training got more support shortly after the Women's Programme began to take root in the early 1970s. At that time, the ECA collaborated with the FAO and SIDA to sponsor a Seminar on Home Economics Development Planning for English-speaking Countries of Africa. That seminar in Addis Ababa was revolutionary in its critique of the prevailing home economics programmes which even FAO staff characterized as 'stitchin' and stirrin'.

The major ECA document challenged home economists, who were believed to have the greatest single vocational education influence on women in Africa, to reject the conventional wisdom by opening up discussions about women's economic activities. The document stressed the urgency of lifting women's burdens and making it possible to increase their productivity in the fields, the markets, and the home. It reminded seminar delegates that women were farmers who performed 60% to 80% of the agricultural work and who often bore the major responsibility for rural development. Calling for the labour-saving technologies that rural women had identified, such as water wells, fuel-saving stoves, fertilizers and improved seeds, the document repeated the ILO's radical 1971 statement that for rural women 'home economics education, while essential, is not enough'.[19]

A second document, on women and rural institutions, also broke new ground at the session with its breadth of information on women's grassroots rural solidarity groups. The paper accorded great respect to such groups and to other organizations that facilitated women's contributions to civil society, production, marketing and community self-help.

Immediately after the seminar, a second mission went to countries in eastern and southern Africa, this time to prepare governments and NGOs for the proposed 'itinerant training workshops' for trainers in home economics. The title 'home economics' was selected because it was acceptable to governments as a subject appropriate for women. The training content, however, was by no means totally traditional.

En route to the countries, a fortuitous airport meeting between the Regional Adviser and doctors Jean Delaney and W. Schulte of the FAO led to an agreement to reassign FAO senior staff person Jean Ritchie (Scotland) from a Uganda appointment that was endangered during the reign of Idi Amin. Ritchie first served as a faculty member for the nutrition and population components of the itinerant training workshops, then became a full member of the Women's Programme under FAO auspices, as its first Programmes for Better Family Living (PBFL) officer, financed by the United Nations Population Fund, UNFPA.[20] Ritchie and Delaney made very substantial and critical contributions to the Women's Programme and later to the ATRCW as two of its founders.

The first series of five itinerant training workshops took place consecutively in Ethiopia, Lesotho/Botswana, and Swaziland, and then in Tanzania and Somalia. The workshops were financed with an initial grant from the Netherlands, and a follow-up grant from the Federal Republic of Germany ($45,000 and DM125,000 respectively). They had as their primary objective the development of skilled and qualified trainers in home economics and other family-oriented programmes.

In organizing the workshops, the ECA became a pioneer in the UN system by insisting that non-governmental organizations should nominate one fourth of the total trainees. This move was exceptional in a UN system that concentrated almost exclusively on governments.[21] The trainees included teachers in rural development and co-operative institutes, nurses, government officials from community development and agriculture ministries, and secretaries of national women's organizations.

Two or more national trainers organized the courses, and in addition to the international team of four persons selected by the ECA, representatives of government ministries of planning assisted in the discussions on the priorities for national development plans.[22] Successful local entrepreneurs such as Kozi Noge of Swazi Flame and a widowed shopkeeper in Monze, Zambia, brought their inspirational life stories to the workshops, and motivated a number of trainees to venture into the business world. The pioneering international training team for the first five countries consisted of Janet Asare (Ghana), and Asmeret Hagos (Ethiopia), with Women's Programme staff Ritchie and Snyder.

Curricula for the workshops expanded traditional home economics subjects by incorporating a broader spectrum of development concepts and methods. In addition to the relevant sections of the national development plans, agricultural productivity, co-operative principles, entrepreneurship, savings and credit societies and local leadership structures were considered as key ingredients for improving family nutrition and income levels.

Projects were developed by the international team, as needs arose. For example, in 1973 in Swaziland, where 48% of household heads are women, the UNDP Resident Representative, Hugh Greenidge, asked the senior team members to write up a rural industries programme for women. With a rough draft, he said, he could pin down enough monies, and the details could be filled in later. This was done, and it became the Nfonjeni Economic Roles of Women project under the initial leadership of a dynamic project leader, Linda Vilakati. The project included training, technologies, and an innovative credit system in the form of a community revolving loan fund that the Voluntary Fund for the UN Decade for Women (later renamed UNIFEM) financed in 1978.

The credit fund idea came from the only extension worker at the time, Dumsile, and it was the first such fund ever provided under the United Nations Development Programme (UNDP) system which channelled UNIFEM's grants to the field. A decade later the credit fund was deposited as a guarantee cum risk fund at the Swaziland Development and Savings Bank, which loans out four times its value. The project employed thirty-seven Swazi women and men by 1988. Swazis and ATRCW staff had designed a small experimental project that now works nationwide, defying the critics of 'those small-scale women's projects', and raising questions as to whether investments in projects with women were ever adequate to the task.

Christabel Motsa, from the Ministry of Agriculture, who assisted an evaluation of the project, spoke to the issue of scale and other effectiveness factors of the project:

> I do believe that starting small is sometimes not the worst thing you can do. Swaziland is a patriarchal society; here gender roles are played out very significantly, much more strongly than in other societies. That made it very difficult to start a women in development project in the first place. But lucky for us, it did start. I think that was a result of conscientization, the workshopping that preceded the establishment of the project itself. So by the time the project really came in 1975, society was almost ready to accept that kind of thing. Some of its features that are really significant, like the revolving loan fund, the brick making and welding and shoe making, other non-traditional activities were added gradually as time went on.[23]

The under-secretary of the Ministry of Home Affairs, Tars Makama, found the Nfonjeni project 'very very effective' and an impetus for activites such as piggery, agriculture and sewing in other parts of the country.[24]

The eagerness of many women to enrol in the ECA training workshops testified to the dearth of opportunities for adult learning that women faced in the early 1970s. In Somalia, for example, despite the decision made between government and the ECA that there would be a maximum of thirty English-speaking participants on the course, the international training team found fifty Somali participants poised to begin; only a handful of them spoke the course language. The team managed to conduct the workshop by adding some Italian, some Tigrinia and *ad hoc* sign language.[25]

The closing speaker at the Zambia training course echoed the demand for training programmes that had been made at ECA regional conferences held in the 1960s and early 1970s. Then she challenged the ECA team to establish an Africa regional training centre for women, reviving the recommendations of the 1969 and 1971 regional conferences.

Back at ECA headquarters in Addis Ababa, that challenge won additional support from Riby-Williams, from Tesha, and from Executive Secretary Gardiner himself. With some studied impatience, Gardiner instructed the training team to go ahead and prepare a detailed design for the proposed Pan-African Research and Training Centre. He then asked them to develop his own idea of creating a 'volunteer corps' among skilled African women; the corps was eventually named the African Women's Volunteer Task Force.[26]

In its annual report to the Conference of Ministers for 1973–74, the ECA was able to announce the completion of three itinerant training workshops.[27] By 1977, following preparatory missions by Jean Ritchie, Suzanne Prosper (Mauritius) and Danielle Bazin (Haiti), twenty-two countries had completed workshops.[28]

These workshops became a vehicle for the World Council of Churches' Commission of the Churches on International Affairs to put pressure on the President of the World Bank, Robert McNamara, on behalf of peasant women. Dr Richard Fagley, representing the commission at UN headquarters, began an exchange of correspondence with McNamara in late 1973. Using the ECA/FAO workshop report that identified development strategies, Fagley continued over time to remind McNamara about the neglected status of peasant women in rural development.

Micro-enterprise

Beyond rural development, a second priority area of the Five Year Programme was employment – both wage and self-employment, although opportunities for the former were slim indeed (see Annexe 3). A special area for research and action that was identified was that of micro-enterprise: handicrafts and other small industries. Through such enterprise, innumerable rural and urban women gained incomes to support their dependants.

In 1973, when a coalition of organizations, including the ILO, SIDA, the ECA and the World YWCA, joined to organize and support a

Workshop on Women's Participation in Handicrafts and Other Small Scale Industries, in Kitwe, Zambia, there was little documented information on women's participation in small enterprises.[29] The method used to solve that problem illustrates the ECA Women's Programme's overall approach, namely to seek information from the field. Today it might be called rapid rural appraisal, or participatory action research.

Tesha of the ECA, Noge of Swazi Flame and Lettie Stuart of Sierra Leone undertook a survey of projects already active in the sector. They visited and interviewed women at a total of 112 projects in 14 countries to prepare for the workshop.[30] The surveys they conducted were the first to pull together information on such projects from around the continent. The results provided an analytical basis for examining the issue of women's participation in the handicraft and small-industry sector, as well as for designing technical and training programmes for the promotion of micro-enterprise. The surveys became the starting point for discussions at the 1974 conference in Kitwe.

The final report on the surveys summarized the findings in certain categories. In the area of government policy, the researchers observed that women in the small-industry sector did not usually benefit from government programmes and policies. Government promotion of business and import substitution was not advantageous to women with small industries, and women active in that sector were usually excluded from co-operatives, loans and training opportunities, because they were not counted in the labour force.

Projects designed to help women involved in the handicraft and small-industry sector often fell short of their objectives for a number of reasons, according to the evaluators. They often lacked trained and committed personnel, and did not have the benefit of professional advice in areas such as production and quality control. They often failed to provide adequate or appropriate training opportunities to project beneficiaries. The beneficiaries themselves became discouraged when they were unable to find secure marketing outlets, or when they identified markets only to find themselves unable to meet demand.

In some instances, women entrusted their business to their sons or other male relatives, thereby limiting their own control over the business and restricting the potential for improvement. Women also tended to concentrate on home-based industries such as sewing, which meant that profitable opportunities such as making soap, furniture, jewellery, shoes, and carpets were not explored or exploited.

In short, the researchers identified a number of problems that limited the effectiveness of existing small-industry projects. The current need for training in management, organization, quality control and, most important, marketing, was verified, as well as the eventual need to replace imported materials with locally produced products. Another important finding was that the expatriate advisers on whom a number of projects depended for technical assistance could be replaced if training programmes were developed for African staff.

The study demonstrated, and the Kitwe workshop concluded, that it is critical for government policies to give proper support to micro-enterprises as distinct from businesses of a larger scale. It suggested that those organizations already active in the field should be included in the design and planning of activities. The information not only provided the groundwork for further analysis and discussion but it also provided a foundation for future partnerships with organizations involved in promoting micro-industrial development for women.[31] Regrettably, it would be a decade before the development experts and planners gave very much attention to the needs and potential of the informal sector. Women's experience fell on deaf ears.

Co-operative approaches to small-scale industry became the subject of two additional workshops in the 1970s. The first, in Mombasa, Kenya, was co-sponsored with the International Co-operative Alliance (ICA). The second was organized by the ATRCW in Yaoundé, Cameroun. This series eventually prompted the ATRCW's design for the Joint ECA/ILO Handicrafts and Small Scale Industries Unit, which drew SIDA support.

Notes

1. As seen in Chapter 1, the human development theme has arisen again twenty years later.

2. The ECA Conference of Ministers, Res. 170 VIII. The programme was entitled Development of Skills and Job Opportunities for Girls and Women in Africa. See E/CN.14/591 1972–1973 para. 171, 23 February 1973. The activities set out included advisory services on vocational and technical training; establishment of national commissions and women's bureaux as a strategy to augment the participation of women in national development; country studies on pre-vocational and vocational training opportunities and institutions for girls and women; a directory of organizations concerned with the participation of women in development in Africa; itinerant national training and workshops for trainers in home economics; and training trainers and programme planners engaged in pilot projects for marketing and service industries. See also ECOSOC Resolution E/1682 (LII).

3. See Chapter 3.

4. ECA/FAO/SIDA, 'The Impact of Modern Life and Technology on Women's Role: Implications for Planning', ECA, Addis Ababa, 1972, p. 15.

5. The womanpower studies were officially titled 'Country Studies on Pre-Vocational and Vocational Training Opportunities for Girls and Women in African Countries'. They were incorporated in the ECA Programme of Work and Priorities for 1971–1973, together with an evaluative study of unemployment among school leavers and of secondary-school enrolment in relation to middle-level manpower requirements.

6. ECA, 'Towards Full Employment of Women in Ethiopia', Addis Ababa,

1972. The idea arose during the first ILO Full Employment Mission to Kenya, whose report took women into account, thanks to the assistance from, for example, Dr Ulla Olin of UNDP, who also invited and received the ECA regional adviser's contributions.

7. Tesha made history at the ECA and brought happiness to its women staff by claiming her husband as her dependant.

8. ECA, 'Towards Full Employment of Women in Ethiopia'.

9. ECA, 'Employment of Women in the Sudan', Addis Ababa, 1975.

10. ECA/FAO/SIDA, 'Impact of Modern Life', para. 26.

11. Ibid., pp. 15–16. The ECA put less emphasis on formal education in its operational activities because another United Nations organization, UNESCO, concentrated in that area.

12. Ibid., pp. 4, 5, 12.

13. Ibid., p. 3.

14. *Canadian Journal of African Studies (CJAS)*, Vol. 6, No. 2, Ottawa, 1972, p. 5.

15. UN Statistical Office, *The World's Women: 1970–1990*, United Nations, New York, 1991.

16. ECA, *The Data Base for Discussion of the Interrelations between the Integration of Women in Development, Their Situation and Population Factors*, Addis Ababa, 1974. E/CN. 14/SW/37. p. 57, Table 14.

17. ECA, *Women of Africa: Today and Tomorrow*, Addis Ababa, 1975, p. 58. Lest African women's view of the long-term societal purpose of development be overlooked, the ECA devised its own definition of the newly popular phrase 'the integration of women in development'. It was 'to have by legal right as well as to have access to available means for self-improvement and the improvement of the society', as stated in *The Data Base*, para. 25. This was a quite different use of the term than was common in United Nations circles at the time, because it indicated not just that women should enter existing, imperfect systems but that society itself needed to be changed if better lives were to be possible for everyone.

18. ECA, 'Women and Development in African Countries: Some Profound Contradictions', *African Studies Review*, XVIII, 1975.

19. ECA/FAO/SIDA, 1972 paras 2–5.

20. The Programme for Better Family Living (PBFL) was established because of the 'relationships between levels of living and family size, aiming at an integrated approach through existing national programmes to improve rural family well-being, by achieving food security and a better life for all families'.

21. Involving the NGO's pleased Executive Secretary Gardiner, who had become an admirer of OXFAM and who assigned the Regional Adviser of the Women's Programme the additional task of acting as Head of the ECA's newly established Voluntary Agencies Bureau.

22. The development plans of the individual participating countries were summarized by the ECA Women's Programme as part of the set of workshop training materials.

23. Interview with Christabel Motsa by Margaret Snyder in Mbabane, September 1993.

24. Interview in Mbabane of Mr Tars Makama by Margaret Snyder, September 1993.

25. Three of the trainers threatened the team leader with mutiny and immediate

return to Addis Ababa, but with the Tigrinia and Italian languages known by two of the trainers, and bits of English and a great deal of informal sign language adopted by all, the training went ahead and was by all accounts a successful workshop.

26. During the follow-up briefing on the recommendations of the first five itinerant training workshops, Gardiner read carefully through the Summary Recommendations – 'What are the Next Steps?' – which included the African Women's Development Task Force; he strengthened the text. Informal memo, Snyder to Riby-Williams, 4 October 1973.

27. ECA, *Annual Report 1973–1974*, Addis Ababa. E/CN.14/619. In Ethiopia, Lesotho/Botswana and Swaziland, and forthcoming in Tanzania, Zambia and Somalia, thanks to a Netherlands grant. Ghana, Liberia, Sierra Leone, the Gambia, and Nigeria were added in 1975, as were Dahomey, Gabon, Congo, Zaire, Togo, Upper Volta, Cameroun and Rwanda. See Annexe 19, 'The ECA's Country-level Activities 1971–77'.

28. See 'Rapport de Mission à Dahomey et Dans Cinq Pays D'Afrique Centrale, de Mme Danielle Bazin, Consultante', ECA, 1974; See also 'Report to the Federal Republic of Germany on Phase II of the Itinerant Training Programme', UNECA, August 1975. M 75-1558.

29. The workshop took place in Kitwe, Zambia, during 9–23 December 1974.

30. ECA, *Selected Projects in Handicrafts and Other Small Industries in English-speaking African Countries*, Addis Ababa, 1974. HR/AF/RG/1974 D.7. See also *Report of a Mission in Preparation for Workshop on Women's Participation in Handicrafts and Other Small Industries in English-speaking African Countries*, ECA, Addis Ababa. HR/AF/RG/1974. The Government of Israel had contributed one of its experts, a Mrs Jacobsen, and a financial grant to assist with these activites, but when the break in relations came about between Israel and a number of African countries, both expert and contribution were withdrawn and Daria Tesha quickly took over the ECA's work, co-operating with Marion Janjic of the ILO and Lettie Stuart of the World Young Women's Christian Association (YWCA).

31. See ILO, *Report on ILO/ECA/YWCA/SIDA Workshop on Participation of Women in Handicrafts and Small Industries, Kitwe, Zambia.* ILO/TF/AFR/R.19, Geneva, 1974.

A Ministry of Social Action and the Family: a conversation with Akila Belembaogo

Q: Madame Minister, your Ministry of Social Action and the Family and the Ministry of Planning have taken exceptional steps in creating a national policy on women and development. What is its history?

ABG: In April 1993 the Burkina Faso Government adopted the National Plan of Action for Strengthening Women's Role in the Development Process. An inter-ministerial co-ordinating group was set up in 1986, to guide the production of a document. It was led by the Ministry of Social Affairs. The ministries of agriculture, social action, planning, environment, education and political co-ordination were represented. With a national resource person financed by UNIFEM, a National Women and Development Strategy was produced; it formed the basis for the Plan of Action.

Government has just set up a National Commission which is chaired by the Minister of Planning, with the Minister of Social Action as Vice-Chairman. The commission meets twice a year to monitor the implementation of the Plan of Action by the various technical ministries. There is a small secretariat in the Ministry of Planning to backstop the commission. In September we organized a national seminar to launch the plan. All this is a beginning that needs to be strengthened.

You also work with non-governmental organizations?

We have a number of women's voluntary associations now. My ministry is in charge of co-ordinating their work, in particular as we prepare for the 1995 Conference of Women. Our government delegation may include NGO representatives. Our reports will reflect the views of NGOs.

Women are already working internationally?

Burkina Faso was recently selected as secretary-general of the West African Women's Association (WAWA), which is affiliated with the Economic Community of West African States (ECOWAS). We are also represented on the Board of the International Research and Training Institute for the Advancement of Women (INSTRAW) and on the UN Committee for the Elimination of Discrimination against Women (CEDAW). I have recently been elected – as an individual – as Vice-Chairperson of the International Committee on the Rights of the Child.

And we have a national committee against the physical mutilation of women and girls that is affiliated with the African committee on female circumcision. It has been said that 75% of women in our country have experienced circumcision. Our national committee was set up in 1975 with forty volunteer members, to plan information and sensitization campaigns.

What is your approach to women?

We work with women as members of families, not as separate individuals. For instance, when we create an educational centre for women, we try to include a kindergarten so that women can be free to learn and to produce. We have an association of widows which has such a centre and kindergarten. All this work comes under the Directorate for the Promotion of the Family. We are preparing a special week of events to honour the International Year of the Family. Issues for discussion will include the single-parent family, population, AIDS, and better family life. The family code will be disseminated.

In 1986, we assisted government with defining priorities, policies and strategies on women and development. Now we are partners in implementing them.

Ouagadougou
December 1993

CHAPTER 6

INSTITUTIONAL CHANGE AND
PARTNERSHIP PROGRAMMES

Having committed itself to a holistic approach to the future of the region, the ECA understood that programmes met contemporary needs but did not, of and by themselves, guarantee long-range systemic and/or institutional change. If women's concerns were to remain an integral part of the development arena and agenda, then women had to be assured a place at the decision-making level within governments, institutions and non-governmental organizations.

The imperative for change emerged in opposition both to deeply ingrained attitudes towards women and to the historic development of systems meant to ensure social stability during the colonial period. Recall that gender-specific, parallel institutions allowed separate interests to be considered, and frequently husbands and wives controlled their own incomes in pre-colonial times. To foster the market economy, men were pressured into the system by taxation policies, education, training, land consolidation and opportunities to join the civil service or other wage employment. The resultant status quo not only assumed but stressed women's dependency on men: a situation reinforced by Western missionary influence.

Well into the era of independence, the presence of women at any level of government or regional organization was miniscule at best, and even rarer in the sphere of policy.[1] The ECA was no exception to this pattern; in 1973, 7.6% and in 1978 fewer than 6% of permanently employed professional staff were women, most of whom served as editors and interpreters. (See Annexe 8.)

The Chief of the ECA's Human Resource Development Division, James Riby-Williams, saw the clear connection between the 'priority needs and aspirations of the nation' and the absence of women as economic actors in three- to five-year development plans. He shared women's vision, which embraced the transformation of the status quo through the creation of organizational units that would fully engage women as well as men. To that end, the ECA Women's Programme sought the establishment of long-lasting governmental and Africa-wide institutions and organizations in which women would assume the power to design policy and to make necessary decisions.

One practical design for achieving that goal was proposed by a special working group at the Rabat conference in 1971. It was drafted into Recommendation 19, and was grounded in previous resolutions of the UN General Assembly, ECOSOC, and the ECA, including resolutions to the 1969 regional meeting on the Role of Women in National Development.[2]

The resolution recommended that member states of the ECA establish four mechanisms. The first would be national commissions on women and development, 'consisting of leading men and women with experience in such fields as government service, policy-making, development planning, employment, social development, education and training and other aspects of public life'. The second would take the form of permanent secretariats of the commissions, or technical women's bureaux, to undertake research, to formulate projects and programmes, and in general to ensure women's integration in all sectors of economic and social development.

The third mechanism would be an Africa Regional Standing Committee on the Role of Women in Development, which the recommendation proposed that the ECA should establish. It would consist of representatives of governments, intergovernmental and non-governmental organizations to co-ordinate the work of the national commissions, advise the ECA Women's Programme, and liaise with international and regional organizations.[3]

The fourth mechanism was based on the ECA's ability to promote national action to create the 'machineries' and to facilitate exchange of experiences. It was proposed that the ECA's Women's Programme be transformed into the 'Pan-African Training and Research Centre for Women'.[4]

To implement these creative and far-sighted recommendations, the Women's Programme began a search for resources. By 1974, it was able to report on initial financing from the US Department of Labor.[5] The funds would support a package of activities to promote the establishment of government machinery, especially national commissions on women and development, plus their permanent secretariats or technical women's bureaux. Included in the project was the dissemination of the tri-annual newsletter *African Women* (the first issue was dated July 1973), a 22-page booklet that explained what national machineries were, how they worked, and how to establish them, and provision for a series of three-day national seminars. Also to be distributed was *Women of Africa: Today and Tomorrow* – the popular version of *The Data Base*.

The ECA's international training teams for the national machineries seminars consisted of one or two women from the region, one ECA representative and another from an experienced women's bureau like those of Canada and the United States. The first national seminars team members were Dr Fatima Mahmoud, a government minister in the Sudan, Phoebe

Asiyo, Member of Parliament in Kenya, Kay Wallace of the US Women's Bureau, and Daria Tesha of the ECA.[6] Seminars were organized in Sudan, Ethiopia, Kenya and Lesotho. The team provided a forum for policy-making men and women representatives of governments, national women's organizations, voluntary and private agencies and others to discuss the national machinery concepts within the very specific context of the individual country and its national development plan.

The country studies of womanpower, and summaries of national development plans were among the resource materials employed.[7] The seminar process later led to the ECA's employment of Dr Agnes Diarra (Niger) as director of the project. Looking back on her participation in the seminars as first head of the Women's Bureau of Kenya, Terry Kantai noted that the seminars 'made great impact in terms of sensitizing and training women in leadership positions'. She also described the Women's Programme as a 'vital source of data and information' and, more important, as 'a sustained contact, which contributed significantly to ongoing leadership growth'.[8]

The booklet *National Commissions on Women and Development and Women's Bureaux* became an invaluable working document for the UN-sponsored Interregional Seminar on National Machinery to Accelerate the Integration of Women in Development and to Eliminate Discrimination on Grounds of Sex, held in Ottawa, Canada, in 1974. African participants at the seminar referred to the booklet as an extremely valuable document for governments to use, and said that the advisory services and national seminars the ECA offered to its member states were also helpful. The ECA Women's Programme was beginning to have a marked impact, they said. Participants from other global regions welcomed this information and hoped that it might be possible to establish programmes similar to that of the ECA in other regions.[9]

The partnership programme

Over time, the Women's Programme continued to co-operate with regional organizations, ECA member states, donor governments, UN organizations and non-governmental organizations, as it built the foundation for what would become a true inter-agency programme, and a prototype for the genuine partnership programme that many women envision. Of special importance among the organizations with which the Women's Programme maintained a close association was the All Africa Women's Conference (AAWC) – the first pan-African network of women on the continent. As we saw in Chapter 1, the AAWC was created in 1962 and was managed entirely by African women.[10]

The organization had three major objectives: to accelerate African women's full participation in the social, political, and economic activities of their countries; to support the trend of political, economic and social liberation of Africa and contribute to the advancement of its peoples; and to promote friendship and co-operation between African women and other women of the world with a view towards promoting progress, justice and peace.[11] To those ends, the AAWC held periodic conferences to share ideas both among themselves and with observers from national and international organizations, especially from the so-called 'socialist countries'. The ECA was regularly represented at these conferences.[12]

In 1974, at the Fourth Congress of the AAWC, its name was changed to the Pan-African Women's Organization (PAWO) and discussions ensued on the possibility of starting a pan-African women's centre for training African women. ECA Women's Programme staff continued to work closely with PAWO. When the Council of Ministers of the Organization of African Unity (OAU) met in Addis Ababa for its 24th Ordinary Session, it officially recognized PAWO as the only 'continental women's organization'. The OAU urged its member states to encourage their national women's organizations to participate in PAWO. It further suggested that special attention be given to increasing opportunities for women in the development of their countries by increasing their access to health facilities, water supplies and other labour-saving technologies, to employment (including self-employment) and to participation on policy-making bodies.[13]

In line with the ECA Women's Programme focus on close co-operation with non-governmental organizations, the programme made contacts with the Arab Women's Commission, the Society for International Development, the International Alliance of Women, the International Council of Women, the International Home Economics Association, ZONTA International, and the Church World Service, among others.

An early association with the Ford Foundation made it the second international foundation (after the German Foundation for Developing Countries) to support ECA Women's Programme activities. When the Ford Foundation was undergoing an internal reorganization in 1972, the development of programmes for women became an emerging priority. The foundation established a Task Force on Women, which began to investigate the possibility of promoting women's programmes in Africa and found that there was as yet inadequate documentation on which to base a recommendation.[14]

Recognizing the critical importance of gaining an understanding of the roles of women before developing programmes to help them, the foundation welcomed an ECA study on the economic participation of women in Africa.[15] The result (already referred to in Chapter 3) was the ECA document 'Women and National Development in African Countries: Some Profound Contradictions'.[16] That study became instrumental to Ford's grant to the ECA for national bibliographies and other research series on women. The message of 'Women and National Development' remained relevant;

nearly two decades later ECA would again press this key point: 'The mobilization of women for development is not just a question of equity but one of economic efficiency'.[17]

The word spreads: representation of the Women's Programme at international meetings

The ECA's Women's Programme was represented intergovernmentally at the ECA's Conference of Ministers and, because of the ECA's status as a United Nations organization, at UN headquarters meetings. One such meeting proved to be very important for the Women's Programme: the Twenty-fifth session of the UN Commission on the Status of Women. Of the 31 member states in attendance, 5 were African.[18] The session prepared for the celebration of the first ever International Women's Year, 1975, with the theme 'equality, development and peace'. When a world conference was agreed upon as a special way of celebrating, delegate Phoebe Asiyo of Kenya, backed by Rhuda Muhammed of Nigeria, proposed that this conference take place in a developing country. The CSW accepted that proposal.

At the same session, Kenya and several other countries identified the ECA Women's Programme as exemplary and as one that should be imitated by other UN regional commissions. Some delegates also spoke of and supported the creation of the proposed ECA-sponsored pan-African Women's centre and African Women's Task Force. The ECA representative urged that all statistics be broken down according to gender and that the definition of the active labour force recognize the economic activities of women. The ECA representatives called for data on both *de jure* and *de facto* heads of household.

The 1974 International Forum on the Role of Women in Population and Development, held at UN headquarters, helped to define women's positions on both the World Population Year, 1974, and the International Women's Year, 1975.[19] The debate at the forum stressed the need for greater diversification of economic opportunity in rural areas, and the importance of labour-intensive technology, and formal and non-formal education, including agricultural training and literacy.

Educated women were encouraged to work with their sisters in rural areas on the grounds that people should help one another rather than waiting for governments to help them. This had a familiar ring for those who had been present at the First Kenya Women's Seminar more than a decade earlier, in 1962, when delegates had pledged their 'united and separate efforts toward establishment of self-help groups, before we ask for assistance from either government or outside sources'.[20]

While it took place far from the African continent, the international forum was important to the ECA Women's Programme for at least three reasons. First, it exposed the programme to a wide audience. The UNDP delegate, Ulla Olin, stated that 'the ECA Women's Programme should be used as a model for this conference'. Judge Jiaggie strongly supported the ECA's programme to establish national commissions and bureaux, expressing the hope that the Rabat and ECOSOC resolutions might be fulfilled.

Second, preparations were made at the forum for the Africa regional seminar that would design a plan of action for the region and encourage the other UN economic commissions to follow the ECA example. Third, the inter-organizational partnership concept of the Women's Programme and the creation of the centre were advanced. Trilateral discussions on collaboration were held with the FAO and UNFPA. The US Women's Bureau expressed keen interest in co-operating under its new Percy Amendment to the US Foreign Assistance Act. UNICEF's new interest in labour-saving technologies and income-generating activities for women was its basis for partnership. The non-governmental women's organizations and later the Intermediate Technology Development Group (ITDG) in London sought association. All of the potential partners began to focus on the ECA Pan-African Women's Centre.[21]

A regional database and a regional conference

June 1974 marked a major milestone in the evolution of the ECA's support of the regional and interregional women and development movement. For the first time anywhere, data on the women of a whole geographical region existed, compiled and analysed. *The Data Base for Discussion on the Interrelation Between the Integration of Women in Development, Their Situation and Population Factors in Africa*, published by the ECA, was unique.[22] The data and research findings had been assembled from the ECA national woman-power studies, from government and international agency statistics, from sample surveys, and from research studies relevant to the current situation of women, particularly rural women. The studies had documented women's tasks and responsibilities in social and economic life, the extent of their integration in development (both in the modernizing rural areas and in the modern sectors of their societies), and the relationship between women's participation, population factors and national development.

The document and its popular version, *Women of Africa: Today and Tomorrow*, quantified women's and men's participation in traditional and 'modern sectors' through a series of 'units of participation'. The document's charts and diagrams (such as Figure 4.1) appeared in innumerable publications over more than a decade. It also presented another opportunity to consult with women of the region and with UN organizations on the proposal to establish a pan-African women's centre.

The Data Base was the basic working document for the Regional Seminar for Africa on the Integration of Women in Development with Special Reference to Population Factors. The 1974 seminar was convened in Addis Ababa by the Centre for Social Development and Humanitarian Affairs of UN headquarters, in co-operation with the ECA, and financed by UNFPA. It was a response both to the concerns of the UN Second Development Decade and to the work programme of the ECA's Human Resources Development Division on popular participation in development.

Significantly, the seminar marked the first interjection of population concerns as key issues on an agenda of an Africa regional women's conference.[23] Child spacing and family planning were discussed in the context of the increased survival rate of children which made multiple births less urgent, and of the too-frequent pregnancies that debilitated women, causing maternal and/or child mortality and morbidity. It became clear that women needed access to family planning information and technologies. (See Annexe 2 for data on health.)

The women at Addis Ababa, aware that many of their governments resisted population issues at the time, handled this potentially explosive subject by stressing in the debate the importance of the conditions under which women raised their families. They pointed to such factors as the availability of water and sanitation, diet, medical services and transport; and they emphasized women's need for resources, incomes, and freedom from uninterrupted childbearing. Their approach was especially appropriate at that time, when the concept of 'basic needs' was just beginning to be formulated in international development circles (it would be presented in detail by the International Labour Organization in 1976).

The *Plan of Action for the Integration of Women in Development in Africa* and the final seminar report drew heavily on the report of the Rabat regional conference and on the ECA *Data Base* paper.[24] They highlighted and thus reinforced the ECA's programme for the creation of 'organizational machinery', by governments and by international and regional organizations, to assist efforts to widen opportunities for women. National Commissions on Women and Development and Women's Bureaux, national Non-governmental Organization Co-ordinating Committees, the Africa Regional Standing Committee, and the Pan-African Research and Training Centre for Women got the full support of the meeting. Women were finally coming to the forefront, and institution building would sustain their concerns.

As 1974 closed, the Women's Programme had strong intellectual, programmatic, financial and administrative foundations, well-established professional contacts and a broad base of support from government officials and non-governmental leaders in all the member states of the ECA. In the brief time of its existence, the Women's Programme had achieved the readiness to be a fully institutionalized component of the total ECA programme. The African Training and Research Centre for

Women (ATRCW) was about to materialize. It would play a unique role in development schemes and have a significant impact on the women of Africa.

Notes

1. See Jane Parpart and Kathleen Staudt (eds), *Women and the State in Africa*, Lynne Rienner Publishers, Boulder, 1990, for further information and case studies.

2. General Assembly Resolution A/RES/2716 XXV; ECOSOC 961 XXXVI; and ECA Conference of Ministers 88 V, 118 VI, and 119 VI.

3. The Standing Committee was established on the detailed recommendation of the Nouakchott conference, 1977, that was adopted by the ECA Conference of Ministers. See Annexe 10b.

4. This action was recommended in various forms at the regional conferences in Addis Ababa in 1969, in Rabat and Libreville in 1971 and, finally, at the Addis Ababa 1974 regional conferences.

5. The initial US contribution was $28,000. Ms Wallace, Mary Hilton, Clara Beyer and Margaret Akroid of the Women's Bureau and Jean Pinder of USAID led those who assisted the ECA. Later assistance was given in the context of implementation of the Percy Amendment to the US Foreign Assistance Act that mandated attention to women when giving foreign aid.

6. See Annexe 19, The ECA's 'Country-level Activities Concerning Women, 1971–1977', for a complete list of countries where seminars, training courses and other activities took place.

7. Seminars were held in 1975 in Tanzania, Zambia, the Gambia, Upper Volta, Togo, Dahomey and Gabon; in 1976 in Libya, Morocco, Tunisia and Nigeria; and in 1977 in Mali and Mauritania.

8. Interview with Terry Kantai by Kathy Larin, Nairobi, December 1992.

9. See E/CONF.66/BPs/4, 18 April 1975, paras 82, 83.

10. Working with Kenyan women at the time, co-author Margaret Snyder attended the inaugural session in Dar es Salaam.

11. Snyder, memo to R.K.A. Gardiner, 16 August 1971. The memo reported on ECA participation in the Seminar on the Preparation of the African Women for Professional Life, Congo (Brazzaville) 17–25 July 1971, sponsored by the AAWC.

12. For example, on those on The Preparation of the African Woman for Professional Life, in Brazzaville, July 1971; and on the Role of Women in the Liberation of Africa, in Dar es Salaam, July 1972. See the 'Statement by the ECA Representative to the Tenth Anniversary of the All African Women's Conference on the Role of Women in the Liberation of Africa, 24–31 July, 1972'.

13. Resolution of the International Women's Year, 1975, adopted by the OAU Council of Ministers, Addis Ababa, 13–21 February 1975; ECA Women's Programme staff were consulted on the drafting of the resolution.

14. Visit by Susan Fischer of the Ford Foundation. Daria Tesha, 'Mission Report: Seminar on Family Life Education, Nairobi, October 16–28 1972'. Dated 21 November 1972.

15. The study was originally proposed by Mel Fox of the Ford Foundation. See Margaret Snyder, 'Mission Report to Europe and USA, 14 July 1972'.

16. The document was later published by the ECA in the *African Studies Review*, Vol. XVIII, No. 3. Other key Ford Foundation staff who continued to work with the ECA in later years were Betty Skelnick, Eleanor Barber, Herschel Challendor, Frank Sutton and Adrienne Germaine. See Margaret Snyder, 'Mission Report: 25th Session of the Commission on the Status of Women, 14 January–1 February 1974'.

17. *Report to the Fourth Regional Conference on the Integration of Women in Development and the Implementation of the Arusha Strategies for the Advancement of Women in Africa: Regional Perspective*, ECA, Addis Ababa. E/ECA/ATRCW/RCLWD 4/3, 5 September 1989.

18. Egypt, Kenya, Liberia, Nigeria, and Zaire; the Central African Republic and Madagascar, also members, did not attend. The meeting was held from 14 January–1 February 1974.

19. The forum was held 25 February–1 March 1974 at UN headquarters.

20. Report of the Kenya Women's Seminar Report, 1962, p. 7.

21. Margaret Snyder, 'Mission Report', 20 March 1974. Among conferees were Dr Jean Delaney of the FAO, Dr Nafis Sadik of the UNFPA; Kay Wallace and Clara Beyer of the US Women's Bureau; Jack Charnow of UNICEF: Esther Hymer of the women's NGOs and Dennis Frost of the Intermediate Technology Development Group.

22. ECA, *The Data Base for Discussion of the Interrelationships Between the Integration of Women in Development, Their Situation and Population Factors*, Addis Ababa, 1974. E/CN.14/SW/37.

23. In doing so the seminar testified to a fact that remains true today: that the link between woman and development is most universally understood in relation to her childbearing functions.

24. United Nations, *Report of the Regional Seminar for Africa on the Integration of Women in Development, with Special Reference to Population Factors*, New York, 1975. ST/ESA/SER.B/6. And *Plan of Action*, United Nations, New York, 1974. ST/ESA/SER.B/6/Add.1.

Views of an entrepreneur: a conversation with
Catherine Mwanamwambwa

Q: What should women's development priorities be today?

CM: Democracy has come into Africa now, accompanied by emphasis on the private sector. There should be a bias, a very very conscious and positive bias, towards helping the private sector to help women. For example, a lot of African governments have some 10 to 15% of their budgets funded by donors. A percentage of that should be given to the private sector, specifically geared towards women in the rural areas. NGOs work towards the collective good, but I think that now, in the rural areas, individuality should be supported, through the private sector.

Where should donors put that percentage of their money?

They should put it in agri-business. If you are going to sustain yourself and feed yourself, you have to be able to store your food all year round. They should create storage depots, where women are responsible, because it's women in our society who take responsibility for storage and processing. They should have ways for women to buy ploughs and pay with crops. This could be managed by the private sector – a company or a private broker, because it is in their interest to buy the crop from the women.

Do you think that accountability is easier that way?

Much easier, and working with the private sector, it is sustainable. When donors give that money to a private sector entrepreneur, they must give a grace period for its use before repayment. So you on-loan to twenty farmers the first year, and forty the next. Part of our problem now is some donor money is never accounted for. The private sector has everything to lose, so has to be accountable. And it provides a secure market.

It is not always true, the assumption that the private sector will exploit. It is very difficult to exploit a farmer, I am telling you. Farmers have a floor price for a crop, and won't sell it for less than that. Still, credit given to the private sector to do a joint venture with women should have many controls.

Is the emphasis on self-sufficiency in food, or on markets?

What we must do more in agriculture is to keep away from a mono-crop like maize and diversify into other crops. Once we do that, we will be able to have cash crops. I do not think farmers should only grow food for consumption; they should also grow food to make a living, to have an income. The farmer needs more than food to sustain the family: school fees, blankets, shoes. Those who are growing just maize can grow a bit of sorghum, a bit of soya beans, sunflower to process, to export.

You have worked with women farmers?

Yes. And I have very great difficulty in getting to women farmers, because when I start talking to them, their husbands butt in. So we are devising a system we call 'turning the home garden commercial'. Women usually have a small portion of land: two or three wives together may have two hectares. We say to them: 'grow 1.5 hectares of sorghum and use 0.5 hectares for a backyard garden, since we give you fertilizer.'

Are grassroots women reached by the women's movement?

Not enough. We are moving very fast towards a free market economy, and that is leaving a lot of vulnerable groups. And the pace at which these people are being left behind is so fast that we don't have the comprehensive programme articulated to meet their needs as yet.

What role do you see for the ATRCW?

Turn it into a centre that will have information, that will focus on one thing at a time. For the first three years work to expand entrepreneurial development at the grassroots level, and then turn to different areas. An economic base makes people pay attention.

Lusaka
November 1993

CHAPTER 7

THE ATRCW: A NEW INSIGHT
ON DEVELOPMENT

The global celebration of International Women's Year was a positive and hopeful sign in the midst of the harsh economic environment facing Africa in 1975. Prompted by those contrasting realities, the ECA moved to establish the African Training and Research Centre for Women (ATRCW). In making that move, the commission affirmed the impact of the Women's Programme training activities and attested to the centrality of women in the arena of social and economic progress. Just as the International Women's Year was the culmination of efforts by women around the world, so too the ATRCW was the realization of what many African women had aspired to. They were the ones who had articulated the need for a centralized training/research facility as a corrective to the conditions under which they often had to struggle to provide for themselves and their families.

A climate for structural change in Africa

As development priorities and paradigms were being reconsidered in the 1970s, dependency theory gained ascendency. Economic colonialism persisted even after political independence was achieved, and the global economy provided the framework for understanding the developing countries.[1] Compounded by falling prices for exports and escalating prices for oil imports, the recession started to savage the flow of foreign exchange. Debt and debt interest owed to overseas public and private lenders began to accumulate.

As these burdens mounted, African states began to revise their strategies in order to emphasize self-reliance, interdependence among developing countries, and the progressive elimination of unemployment and mass poverty. Over-reliance on external markets with their uncontrolled price fluctuations simply did not work. Economic co-operation was seen 'not merely as a means for market expansion but primarily as an instrument for the transformation of the structure of production and distribution', as was later stated in the ECA's 1976 'Revised Framework of Principles for the Implementation of the New International Economic Order in Africa'.[2] To promote that transformation the ECA proposed to encourage interaction among three strategic sectors: the agricultural, the rural and the industrial.

In agriculture, emphasis was placed on food production because food supply was not keeping pace with population growth. That imbalance resulted in too much foreign exchange being spent on importing food. Finding little evidence that serious consideration was given to 'the roles of women and children in agriculture, particularly food production, processing and marketing', the ECA called for a 'comprehensive research programme' on the micro-economics and micro-sociology of rural societies. In the area of industrial development, questions were raised as to which technologies were appropriate to individual societies and tasks, since economic models from industrial countries were judged by that time to be of little use.[3]

The action proposals that flowed from the defined linkages between the agricultural, rural and industrial sectors contained the priorities of the ECA Women's Programme and expedited its evolution. The concept of the ATRCW emerged naturally from the interface between the changing strategies of African states and the strategies of the five-year Women's Programme. The International Women's Year (IWY) 1975 provided the ECA with the unique opportunity to set forth formally in a comprehensive project description the evolution of the Women's Programme into the ATRCW.[4]

The ECA's blueprint for the ATRCW

The ATRCW was envisioned not as a bricks-and-mortar structure, but as a 'concept and a programme' by which activities would take place throughout the continent. Using the resolutions of regional conferences and *The Data Base*, the ECA secretariat formulated a statement of aims for the centre.

> To assist Governments and voluntary agencies by serving as a focal point for the mobilization of African women, to broaden their horizons and strengthen their skills.[5]

An 'African women's volunteer task force' component would allow skilled women from one part of the region to serve in another when requested. The rationale behind the task force was to stimulate the spirit and potential of voluntary service, by creating opportunities for women who would otherwise never meet each other to come together in mutuality of service. Volunteers could choose to be placed in other countries as qualified trainers in business or women's organizations, as providers of technical assistance, or as reseachers. Intra-African technical co-operation and assistance would be encouraged.

The centre and task force, working together, would concentrate on ways to lighten women's workloads and to increase their work efficiency. Methods to improve administrative procedures within women's co-operatives, trade unions and other organizations would be a priority. Working with women in different areas, the centre staff and volunteers would design income-producing ventures. Programmes already under way, such as the itinerant national workshops for rural trainers, and the seminars on national commissions, were to be continued and expanded. Through all those efforts, special attention would be paid to the goal of setting up the recommended national institutions that would perpetuate this work in every country. The term 'national machineries' was adopted to describe them.[6] (See Annexe 4.)

Also built into the ATRCW's design was an innovative apprenticeship programme to assist a variety of individuals. University women seeking skills for rural development; national and project-level planners; trainers; business administrators and others: all could take advantage of the programme's benefits. Applied research projects would be relevant to the ATRCW's concern for rural life and to such issues as self-employment, national planning and the evaluation of training and teaching methods.

Provision was made for the information gathered from the programmes and research to be disseminated throughout the whole African region. *African Women*, the newletter initiated by the ECA's Women's Programme, served as the vehicle for that exchange and for communicating other items of interest.

To ensure that the collaborative nature of the ATRCW would be maintained, the proposal called for the formation of a permanent committee. It was to be composed of representatives from women's national commissions and bureaux. That intention would become a reality when the African Regional Co-ordinating Committee was established in 1977, as the final component of the regional structure.

To create the centre, the ECA sought the active participation of the groups and organizations that were already co-operating with its Women's Programme – the FAO, ILO, the NGO community and donor governments. The resultant multi-agency coalition became fully integrated into the establishment of the ATRCW and into the planning and implementation of its activities.

That unparalleled coalition constituted a co-operative, non-hierarchical, and participatory structure that was positioned to meet the needs of African women. Its inclusive programmatic strategy capitalized on the expertise and interests of each of the groups involved. It made the ATRCW the only genuinely inter-agency partnership programme within the UN system. This was a unique contribution by the ECA and the ATRCW to the conceptualization of development institutions – a contribution that deserves serious consideration as civil society and the private sector gain prominence and power in national and United Nations forums today.

When all the discussions were over and the suggestions had been considered, the ATRCW's profile was put together: it contained fourteen sub-projects groups under four subject headings: National Planning; Work Efficiency; Quality of Life, and Communications. (See Annexe 17.) Each of the major subject areas comprised training, applied research and information activities.

In its final form, the ATRCW proposal was enthusiastically endorsed by the 1974 Regional Seminar for Africa on the Integration of Women in Development with Special Reference to Population Factors, held in Addis Ababa. That seminar set out in its Plan of Action for the Integration of Women in Development in Africa the organizational machinery that had been recommended at Rabat three years earlier, including the proposals for the ATRCW. The proposal was formally approved by the ECA Conference of Ministers in its Resolution 269 (XII) in February 1975.[7] (See Annexe 10a.)

Substantial and broad-based support came from donors, starting with USAID's leveraging grant of $65,000. The other early contributors included UNICEF $65,000, UNDP $678,000 (the contribution was delayed for several years due to the organization's liquidity crisis), the Federal Republic of Germany $92,000, the ITDG – (which contributed a professional staff person), ZONTA International $100,000, UNFPA/FAO $420,000, SIDA $582,000, and ILO $300,000.[8] (See Annexe 9.)

31 March 1975, was a day of celebration.The ECA's Executive Secretary, Robert K.A. Gardiner, declared the ATRCW officially established. As it turned out, bringing the process to closure was Gardiner's final official act before his retirement from the ECA. He took that opportunity to speak with celebrating staff about his mother's entry into the business world when he was just two years old, after the death of his father. Her savings made his studies at Cambridge University in England possible. He explained his deep respect for women's economic activities and their very significant contributions to their communities through self-help groups.

The International Women's Year, 1975

The creation of the ATRCW lent strength and excitement to the ECA's delegation to the most significant event in the international women's movement of the twentieth century. The World Conference of International Women's Year (IWY), and its parallel NGO meeting, the International Women's Year Tribune, were both held in Mexico City, from 19 June to 2 July 1975. The objective of IWY was set out:

> To define a society in which women participate in a real and full sense in economic, social and political life and to devise strategies whereby such societies could develop.[9]

The themes of the conference were equality, development and peace. Among its strategies were the following:

> to examine to what extent the organizations of the United Nations System have implemented the recommendations ... made by the Commission on the Status of Women since its establishment, and to launch an international action programme including short term and long term measures aimed at achieving the integration of women as full and equal partners with men in the total development effort, and eliminating discrimination on grounds of sex, and achieving the widest involvement of women in strengthening international peace and eliminating racial discrimination.[10]

The delegations from 133 member states of the United Nations included 37 from the Africa region who participated in the official governmental conference. The Organization of African Unity (OAU), 98 nongovernmental organizations and 6 liberation movements from Africa were observers.[11]

African delegates were delighted to hear familiar, supportive statements at the opening session of the conference. The President of Mexico, Luis Echeverria, referred to the indisputable fact that women in all countries were treated as minorities. He warned that if the status of women was to be improved, social transformations were necessary in both the internal (national) and the international order. 'Only a critical, radical effort will make possible the true liberation of women, that is the liberation of humanity and the transformation of the world economic order,' he said. He added that no woman was more discriminated against or more exploited than the woman who was without bread, school, or medicines for her children.[12]

The Mexican President thus set the stage for a comprehensive consideration of the subjects of women, of poverty, and of the relationship of women's situation to national and global issues, especially economic and political ones. He endorsed a New International Economic Order (NIEO), that Africa's regional conference of women would discuss two years later.[13]

Many participants from developing countries, including African delegates, agreed with the President's macro-political and economic context for discussion of women's issues. They found that 'the very condition of underdevelopment imposed a double burden of exploitation on women', who were subject to the effects of their countries' poverty as well as the effects of gender discrimination. Consequently, they said, both a more equitable system of international economic relations and women's full participation in national and international life were preconditions for the progress of societies.

Many industrial countries' representatives did not agree with the macroeconomic premises of those assertions. The dominant strains of Western feminism at the time had relations between the sexes as their overriding concern. They failed to embrace macro-political and economic issues as 'women's issues'. For these reasons the Declaration of Mexico was drafted separately from the plan of action that would be the major output of the conference. The declaration contained the key concerns of the Group of 77, the developing countries, about issues such as the proposed NIEO, which was also under heated discussion at two special sessions of the United Nations General Assembly at the time. The declaration stated:

> the issue of inequality, as it affects the vast majority of the women of the world, is closely linked with the problem of underdevelopment, which exists as a result not only of unsuitable international structures but also of a profoundly unjust world economic system. ... It is essential to establish and implement with urgency the New International Economic Order (NIEO).[14]

While many participants were adamant in their calls for a new world order, they also recognized that it would have to come hand in hand with other basic changes in national social and political systems. They therefore devoted time to highlighting ways in which women could increase their access to available resources and their participation in decision making. They defined areas for national, regional and international action. Political participation, education and training, employment, health, nutrition, family life, population and housing were all areas of specific concern.

In line with Africa's priority attention to rural development and to food security, African delegates joined with others in clear and firm statements about women who lived in rural areas. The work of women in the countryside was overburdensome, underproductive and harmful to present and future generations. Most delegates agreed that women's legal position was on the whole healthy, although women did not always make use of the laws in their countries. But as women had said time and time again in African regional conferences, and the ECA had echoed in its policy premises, the attitudes of both women and men needed transformation, and illiteracy had to be wiped out if the impediments to women's work were to be removed. Several delegations and representatives of OAU and United Nations agencies mentioned the ECA/ATRCW in the plenary sessions, offering it as a model for activity in other regions.

The leader of the ECA delegation, Riby-Williams, cited the ECA document that was presented to the conference, and spoke about the Africa region governments' awareness of the necessity to involve women in the planned development effort, especially the women living and working in rural areas.[15] An African caucus of delegates from member states in the region met frequently under OAU auspices with ECA assistance over the course of the conference. Its first session reviewed the establishment and functioning of the ATRCW, while subsequent sessions discussed resolutions and other conference matters of special interest to Africa. African delegates used every opportunity to influence the conference debate.

Jean Martin Cisse, who was not only the president of PAWO but also the Permanent Representative of Guinea to the UN, chaired Conference Committee One. That committee was responsible for drafting the World Plan of Action for the Implementation of the Objectives of the International Women's Year.

This plan was the most influential document to emerge from the conference. It was the first multilaterally supported document the world had seen that concentrated so comprehensively on the problems and concerns of women. Covering all possible aspects of women's lives, from food, health, education and family planning to political participation, it included the full texts of the African and Asian plans of action that had been drafted at the earlier regional conferences; the African plan contained the blueprint for the ATRCW, the regional standing committee and the African Women's Development Task Force.

The plan and a companion resolution challenged existing multilateral and bilateral operational organizations, foundations, international and regional development banks, and other international financial institutions:

> to make a deliberate and large scale effort to ensure high priority was placed on giving women the skills, training and opportunities necessary to improve their situation and enable them to participate fully and effectively in the total development effort.[16]

The repercussions of such obligations later penetrated the entire UN system, including the ECA. The plan became the ammunition for staff of the UN organizations to insist that resources reach both women and men. But neither delegations, NGO representatives nor staff of United Nations and bilateral aid-giving organizations foresaw the enormity of the task they had defined. No estimation was made or consideration given to the magnitude and type of resources that would be needed, or to the number of decades that it would take to transform vast bureaucracies.

That failure to consider questions of scale would prove costly. Some fifteen years later, the situation would remain sobering.

— In the World Bank, just 15% of the 1989 financial year's operations are judged to have the potential for substantial effect on women's well-being.[17]
— In UN organizations it is estimated that ... 3.5% of projects benefit women, representing 0.2% of budget allocations, and less than 1% of FAO projects actually contain strategies to reach women.[18]
— A Norwegian evaluation stated that information on how women have so far gained from NORAD programmes is poor and scanty, but what is available indicates rather few benefits for women in general.[19]
— Only 10% of USAID's agriculture projects specified a women's component.

At the Mexico conference, simultaneous with the call for a reorientation of existing global and regional institutions came a call for the institutionalization of women's interests at national level. African delegates took the opportunity to report that national commissions on women and development and/or technical women's bureaux had been set up in seven countries of the region – five of them during IWY – and many others were soon to follow. One example came from Ghana, where by decree the ruling National Redemption Council had created the National Council on Women and Development the previous April.[20] The prime mover of that decree, Justice Jiaggie, led her country's delegation to the conference.

New institutions were considered to be necessary at the global level also. Delegates from several African countries contributed to discussions on the urgency of channelling new resources to women through creating a women-specific development fund within the United Nations system. The Voluntary Fund for the UN Decade for Women (VFDW, renamed UNIFEM in 1985) was later created by the General Assembly, based on the resolution adopted in Mexico.[21] VFDW/UNIFEM soon became a significant source of support for senior posts and field projects of the ATRCW, and for creating and supporting women's programmes at other regional commissions as well.

Delegates from Egypt, Ghana and Senegal were among the thirteen sponsors of a resolution which proposed to establish the companion International Training and Research Centre for the Advancement of Women (INSTRAW). Like UNIFEM,[22] INSTRAW was later created by the UN General Assembly and would become a co-operator with the ATRCW.

A resolution on women's access to credit was inspired by a delegate from the Africa region at a pre-conference workshop.[23] There, entrepreneur Esther Ocloo remarked on the failure of banks to extend credit lines to women, and stated firmly: 'What we need is a women's bank.' 'Yes,' commented a UN representative, 'a world bank for women.' After several informal meetings at the NGOs' meeting (the IWY Tribune), the government conference delegates, including Jiaggie, Cisse, Mohamed (Nigeria) and delegates from Côte d'Ivoire and Kenya, proposed a draft resolution that became the basis for the creation of Women's World Banking (WWB).[24]

The ATRCW later surveyed selected member states and banks in its region on women's access to credit and repayment records, as a contribution to WWB's knowledge base. Follow-up collaboration between the ATRCW and UNIFEM resulted in the pioneering community revolving loan fund of the United Nations Development Programme system: the ATRCW/UNIFEM grant in Swaziland.[25]

Several other resolutions adopted by the conference were of special interest to African delegates and to the ATRCW. They ranged from welcoming the decision of the ECA Conference of Ministers to create the

ATRCW, to a call for all governments to apply economic sanctions against South Africa, Namibia and Southern Rhodesia. There were further calls for research towards the formulation of policies and programmes on women and development, followed by a request that national machineries for women and development be established at the highest political levels. The UN system was asked to provide staff and resources to implement the World Plan of Action.[26]

It is interesting to note that the World Plan of Action and a set of IWY World Conference resolutions that were adopted by the UN General Assembly in its Resolution 3520 (XXX) in December 1975 spelled out global development priorities that reflected those of women in the Africa region. They also called upon the UN regional commissions to further the objectives of the World Plan of Action at regional and sub-regional levels. Together the plan and resolutions:

— opened a fresh perspective on women as farmers, farm managers and entrepreneurs, and articulated previously poorly understood concerns such as women's need for land and credit;
— recognized the integral relationship between women's situation and national and global economic and political issues;
— reaffirmed the vital empowering and leveraging roles of women-specific organizations in the UN, in governments and in intergovernmental organizations;
— mandated all development-oriented administrative bodies, from local to global levels, to recognize women's present and potential contributions;
— confirmed the position of the UN as proponent and guardian of human-centred development and thus a major advocate and source of strength for the fledgling women and development movement;
— called for support, understanding, mutual respect and trust among women of the world, despite the political and other boundaries artificially set between them;
— enhanced the ATRCW as a partnership programme, and as a model for other world regions.

African women celebrated IWY throughout the continent. They took the opportunity to compile information on women's contributions to self-help and other development projects in their countries. Women's organizations reported on the conference and convened meetings locally and nationally, using local languages, in country after country. They emphasized women's centrality to social, economic and political development, to education and to family life. Traditional cloths on sale at local markets featured the IWY symbol – the dove that represented peace, development and equality; jewellery was made with the same motif. The local press interviewed innumerable women.

The outcome of that momentous year was beyond anyone's expectations. At Mexico City, the women and development concept was transformed into a global movement. The themes of IWY and the conference were felt by women at all levels of society, from farm to village to city, throughout the world. For the first time, women were given global recognition for their contributions, and they had an opportunity to celebrate. Women who had never looked upon their own achievements as important were suddenly lauded as the mainstays of their societies, and they took the recognition as a cause for rejoicing. They welcomed the UN General Assembly's decision to continue the work of IWY through the United Nations Decade for Women: 1976–1985. The momentum of the conference gave African women and ATRCW staff both an affirmation of the value of their work and a stimulus to renewed effort.

The ATRCW matures

The energy generated by IWY and the UN Decade for Women continued to affirm and support the ATRCW's work during the early years of its existence. That work was transformed from being a programme to a full-fledged inter-organizational centre with a staff of eleven professionals, which later grew to seventeen. (See Annexe 15.) One by one, the different segments of the centre were put into action. The volunteer task force, the information activities, and the appropriate technology unit all became operational. New specializations, such as handicrafts and small business enterprises, continued to be put in place. (See Annexe 11).

Earlier emphases on training and on national planning continued, as did co-operative efforts that brought human resource concerns, particularly those of women, into the many substantive divisions of the ECA, such as those for agriculture, statistics, and planning.[27]

The ATRCW also participated in global inter-agency meetings for the Decade for Women, presenting the draft of a policy statement on co-ordination and co-operation between UN headquarters, agencies and regional commissions, towards the implementation of the World Plan of Action. Early in 1976, Mary Tadesse of Ethiopia was appointed by the ECA to be the first Chief of the ATRCW.[28]

The breadth and scope of its activities illustrate the ATRCW's holistic approach to development.

Appropriate technologies

Village technology (sometimes called intermediate or appropriate techno-logy) was a term used by the ATRCW to refer to any tools, equipment, or methods that eased the burden on rural women by reducing their workloads, increasing their incomes, or improving their home environ-ments. Typically less complex than most industrial technologies, they could

be produced by skilled local artisans, and/or knowledge about their use
and availability could be spread by extension workers. Widely acknowledged
as useful by women in Africa, they represented an important means of
improving the living standards of rural women.

The village technology programme of the ATRCW was based on a
survey of member states in 1973 that followed up on the recommendations
of the Rabat (1971) and Addis Ababa (1972) conferences. The programme
began in earnest with the secondment to the ECA of the economist Dr
Marilyn Carr of the ITDG in 1975.[29] It had several different aspects, and
became an integral part of other ATRCW programmes, such as the
itinerant training workshops that were used to introduce technologies, to
exchange knowledge and ideas, and to identify ways in which the chosen
technologies could best be incorporated into rural development projects.

The value of the ATRCW's programming lay in its ability to assist the
implementation of policy decisions. The design ideas for the village technology programme materialized in specific components which remained
consistent throughout the region: research (for example, on technologies
already in use), pilot projects, and workshops for government officials,
extension workers, and NGO representatives. The scholarships that accompanied the programme were an added incentive to persons involved
with training African women and engineers in the field.

One of the earliest research activities was a survey of rural technology
in Sierra Leone.[30] The survey was conducted by students of Njala University College and included comprehensive analyses ranging from
preservation and processing of foods such as cassava, nuts, corn, onions
and fish, to production of consumer goods like laundry soap and tyre
sandals. Perhaps the most useful consequence of the survey was that it
was fed into curriculum development for schoolchildren in Sierra Leone.
Similar surveys done in other African countries added to the knowledge
base and helped to identify new methods for introducing innovative
technologies.

In conducting research on village technologies, one of the first lessons
learned by the centre was that new technologies were often introduced to
solve a particular problem without any evaluation of potential secondary
or tertiary effects. The ATRCW sought to fill that gap by conducting a
series of in-depth studies which focused on the socio-economic impacts
of ongoing projects. For example, in 1975, a study was done on the impact
of water wells in ten villages in Ethiopia to examine whether there were
secondary effects on the division of labour, time allocation, and decision
making within households, as well as on village attitudes about benefits.

A critical finding of that study was that improved or new sources of
water supply were not priorities in the highlands but they were an acute
need in the lowlands. It turned out that villagers had not been asked
about their own priorities. The actual economic conditions of the area

called for an integrated rural development approach, one that simultaneously tackled problems of land scarcity, soil infertility, chronic malnutrition, plant diseases and so on. 'Otherwise the development of surface water supplies would not be sufficient to result in a dramatic impact on the lifestyle of the people,' the study concluded.[31]

In addition to research, the ATRCW also supported pilot projects to test the acceptability and usefulness of new technologies in selected villages. Diversified in content, projects ranged from the introduction of hand-operated grinding mills for sorghum and millet in Upper Volta, to hand-operated oil presses for palm fruits in Sierra Leone, and post-harvest and crop processing equipment in the Gambia.

In many cases, projects encompassed the entire process of technological development and application. First, researchers identified areas in which new technologies were needed; then, project staff worked with women in villages to identify their specific needs. Afterwards, technology was developed, introduced, and tested. For example, in Niger, project staff worked with women involved in salt extraction to develop improvements which would not only reduce their workloads and the health hazards involved in processing, but would also serve to increase their income.[32]

A major impediment to the introduction of new technologies was the lack of access to information about methods or equipment that had proved effective. To address that problem, the ATRCW conducted a series of workshops for planners, extension workers and government officials. Some of the workshops, such as the Food Storage and Preservation Workshop in Tanzania and the Village Technology Workshops for Extension Workers in Kenya, brought together experts from around Africa to exchange information on specific subject areas.

The ATRCW provided scholarships to nationals for research that would contribute to their work at university or with government agencies. Taking advantage of such opportunities, officials from the Gambia and Sierra Leone went to Kenya, where great strides had been made in the development and dissemination of village technologies. An African woman was apprenticed for a month at the ITDG in the UK, the world centre for the advancement of appropriate technologies at the time, and a Gambian engineer studied at the long-established Technology Consultancy Centre in Ghana for three months.

Whilst the identification and development of effective technologies was the primary objective of the Village Technology Section of the ATRCW, the documentation of problems encountered in introducing those technologies turned out to be of equal importance. Evidence showed, for example, that the effectiveness of innovative methods or tools is highly sensitive to cultural attitudes and specific village conditions. Outsiders did not always take that fact into account. The ATRCW also uncovered logistical problems that hamper successful adoption of technologies that would otherwise be appropriate for a given community. Fortunately, the ATRCW project was designed to address such dilemmas.

Another important ATRCW project in the field of technology was the compilation of a manual. Entitled *Appropriate Technology for African Women*, it collected examples of experiences with various technologies in Africa so that those which had proved effective could be adapted for use elsewhere.[33] The information gathered in the process also led to the reintroduction of traditional technologies that had been lost over the generations. The manual listed ways in which women's productivity could be increased and their workloads eased by the introduction of new technologies, and examined the experiences of introducing them.[34]

The African Women's Development Task Force

The task force initiated by the ATRCW was an innovative approach to providing training and technical assistance to community groups, organizations and governments involved in activities for women. It shared the goals of Africa's revised framework of principles with its emphasis on interdependence among developing countries.[35]

In accord with the vision of Executive Secretary Gardiner, the task force was composed of African women who volunteered to take time from their careers to share their expertise in sectors ranging from agriculture, nutrition and medicine, to engineering and law. They initially agreed to spend anything from a month to two years working in another African country. The ATRCW co-ordinated the placement of the volunteers and provided logistical support.[36] As it turned out, the demand was heavily weighted toward volunteers with skills in micro-enterprise, and West African businesswomen became very popular indeed.

The UNDP Representative in Lesotho described task force volunteer Rebecca Agroh (Ghana) as the most outstanding United Nations ambassador ever to visit that country. Agroh's assignment as the first volunteer came in 1975 when the government of Lesotho requested an expert in tie-dye and batik printing.[37] She travelled up and down the Lesotho mountains for six months, teaching women and learning from them. She worked in sixteen rural centres and trained some 2,000 women, returning a year later to conduct more intensive training. A two-week course in the capital city drew forty-four trainers, including Lesotho's Queen. Among their products were clothing and calendars that were sold locally.

The second African Women's Development Task Force assignment was to send organizers of women's programmes from Mali, Mauritania and Upper Volta to train in the Cameroun for two months. They worked with volunteer trainers Michel Meneault and Olga Tovomov, joint owners of a Yaoundé workshop, learning fabric printing skills and organizational techniques.

By 1977, the demand for volunteers had multiplied, and Ghanaian Dr Agnes Aidoo took over as manager of the task force at the ATRCW. She found that some of the skilled women who expressed a willingness to serve were unable, or unwilling, to leave their own businesses for an extended length of time. In such cases, women were brought from other countries to the volunteer's own business to learn the trade. Barbara Baeta, owner of Flair Catering, and Esther Ocloo, owner of Nkulenu Industries (food processing) in Ghana, were among those who accepted 'apprentices' from East Africa. Baeta demonstrated what could be done in business with a minimum of money; her apprentices found that possible on their return home, where they set up businesses and kept in touch with her for some years.

Often there were short follow-up visits to trainees by volunteers who provided on-site technical assistance and made sure that the skills learned during the training were being applied. One observer of the programme cited a range of benefits that went beyond mere skills training. Commenting on the experiences of Ghanaian women who travelled to Kenya for training, she noted:

> the exposure to a different environment and the confidence that comes with successfully adapting to a different culture had a noticeable liberating effect on them and they are performing very effective leadership roles in their communities.[38]

Research and publications

Much of the credit for the striking visibility given to women farmers and the surge in research about them in the 1970s and 1980s was attributed to the ECA's 1972 article 'Women: the Neglected Human Resources for African Development'.[39] As detailed in Chapter 3, a companion series of landmark overview documents was published in the early 1970s. Because they described and quantified the serious imbalance between women's labour and women's access to resources, these documents were 'widely disseminated and nearly etched in stone'.[40]

The Women's Programme/ ATRCW itself engaged in secondary research and conducted surveys. While the centre continued to support primary research on customary issues of employment and planning, it also endorsed national studies of the mass media's effect on attitudes towards women and towards population issues. Concerned with closing the knowledge gap and with the lack of reliable micro-economic and micro-sociological data, the centre set specific criteria for research topics; they had to relate to the development priorities of particular countries and to the centre's programme. Research also had to be in a field in which significant data were missing and had to facilitate comparative analysis among member states.[41]

As a basis for its research and publications programme, the centre sought to measure and monitor the participation of women in development activities as compared to that of men – a process later defined as 'gender analysis'. A working definition of the internationally popular phrase 'the integration of women in development' was adopted before a set of indicators was created. To be 'integrated in development' was defined as having both the legal right and access to existing means for the improvement of oneself and of society.[42] That definition was deemed necessary because the phrase had been encrusted with implications that women were not working for development and that the development goals that governments spelled out were always the ones that women wanted. Pala-Okeyo articulated this criticism.[43]

By 1977, a methodology to assess women's contributions to GDP was devised in consultation with the ECA Statistics Division. Using data from a case study of Lesotho, the system estimated the monetary value of the female labour expended. Countering traditional assumptions, it showed that women's work actually amounted to two-thirds of the total value of the labour output in the country during a three-year period.[44] The ATRCW went on to draft a set of socio-economic indicators to verify the participation of women in development and their access, or lack of it, to its means and rewards.[45]

These measurement systems were set out in the ATRCW's policy document for the Nouakchott conference of 1977: *The New International Economic Order: What Roles for Women?*[46] This document was the centre's first major effort to bring women leaders into discussion of macro issues that appeared to be outside pragmatic concerns.

The NIEO discussions at the UN General Assembly and the ECA's 'Revised Framework of Principles for the Implementation of the New International Economic Order in Africa, 1976–1981' had not captured the very real relationships of women to the global economy.[47] Using case studies of women's economic activities in each area, the document set out strategies for rural transformation, international trade, transfer of resources for development, science and technology and co-operation among developing countries. Discussion of the document opened new perspectives on the linkages between women's needs and the priority needs of the nation.

Research sponsored by the ATRCW was edited and published by the ECA with the professional assistance of Dr Nancy Hafkin.[48] Titles of the Research Series ranged from *Law and the Status of Women in Nigeria* to *Marketing in Ghana*. Another major contribution of the ATRCW, in its role as a clearing house for information, was the publication of a Bibliography Series, the first of which, written by Hafkin, was entitled *Women in Development in Africa: An Annotated Bibliography*.[49] Each volume in the series compiled references according to subject areas, as a resource for researchers and practitioners in a given country. The bibliographies, initially a study of Tanzania by professors Marjorie Mbilinyi and Ophelia Mascarenhas, were the first to assemble citations from works centred on women, government data, and other resources; they demonstrated the diversity and extent of information available.[50]

A Workshop Series published reports of training workshops so that participants could have what amounted to a training manual to keep. This made it possible for women who were unable to attend to benefit from the material presented for discussion at the workshops.

The ATRCW Review Mission of 1978 identified several factors that enhanced the ECA's comparative advantage for conducting research on women in Africa. The centre was uniquely situated to co-ordinate comparative studies, involving several countries, on a given topic. Further, ATRCW staff were well positioned to know which subject areas were of critical importance to the majority of member states.

To policy makers, the centre's research carried the prestige of the ECA, and it could tap international support to national research institutes and individual researchers. Reflecting the impact of the initial policy documents of the Women's Programme, the review mission observed that the centre's 'unique role as catalyst for research on women should not be underestimated'.[51] (See Annexe 14: 'List of Publications/Documents by Subject Area'.)

Skills development: training courses

The second series of itinerant training programmes to improve the quality of rural life had begun in 1975. One of these was the national workshop on food preservation and storage for rural development workers in Tanzania. It was held in conjunction with that country's grow-your-own-food campaign, and with the co-operation of UNICEF. Another Round Two workshop, as they were called, was held in Zambia. That one was entitled Planning Techniques, Communication and Adult Education.[52] Others concentrated on day care for children in Kenya, and co-operatives in Cameroun, the latter assisted by PAWO.

Round Two workshops arose from the 1975–76 evaluations of the original itinerant training workshops.[53] Even though the information showed that the original two-week format was too short a time for participants to get a real grasp of the subject matter, the evaluators, Thelma Awori (Liberia), Daria Tesha and Jean Ritchie, also discerned that the participants' willingness to try out at least some of the ideas was a positive outcome. They found, for example, that participants had indeed practised group planning and evaluation, and that they were teaching food preservation techniques, such as sun-drying, salting, bottling, and jam making, and sharing transport with other ministries and NGOs. Although their attempts to use a systems approach to planning were not always successful, the participants were using the basic principles they had learned at the workshops. The evaluators recommended follow-up training in order to profit from those gains.

The evaluations of Round One, together with the end-of-training assessments by participants in Round Two, led to the institutionalizing of the in-service training for intermediate-level trainers. The ATRCW organizer for French-speaking countries, Marie-Suzanne Prosper of Mauritius, FAO/ECA Population Training Officer, and consultant Danielle Bazin reported the opinion of participants that the length of the training was inadequate to prepare intermediate-level personnel to assist the transformation of rural life in Africa.

Thus, in January 1978, ECA, FAO and UNICEF representatives met at Africa Hall in Addis Ababa with a representative of the Pan-African Institute for Development (PAID) with which the ECA already had an Agreement of Co-operation for Training and Research. The project on the agenda provided for three three-month workshops. Agreement was reached at the meeting and the project was launched with a grant from UNIFEM.

Another programme that followed was in response to senior women, who observed that while they had chances to visit Europe or America, they rarely were able to visit and learn from other African countries. The first study tour took senior women from Tanzania, Uganda, Burundi, Cameroun, Rwanda and the Comoros to Kenya for eleven days in 1977, to see and discuss activities related to women and development, in particular those of the FAO/UNFPA-assisted Programme for Better Family Living. A second study tour for senior officials took place in Freetown, Sierra Leone, with participants from Kenya, Tanzania and Ghana.

Meanwhile, ATRCW staff continued to share their expertise at seminars sponsored by other organizations. The centre sent Sori Bai Bangura (Sierra Leone) to a West African seminar on 'The Role of Women in Marketing Local Farm and Marine Produce'. Participants were market women and farmers from Nigeria, Gambia, Sierra Leone and Ghana. Communication was facilitated by simultaneous translation of local and English languages.

Bangura said that this very down-to-earth participation 'lent an unusual insight into problems of the women farmers and traders and their relationships in the marketing system'. When he returned to Addis Ababa, he affirmed the role of the traders as the dominant force between food producers and consumers in all of West Africa. He shared his view that the women were characterized by 'experience, skills, courage, perseverance and a hard-working, dependable professional attitude'.[54] Although they were the dominant force in West African trade, the women faced constraints which included lack of road networks and transport. Storage, sanitation and security were inadequate, childcare needs were unmet, and access to credit was negligible.[55]

Like the Women's Programme's region-wide survey of handicrafts and small industries in 1973, the findings of the market women's seminar verified the significance of women's participation in what became known as the 'informal sector' of national economies. It would prove to be one of the centre's key concerns over the long term, as the economic crisis deepened and African women sought incomes as entrepreneurs.

Human resource development was among the top priorities for African governments, and the training of trainers was the Women's Programme's response. As described earlier, it had become the first operational activity, back in 1973, and attracted significant external support.[56]

National institutions

The influence of United Nations decisions on the nascent governments of African countries was a positive factor in the gains made by women. At the time, and even today in many African countries, the state's role was dominant because the private and non-governmental sectors were not as yet fully developed. The ATRCW's status as part of the United Nations ECA therefore was a distinct asset for women, one that prompted a willingness on the part of national politicians and civil servants to co-operate.

Women leaders in member states of the ECA understood this well, and would invariably set appointments for ECA/ATRCW staff to meet with the heads of their states, vice-presidents or parliamentarians to discuss the UN perspective on a proposed undertaking. That approach was used in particular when women sought to establish durable institutions such as women's commissions or bureaux which would give official recognition to their concerns within the government structure.

The national machineries seminars sponsored by the ATRCW proved to be an effective tool for collaboration because they gave government officials and representatives of national women's organizations and other voluntary agencies opportunities to 'discuss and exchange ideas on the nature and type of machineries needed at the national and international levels to assist in promoting the full integration of women in the development process'.[57] The ECA's early commitment to institutionalizing women's concerns as a primary policy concept drew impressive external support. Louise Njai, who later became a Member of Parliament in the Gambia, described one positive aspect of the seminars: the ATRCW team brought information but, she said, they did not tell us what to do.

Governments began to demonstrate a genuine readiness to participate in the planning and establishment of national machineries for women. It was soon seen that the types of national machineries were as varied as the countries of the African continent. An ATRCW survey of governments of member states in 1976 showed a variety of patterns that ranged from a ministry for women's affairs, to a women's wing of the national political party. Some took the form of a national commission and/or women's bureau, an *ad hoc* committee with a select purpose and/or duration, or a non-governmental national council of women's organizations. While some countries had just one type, others had two or more.

Countries having 'women's wings' in political parties tended to consider these to be adequate for the intended purposes, and thus to reject the establishment of new offices within their governments. Of note concerning this rejection is that the political party was in a superior position to the government, and was thus the higher authority.

Another obstacle to the creation of the machineries concerned their potential relationship with existing non-governmental organizations. In many countries, trainers found a need to clarify the respective responsibilities of the new government offices and those of, for example, the national councils of voluntary women's organizations that had represented women's interests over the years.

The concept of national machineries gained momentum as pressure rose to establish sub-regional offices of the ATRCW and a regional advisory committee; *their* effectiveness would depend heavily on the strength of women's offices at national level. In turn, that strength would be enhanced by the ATRCW's databases, and the set of indicators that the centre had developed.[58]

By 1978, ATRCW-assisted seminars had been held in seventeen countries, twelve of which had actually established the machineries. There was wide agreement on the message of Lesotho's Queen Manohato at the closing of the seminar in her country: 'As are women, so is the nation.'[59] After visiting several countries in 1978, an ATRCW review mission included among its recommendations that the centre 'broaden the definition of national machinery' and increase its advisory and technical services to governments.[60]

As was often the case in the history of the ATRCW, individual women emerged who lent their stature and energies to the promotion of women's concerns. In Ghana, for example, the success of the national machinery process was due in large part to the determined efforts of Justice Jiaggie. She explained that she got the idea for the Ghana council when she represented her country on the UN Commission on the Status of Women for several years. Justice Jiaggie became the first Chairperson of the Ghana National Council on Women and Development. Among the council's twenty members were representatives of eight ministries, the Attorney-General and the Chair of the Public Service Commission; women held fifteen of the council seats.

Justice Jiaggie recalled that a legal instrument was created to make it possible for women who worked full-time to give time to the council, and women who were housewives, and a number of men.[61] On all matters relating to women and development, the council both advised the government and served as its representative to the people of Ghana and other countries. Working collaboratively, the members set up research programmes and a system to review and evaluate women's progress in every sector of development.

Through a technical team, the council also became involved in technological innovation, in improving women's productivity by mechanizing some of the processes, for example in making gari (processed cassava). Justice Jiaggie explained that the council first thought that literacy should be its primary concern.[62] Consultations with women from all over the country was enlightening: raising incomes became the highest priority.

Reflecting on the origins of the council and other development work, Jiaggie told us:

> One would wish to see development going at a faster pace. But it is going on, and if it hadn't started, this world would have hurt women so badly. There's a lot left to be done, but something was done; a start was made.[63]

The ATRCW collaborates with other
ECA divisions

All the work of the centre had as a key dimension the ECA itself; it involved mutual support between the ATRCW and the divisions of the ECA. Using early drafts of the ECA Programme of Work for 1978 and 1979 as a basis, the staff of the ATRCW identified areas of ongoing co-operation. In the Agriculture Division, for example, a joint research project was put in process in the mid-1970s to improve the technology that West African women needed to increase their rice production. ECA/ATRCW studies on women as food producers were undertaken in Nigeria and Ghana. In the field of manpower, a similar study on national development planning got under way.

ATRCW staff also participated in rural development comparative evaluation missions to Zambia, Uganda and Tanzania with their colleagues from the ECA Social Development Division. The Statistics Division and the ATRCW worked together to produce the already noted study of women's contributions to GNP in Lesotho. Further formal co-operative mechanisms took the form of inter-divisional studies, for example with the Manpower Division.

In both ATRCW-led activities and those of other ECA divisions, emphasis was increasingly given to human resource development (see Annexe 19).

Notes

1. See *The New International Economic Order: What Roles for Women?*, ECA, Addis Ababa, 1977, Chapter 1. The dependency theory was also coming under heavy criticism. Of interest a decade and a half later is a 1979 observation by Tony Smith of Tufts University in his article 'The Underdevelopment of Development Literature', in Atul Kohli (ed.), *The State and Development in the Third World*, Princeton University Press, 1986, p. 29. Having severely criticized dependency theory, Smith added that the threat of withdrawal of the international economic system from a country was the greatest threat – far greater than the threat of intervention. 'Implicit in dependency analysis', he said, was that withdrawal would 'abandon these dependent regimes to civil and regional conflict'. In the light of the near-collapse of countries like Liberia and Somalia, Smith appears as simultaneously iconoclast and prophet.

2. ECA, 'Revised Framework of Principles for the Implementation of the New International Economic Order in Africa, 1976–1981', Addis Ababa, 27 June 1976. E/CN.14/ECO/90/Rev.

3. Ibid.

4. ECA, 'Comprehensive Project Description: Pan-African Training and Research Centre for Women and African Women's Development Task Force', Addis Ababa, 1975. M75-629.

5. ECA, 'Presentation of the Pan-African Training Centre for Women, Donors Meeting, United Nations, New York, 28–29 January 1975'. The meeting, to be convened by Assistant Secretary-General Helvi Sipila, was postponed.

6. ECA, *The Data Base for Discussion of the Interrelationships Between the Integration of Women in Development, Their Situation and Population Factors*, Addis Ababa, 1974. E/CN. 14/SW/37, p. 86. The United Nations Branch for the Advancement of Women defines 'national machinery' as 'any organizational structure established with particular responsibility for the advancement of women and the elimination of discrimination against women at the central national level. These include governmental, non-governmental or joint governmental/NGO bodies, and could consist of one or several agencies. All are recognized by the Government as the national machinery for the advancement of women.' See *Directory of National Machinery for the Advancement of Women: 1993*. United Nations, Division for the Advancement of Women, Vienna, 1993.

7. *Resolution Adopted by the Conference of Ministers, Integration of African Women in National Development*, Nairobi, 24–28 February 1975. ECA, Addis Ababa, E/CN.14/RES/269(XII).

8. Letter to Mr Murray Mould, USAID, from M. Snyder, 6 March 1975. Subject: agencies that have pledged funds to the ATRCW to date.

9. United Nations, *Declaration of Mexico and Plans of Action*, United Nations, New York, December 1975, para. 14.

10. See *Report on the World Conference of International Women's Year*, 20 August 1975. E/CN.14/ECO.

11. The IWY Conference was the first UN conference at which the majority of the delegates were women; 113 delegations were headed by women. The ECA observer delegation, led by Riby-Williams, included Ritchie, Bazin, Okello, Snyder, Juliana Sendi and Rosita Armerding.

12. Louis Echeveria, President of Mexico.

13. See *The New International Economic Order: What Roles for Women?*

14. *Declaration of Mexico*, paras 14 and 18.

15. ECA, *The Role of Women in African Development*, 10 April 1975. E/CONF.66/BP/8.

16. UN, *Report of the IWY*, New York, 1975, pp. 48–50 and Resolution 27 entitled 'Measures for the Integration of Women in Development'.

17. World Bank, *Women and Development*, Washington, DC, 1990, p. 14. While this figure was said to rise in the following year, it still contained inputs rather than results.

18. Kathleen Staudt, *Women, International Development and Politics: the Bureaucratic Mire*, Temple University Press, Philadelphia, 1990, p. 9. See also p. 310.

19. Royal Ministry of Foreign Affairs, *Evaluation Report 3.91*, Oslo, 1991, p. 11.

20. Decree No. 322 of 2 April 1975. The Ghana Council became one of the models used by ECA's national machineries seminar teams.

21. Resolution 12, entitled 'Special Resources for the Integration of Women in Development'; the remaining IWY conference funds that remained after IWY became the first resources for VFDW (UNIFEM).

22. Resolution 26.

23. The American Association for the Advancement of Science (AAAS) and the UNDP sponsored a seminar on Women and Development, during the week that preceded the IWY Conference in Mexico City, 1975.

24. Resolution 10: 'Women and Credit'.

25. The UN regulations for technical assistance were interpreted as prohibiting giving financial grants as community credit funds; it was necessary for UNIFEM to pressure for the reinterpretation of both UN and UNDP trust fund regulations to open the possibility of such a facility.

26. There were 34 resolutions in all, each touching on some aspect of women's reality and intended to strengthen their future security and well-being. Those most relevant to the work of ATRCW were numbers 1, 3, 4, 12, 14, 21.

27. The Joint ECA/FAO Agriculture Division, Statistics Division and Socioeconomic Research and Planning Division.

28. Mary Tadesse, former Vice-Minister of Education in Ethiopia, had been a consultant in 1975 for three months; she was appointed Chief of the ATRCW on 16 February 1976.

29. Financial assistance was given by Christian Aid in the UK.

30. Marilyn Carr, Report on Visit to Sierra Leone, 15 April–3 May 1976, ATRCW, Addis Ababa, Ethiopia. Further studies were conducted in West African countries to identify ways in which agricultural output could be improved through better understanding of women's roles in agricultural work.

31. *Improving Village Water Supplies in Ethiopia: a Case Study of the Socio-economic Implications*, ECA/UNICEF, Addis Ababa, 1978. ECA/SDD/ATRCW/VTWATER/78.

32. Pilot projects recommended by Kenya are described in the 'Report on a Mission Undertaken at the Request of the Ministry of Housing and Social Services, Nairobi, Kenya, 21 June to 5 July 1976'. For other pilot projects, see 'Report on Activities for Nov. 1975–June 1976', ATRCW, Addis Ababa, July 1976. In many cases, projects encompassed the entire process of technological development:

researchers would first identify areas needing new technologies; village women, assisted by staff, would identify their specific technological needs; then the technology would be developed and put into use. In Mauritania, for example, when a need was identified, the project worked closely with nomadic women to develop new technologies for food preservation which included tools to ease the labour of pitting and drying dates. In Niger, project staff worked with women involved in salt extraction to develop technological improvements which would not only reduce workloads but would also reduce health hazards and increase incomes.

33. Marilyn Carr, *Appropriate Technology for African Women*, ECA, Addis Ababa, 1978. ECA/SDD/ATRCW/VTGEN/78.

34. Besides the ITDG and Christian Aid, the Appropriate Technology Unit activities were later financed by UNICEF, the Ford and Rockefeller Foundations and UNIFEM.

35. ECA, 'Revised Framework of Principles'.

36. See *African Women's Development Task Force*, booklet published by ECA/UNICEF/ZONTA International, May 1976.

37. 'Progress Report on the African Women's Development Task Force', ATRCW, Addis Ababa. Not dated.

38. Florence Abena Dolphyne, *The Emancipation of Women: an African Perspective*, Ghana Universities Press, Accra, 1991, p. 100. Sweden was the initial donor, contributing nearly half a million dollars for the task force. ZONTA International and UNICEF also contributed.

39. *Canadian Journal of African Studies*, Vol. 6, No. 2, Ottawa, 1972.

40. Kathleen Staudt, 'Women Farmers in Africa', in *Canadian Journal of African Studies*, Vol. 22, No. 3, Ottawa, 1988, pp. 567–8. Referring to the early ECA documents, Staudt says, 'These important, landmark overview documents began to prod more research and more institutional action', and 'over the last fifteen years, researchers have increasingly differentiated women farmers' experiences'. The ECA argued in 1972 that women, who were 'responsible for 60 to 80 percent of the agricultural labour', went 'unrecognized, unresourced, and unrewarded'.

41. See Annexe 14.

42. Snyder to Aiyegbusi, informal note, 1974.

43. Achola Pala-Okeyo, 'Definitions of Women and Development: an African Perspective', *Signs*, University of Chicago Press, 1977, pp. 9–13.

44. ECA, *The New International Economic Order: What Roles for Women?*, pp. 26–8.

45. Ibid., pp. 29–31.

46. Ibid.

47. ECA, 'Revised Framework of Principles'.

48. Hafkin edited some 115 Women's Programme/ATRCW documents assisted by Mekdes Gebre-Medhin, before joining the ECA's Pan-African Development Information System (PADIS) where she is currently Chief.

49. ECA, *Women and Development in Africa: an Annotated Bibliography*, Addis Ababa, 1977. This was Bibliography Series No. 1 of the ATRCW.

50. The annotated bibliography was edited and republished in 1983 by the Scandanavian Institute of African Studies in Uppsala as *Women in Tanzania: an Analytical Bibliography*, by Ophelia Mascarenhas and Marjorie Mbilinyi.

51. ECA, *Report of the Review Mission, African Training and Research Centre for Women*, 1978, Addis Ababa, 1978, p. 46, M78-809. The research programme of the centre

was initially financed by the Ford Foundation (legal status, village technology, national bibliographies and development indicators), and later also by the Rockefeller Foundation (women in agriculture), UNICEF (village technology and day care), the FAO and UNFPA (bibliographies and co-operatives), the VFDW (UNIFEM) (village technology, mass media, and small-scale industry), the ILO (small-scale industry) and the governments of Sweden (small enterprise) and the USA (employment).

52. Financed by the Finnish UN Association (Hilkka Pietella, Secretary-General; Helvi Saarivien, President), in co-operation with the Finnish National Committee for International Women's Year.

53. See Evaluation Series No. 1: *Report of Missions to Review and Follow-up the Results of Itinerant Training*, ECA, 1976.

54. Sori Bangura, Report 12–16 December 1977, ECA, Addis Ababa.

55. ECA, *Marketing in Ghana: an Analysis of Operational and Environmental Conditions*, Addis Ababa, 1984. E/ECA/ATRCW/81/07. The ATRCW financed the study by Elizabeth Ardayfio with a grant from the VFDM (UNIFEM). The study was proposed by the Ghana National Council on Women and Development.

56. Belgium and the Federal Republic of Germany were early contributors, as was the FAO/UNFPA which supplied the population and nutrition components, with input from the International Planned Parenthood Federation (IPPF). The United Nations Association of Finland contributed to workshops in new fields, communications and co-operatives.

57. ECA, *Report on Seminars on National Commissions on Women and Development and Women's Bureaux*, December 1974. USAID assisted for several years; Belgium also contributed to launching the national seminars.

58. ECA, *Report of the Review Mission*, p. 17. Recall that, in the mid-1970s, the ECA Women's Programme/ATRCW database and indicators were unique instruments and thus contributions to the knowledge and policy bases for governments. By 1977, support was being provided for national researchers to compile and publish the annotated bibliographies on women in their countries, both as an information base for the national machineries and researchers, and to evolve a set of 'quantified indicators to measure women's changing position *vis-à-vis* access to the tools and rewards of development'.

59. ECA, *Report on Seminars*. See also 'Mission Report: Seminar on National Commissions on Women and Development', December 1976.

60. ECA, *Report of the Review Mission*, pp. 19–20.

61. Interview with Justice Annie Jiaggie by Margaret Snyder, Accra, October 1993.

62. Ibid.

63. Ibid.

A Training Centre for Women: Conversations in Ethiopia with Etetu Zewdie, Terhas Berhane, Etagengn Ayele and Sister Carmelita

Q: The ATRCW got a grant from UNIFEM for the Bethlehem Centre to teach carpet weaving to young women. How many trainees were here when you started in 1977?

EZ: There were eighteen, but now we are about two hundred. I used to work in a coffee organization. I was not educated. When I started to work at Bethlehem I started going to school, and now I have completed. And I have a lot of skills, making floor carpet, tapestries, wall hangings. I am married, with two children, and we live a good life.

Do the single mothers who work here earn enough to support their families?

EZ: Yes, they do. They bring their children to our daycare. They earn enough to pay rent – not for a villa, but a simple house, made of wood and mud. When they complete their studying here for one year, they get a certificate, and go back and start their own work.

I think Bethlehem is a good example for Ethiopia. Bethlehem gives a lot of help to the poor. We take the children of the very poor in this area and keep them in daycare. We feed them. Besides that, when we get some things from outside, we distribute them to some women who stand at the gates. We distribute clothes, food, flour, whatever we can get. Bethlehem has a good name.

TB: I learned from Bethlehem, that if I had money, I would like to help others like Bethlehem does. Bethlehem is like a family to me.

Bethlehem is self-sufficient, from its sales, since 1985. More than two hundred women earn enough to support their families. What is the situation for young women seeking jobs?

SC: It's terrible. There are times when I wake up in the middle of the night and I think, poor thing, what is she going to do, and what will she eat, and with two or three children or sometimes four.

Is it harder for young women now than a few years ago?

SC: There is improvement with the women who are here. I visit their homes every now and then. There is improvement in the house, and in the way they dress. Many of them have finished the twelfth grade, because we ask them to go in the evenings. But I have only one who was entitled to university, out of so many.

How is the overall employment situation?

SC: Government is sending people away from their work. The different textile factories are retiring people, or don't have jobs for them. They have closed corporations and left hundreds and hundreds without jobs. So with the tradition, men are hired and the women have very little opportunity.

Most of the graduates of Bethlehem last year are working. There are just a few that have no jobs. We are trying to assist them.

If there were just one thing you could do for women, what would it be?

SC: That's very hard to answer. I vision and I dream that the government could open a lot of factories; investors could come and give women work. The creation of employment would be the answer to many problems.

Addis Ababa
November 1993

CHAPTER 8

OPERATIONAL OBSTACLES

Unfortunately, as happens in almost every organization, administrative obstacles began to appear as the ATRCW programme expanded. One such obstacle that arose jeopardized the centre's peaceful existence within the ECA. During the exciting months that followed the IWY Conference, ATRCW's immediate supervisor acknowledged that the Women's Programme had 'gathered momentum and has been making its presence felt widely both in the region and outside', due to its 'enthusiasm, competence and leadership, and the support of Unit staff'. None the less, despite that admission, he called for 'proper administrative procedures', meaning bureaucratic ones.[1] By June 1975, after a new Executive Secretary arrived at ECA, difficulties began to emerge.

The location of the ATRCW

During a briefing on the ATRCW, the Executive Secretary expressed his fear that, after the initial contributions generated by the concern of the moment and the celebration of 1975 as International Women's Year, there might not be constant sources of funds over the long term. He added that some donors might not be prepared to contribute to the centre in the future if it continued as a United Nations programme. A second senior official asserted that some donors (later shown to be a single donor, i.e. USAID) had begun to question the centre's future status. Was it to be in ECA, or was it to be independent and loosely attached to ECA?

ATRCW staff, surprised by such views, referred to earlier intergovernmental resolutions and proposed that consideration be given to making the centre semi-autonomous and to draw African governments more closely into its planning and administration, in the hope that they might also contribute to its finances. The decision was made to convene a regional meeting to discuss with African governments and donors the future status of the centre. A working group was appointed to prepare the proposals for that conference.

The issue of the ATRCW's relationship with the ECA remained open until March 1976, when the centre was presented with a 'First Draft Constitution of ATRCW' that was based on a new-to-ATRCW premiss that the centre should become autonomous and be located elsewhere, in a member country. Nigeria was mentioned informally as a potential location. However, a second working document introduced was one prepared by the Women's Centre legal expert and research assistant Nellie Okello and titled 'Status, Organization and Standing Committee of the African Training and Research Centre for Women'.[2]

The first section of Okello's document described the centre's philosophy as that of ensuring that women's concerns were integrated in all development efforts. It also recognized 'that special programmes may be necessary on the short-term basis to recover the lag in women's opportunities as compared with those of men'. That philosophy was cited as a major reason for continuing the location of the centre within the ECA as part of its human resource concerns. Juridically as well, the paper said:

> ECA is bound by resolutions of ECOSOC, the General Assembly, the ECA Conference of Ministers and the Conference of IWY, to intensify its activities directed toward women's roles in development.

Okello's paper then set out in detail the relevant paragraphs of the resolutions of each of those bodies. In addition, the objectives and organization of the centre itself were shown to lead to continuing its location in ECA. The document went on to justify the creation of an 'Africa Regional Standing Committee' that would open opportunities for governments to advise the ECA on the work of its women's programme and that would serve as a co-ordinating body for national commissions on women and development. Terms of reference were carefully delineated.

OAU, PAWO, and UN headquarters representatives were added to those from other groups who would attend the Africa Regional Standing Committee. This technical, legal document also served the more practical concerns of the staff of the ATRCW, who deemed the ECA's association with the United Nations and its procedures, especially staff recruitment, as critical to the professional and technical nature of the ATRCW's work.

In discussions, ATRCW staff recalled the centre's origins in ECA and its relationship with the United Nations. The view of the UNDP was cited; that organization had no desire to support the creation of an institution independent of the ECA. The most persuasive discussion points, however, were on PAWO's plans to establish its own Africa-regional training centre in Algiers.

In the end, it was recommended that the ECA should not create a parallel institution to that of PAWO, and that ATRCW should continue to have its present status as an integral part of the ECA within the proposed Social Development Division. In response to the evidence and discussions, no need was found for the ATRCW to have a constitution. It was advised, however, to establish an intergovernmental advisory committee for the ATRCW, on the model of the Conference of African Planners that advised the Conference of Ministers.

Thus the protracted effort by a few ECA officials to remove the centre not only from the ECA, but from the United Nations was nearly ended. Its complete demise would have to await discussion of the 'Africa Organization for Women and Development' that was presented as the alternative to the Africa Regional Standing Committee at the Nouakchott conference of 1977. That option attracted no attention whatsoever.

The stratagem for removing the centre appeared to arise within the ECA secretariat. One member of the external review mission that visited the ATRCW early in 1978 made a telling comment:

> The problem, I fear, is that the Centre has quietly, and almost entirely on its own resources, gone about its business rather more effectively than its fraternal partners in other divisions. As comparisons of the Centre's work with that of other elements of the Commission are thus often embarrassing to the latter, and partly also because the Centre has been so successful in attracting outside donor support, the 'ladies' (as the Centre was called by one high ECA official) are a rather successful bundle of energy and drive who sometimes appear to threaten less progressive elements of the ECA bureaucracy.[3]

Grateful for the demise of the would-be internal coup, ATRCW staff were finally able to get on with the centre programmes in the region. None the less, as will be seen, the vanquished few ECA staff who were behind the effort for relocation would seek opportunities to divide and conquer on the issue of permanent posts – even for the Chief of the centre – and on the course of the ATRCW's decentralization to the sub-regions.

Ironically, another obstacle to be overcome in the early life of the ATRCW arose from the multiplicity and types of donors to its programme, who ranged from multilateral and bilateral entities to NGOs. Most of the donors had their own accounting and reporting systems, and they often had different fiscal years. Project-directed grants arriving at different times made the creation of a holistic programme difficult because they left gaps in funding schedules. When ZONTA International was prepared to finance task force volunteers, for example, another donor had not yet transferred the funds to hire the task force officer who would run the programme.

The ECA itself, as a UN regional commission, relied mostly on the United Nations regular budget, although it had some supplementary, mainly large scale, grants from bilateral donors. Given such reliance on a single source of support, the ECA was not administratively attuned to reporting to a variety of relatively small-scale donors. The ATRCW thus faced the wrath of its own donors when their accounting schedules were ahead of the ECA's. For example, UNICEF provided continuing grants on a rotating basis, following expenditure reports. When there were no reports, there were no further allocations. The solution for the ATRCW was to have its own accountant; Tekkie Gebre-Medhin was hired.

The increasing number and types of ATRCW operational programmes involved both individual and multiple-country activities which varied from study tours to installation of technologies. In contrast, the ECA itself was administratively structured to carry out inter-country – rather than country-specific – activities, and they were generally limited to meetings, technical advice and research. An example of the implications of these differences in type of activity comes from the ATRCW's effort to have the ECA ship trial grain-grinding mills from the UK to West Africa. It took over a year, and a well-honed sense of humour, to get them delivered.

The deviation in funding sources and in modes of operation between the ATRCW and the ECA posed innumerable obstacles to the efficiency of the ATRCW activities. Nevertheless, staff preferred the challenge of overcoming those administrative obstacles to having the centre become a country-based operation whose ties to the UN would be weakened or severed.[4]

The centre also encountered gender-related technical problems. One clear example can be drawn from the experience of projects intended to introduce efficient maize shellers to rural women. Several versions of hand-held maize shellers were invented (by men) to reduce the workload of women. This was not ordinarily men's work, and as a result the devices they made actually increased the time and energy women expended and therefore were never used. Next, a pedal-operated maize shelling machine was invented, one that was low-cost and easy to repair. It too was never used because in the village where it was introduced, it was culturally inappropriate for women to sit astride a machine. Similarly, efforts to get women to harvest crops with scythes rather than small knives failed because scythes required that the crops be cut lower on the stalk – something the men had not considered. The new devices increased the deadweight of women's burden and left short stumps on which they cut their feet.[5]

Staffing and financial support

From its inception as the Women's Programme in 1972, the ATRCW faced the formidable task of securing adequate funds to hire staff and to support its activities. This was due in part to the ECA's own traditions, in which women had played insignificant roles. The three professional staff employed at the newly established centre were not included in the regular ECA budget but were provided for from external resources.[6] Additional posts were created by inserting staff components in nearly every external grant proposal for operational activities.

The two major, long-term contributors to senior management and staffing were the very foresighted SIDA, whose initial two posts of 1970 continued for more than five years, and the persistent VFDW/UNIFEM, which financed two senior posts for the ATRCW from late 1977 for several years. Both organizations also gave extensive support to operational activities.

By 1978, the centre's professional staff had increased to eleven and its supporting staff to eight as its activities multiplied.[7] Despite that obvious success, only one of those positions was funded by the ECA. In fact, Daria Tesha of the ATRCW was the only African woman at professional level in the whole ECA enterprise at that time. The review mission members were 'frankly stunned' when they examined that information. They found that the situation created insecurity, blocked promotion opportunities for staff, and jeopardized staff continuity.[8]

The ECA, not unlike other bureaucracies, was very slow to consider gender issues in employment practices. In response to the ECA's Conference of Ministers' Resolution 269 (XII) (see Annexe 10a), Executive Secretary Adebayo Adedeji announced his commitment to provide the centre with posts financed from the regular United Nations budget by 1980. Adedeji regretted what he saw as an inevitable time lag between commitment and actual financial support, and he called on the ATRCW's partners and potential partners to institutionalize the centre's posts in their own annual budgets.[9]

The uncertainty about resources, due to dependence on external financing, left the ATRCW in a risky situation even though Adedeji assured the staff that such dependency was normal for any newly initiated programme. Despite his confidence, the review mission observation prevailed: it was impossible for the centre to offer job security or promotion. One solution might have been to recruit the spouses of the ECA staff, but such a policy was frowned upon by both the UN and ECA at that time. As a result, the centre could not give full-time employment to such qualified persons as Danielle Bazin of Haiti, with a PhD from the Sorbonne, and Juliana Sendi of Uganda, with an MSc in Agriculture.

Adding to the staffing difficulties was the geographical location of the ECA. Ethiopia was undergoing civil unrest in the 1970s which made the prospect of living and working in Addis Ababa unappealing to recruits from other places – especially if they had young children. Eventually, in the early 1980s, the United Nations set a policy in favour of hiring spouses.

The review mission 'deplored the fact' that the ECA had allocated insufficient funds to support the centre: a bare 2.6% of the ATRCW's total resources came from its parent organization. At the same time, the ECA subtracted the standard 14% from donor contributions for administrative expenses.[10]

Finding the centre's future to be 'clearly precarious', the review mission recommended that six posts be deployed to the ATRCW from the ECA's regular UN budget. Following that lead, women's groups, donor organizations, and the Consultative Committee on the Voluntary Fund for

Women (UNIFEM) continued to pressure the ECA and the finance committee of the UN General Assembly to channel additional UN resources to posts for women at the regional commissions.

The issue of ECA support to the ATRCW, and at the very least the assignment of a core group of regular budget posts to the centre, would escalate in importance among donors in the 1980s. Partners would continue to play their part, they said, if the ECA played its own part. That perception of the ECA as uninterested was later exacerbated by the commission's prolonged reluctance officially to appoint a head of the ATRCW even after a permanent post was created by the UN General Assembly.

One bright spot in all the uncertainty was that nearly all of the external financing had come to the Five-year Programme and the ATRCW *after* the master plan for their activities had been designed. Donors thus responded to the programme/centre's own priorities, ones that flowed from the decisions and requests of the women of the region. Based on that fact, the ATRCW was able to negate the charge made by its critics that the donors had dictated the centre's priorities. In reality, as the entire history of the centre proves, African women themselves had set the agenda and determined the priorities.

It was with a great deal of satisfaction that the ATRCW heard itself called 'the star in the ECA crown' with respect to donor support. By 1978 numbering fifteen who participated actively, the donors represented bilateral, multilateral and private non-governmental organizations. Having secured US$4.3 million between 1973 and 1978, the centre earmarked 83% of its funds for operational activities. The diversity and level of support was considered 'both an extraordinary accomplishment and a significant factor' contributing to the centre's effectiveness.[11] (See Annexe 9.)

Some recognition and a final step

As the decade of the 1970s came to a close, the ATRCW had not only survived the threat to its status within the ECA, but it had also achieved a level of maturity and stability. Its policies were implemented in significant programmes and its built-in evaluation process assured that it had the flexibility to adjust to changing needs and circumstances.

In addition, thanks to a broadened database and consultations in the region, progress had been made in understanding local, national and international perspectives and influences on the effectiveness of women's contributions to development. Helvi Sipila, the Assistant Secretary-General of the UN, observed that Africa had taken the lead in the whole world, and described the ATRCW as 'the pride of the UN system'.[12]

The review mission of 1978 summarized some of the challenges the centre was successfully facing:

As the first regional centre for women in the world, the ATRCW is recognized as a bold and imaginative experiment. It has had no model to follow, but rather has itself become a model for other regions. Moreover, the region served by the Centre is a vast area, comprising no less than forty-nine countries, and is culturally characterized by a multiplicity of languages, cultural institutions, political systems and levels of economic development. Any assessment of the Centre's success in fulfilling its role during the first few years of its existence must start with an appreciation of the constraints imposed upon it by virtue of the diversity of the context – Africa – in which it is located.

There is no question that the achievements of the Centre to date ... would not have been possible had it not been for the extraordinary versatility, skills and commitment of its staff to the development, implementation and evaluation of programmes. The staff are to be commended for their achievements, given the general constraints ... as well as those imposed upon them by the precariousness of their job security, the lack of promotion opportunities available to them, and the difficult working conditions in which they must operate.[13]

That bit of praise led Deputy Executive-Secretary David Ganao to challenge the agencies of the United Nations system to take another step toward co-ordination:

It is our hope that those agencies which are already contributing to the Centre's work will at the appropriate time consider regularizing their participation and that those not already involved will one day join us. The suggestion I am making is that the ATRCW should become officially an interagency Centre, as it already is in fact. Thus it will later be able to become a joint division of ECA, just like those we already have with FAO in agriculture and UNIDO in industry. ... [O]nly through teamwork can we eliminate waste of all kinds. Only through teamwork can we fight more effectively against poverty, inequality and prejudice in Africa and throughout the world.[14]

Set up as a genuinely inter-organizational centre, the ATRCW was now positioned for the creation of the final element of the institutional structure foreseen at regional conferences a decade earlier, the intergovernmental body that would co-ordinate a flow of information among governmental machineries for the advancement of women, and guide the policies of ATRCW. The instrument for accomplishing those tasks came to be known as the Africa Regional Co-ordinating Committee (ARCC). Its work and that of the ATRCW itself would be strengthened by the location of centre staff in the ECA's sub-regional offices. The centre could then reach out more easily to the women it was created to serve.

Notes

1. Memo to M. Snyder, 1 November 1974.
2. The ATRCW document was dated 22 March 1976. Its two parts were entitled

'Status, Objectives and Organization of ATRCW', and 'Justification and Terms of Reference of the African Regional Standing Committee'.

3. ECA, *Report of the Review Mission, ATRCW*, 10 April 1978.

4. Of interest and affirming the ATRCW staff view is the case of the Women's Centre in Asia. Initially located in Iran, it was moved to Bangkok, located with ESCAP, following the fall of the Shah. With the demise of autonomous regional centres in the Asia-Pacific region when UNDP ceased its funding of them, the Women's Centre was shifted to become a small unit in the Asia Pacific Development Centre in Malaysia.

5. Marilyn Carr, *Appropriate Technology for African Women*, ECA, Addis Ababa, 1978, pp. 28 and 68.

6. Each subject-specific project included its own staff. It will be recalled also that programmes like Itinerant Training and National Machineries Seminars made use of a number of short-term consultants in the early years of the Women's Programme, while SIDA and the FAO/UNFPA financed the first three professional positions.

7. Four of the eleven professionals had PhDs and one had an LL B. Most of the others had masters' degrees. A fifth PhD was under recruitment.

8. ECA, *Report of the Review Mission, ATRCW*, Addis Ababa, 1978, p. 51.

9. Presentation of the ECA Executive Secretary to the Opening of the ATRCW Review Mission, 7 March 1978. The UN organization partners in 1978 included the FAO, UNFPA, UNICEF, UNOTC, the UN Voluntary Fund for the Decade for Women, and the ILO, while the UNDP and UNESCO expected to have similar affiliation in the future.

10. ECA, *Report of the Review Mission, ATRCW*, pp. 62–3. Some quipped that two thirds of the centre's operating budget came from outside donors, close to one third from member states, and the remainder from the ECA.

11. See also 'Summary of Grants: ECA Women's Programme and ATRCW, 1973–1978', in ECA, *Report of the Review Mission, ATRCW*, p. 67.

12. Message from Helvi Sipila, Assistant Secretary-General for Social Development and Humanitarian Affairs to the Review Mission of the ECA/ATRCW 7–28 March, 1978, mimeo.

13. ECA, *Report of the Review Mission, ATRCW*, p. 51.

14. Opening statement by Mr David Charles Ganao, Deputy Executive Secretary, on behalf of the Executive Secretary, in 'Report of the First Meeting of the Interagency Working Group on the Integration of Women in Development in Africa, 30–31 March 1978', ECA, Addis Ababa, Annexe II.

The Africa Regional Co-ordinating Committee and Women: a conversation with Selina Taylor

Q: In the 1960s, women were already calling for a region-wide women's committee. Why was that so important for so long?

ST: In those days women searched for ways to improve their lives. When the ECA ministerial body was established, women also wanted a mechanism to address specific issues of women.

You were Chairperson of the ARCC. How was the ARCC a mechanism for change?

The structure of the ARCC itself brought a number of changes. The ARCC was composed of women who represented their national machineries. They then chose a president, executive members and secretaries. Each member brought a report on activities in her country; there were new ideas on health, education, community development, poverty alleviation. The reports were so rich in themselves and so frank in their compilation that the ARCC offered opportunities to learn from one another.

The ARCC and the ATRCW worked closely together?

Yes, the ATRCW is the lifeblood of the ARCC, it is the executive arm of ARCC. Whatever the Committee has been able to do has been effective because the centre supported it administratively and morally.

What do you think of 'mainstreaming' – making sure that women are represented in larger organizations?

If planning for women were done at the central level, then there would be no need to have national machineries that are specifically concerned with women. Each ministry would monitor its provisions for women. But that isn't feasible now, because in time, nobody would be interested and that would be the end of it. In some countries national machineries have the technical capacities to follow programmes in health, housing and other sectors, and estimate their benefits to women. In most countries, however, the machineries are appendices of strong ministries and they are not empowered enough.

There is a democratic political wind blowing over Africa. This is an instrument of change. Women should seize the opportunity to strengthen their national machineries – they can create women's ministries.

Do you think the attitudes of men towards women and development have changed over the past decade?

Yes. I do not know the exact degree. But we can use the ARCC as the measuring point. Since the ARCC came into being some fourteen years ago we have tried to put the cause of women on the doorsteps of men at national forums. Women have been able to make inroads into country planning and to get their views heard. Without the support of women, Ghana wouldn't have been able to reach as far as it has at the moment. The aspirations of the women of Ghana have never been lost.

Is life more difficult for young women today than in the past?

Youth today, especially young women, leave the hinterland, and rush to the big cities in search of jobs that are nonexistent; they travel across national borders. Because they don't have money, they fall prey to prostitution and deadly diseases. My advice to young people, especially young women, is to ensure that they keep to their partners, keep the jobs they have, observe the rules of health and hygiene. Make money through employment, not selling one's self.

What of the ATRCW in the future?

These days, women are calling on their governments to create ministries for women. The centre is the only, most important institution on the continent that has the technical know-how to help them. There is a critical need to improve the capacity of the ATRCW to absorb the problems that such national machineries face.

Accra
December 1993

CHAPTER 9

OUTREACH AND INFLUENCE:
A REGIONAL NETWORK

By the late 1970s the ATRCW had come of age. Over the years it had been successful in gaining respect for women's contribution to the economic development of their countries and of the Africa region as a whole. More important, through the centre's efforts, the role of women in the food cycle was now held in high esteem. The centre's goal remained constant throughout the 1980s; the systematic collection of data on the conditions of women and upgrading of skills continued, but there were profound changes in its work.

The ATRCW became, unquestionably, a core part of the activities of the ECA, and from that position of strength it sought to exploit more of the commission's human and material resources. New collaborative arrangements were also made with regional bodies and global organizations such as UNIFEM and INSTRAW.

The 1980s also saw the ATRCW promoting sub-regional and regional networking systems for the advancement of African women. Following the decision of the ECA to decentralize, policy organs were set up in regional and sub-regional bodies, complementing those at national levels. Regional conferences were regularized, and global and regional mandates continued to be articulated. Some of those were directed solely to the condition of women, whilst others brought women's influence to bear on overall strategies laid down to promote the socio-economic development of Africa.

All this took place in the context of a disturbing and serious economic crisis and at a time when political instability was further aggravated by the drought and famine that affected all segments of society. Thus, since 'the issue of women's development in Africa is inextricably bound up with the problem of peace and Africa's development', the general condition of women during this period improved little, and in some cases deteriorated.[1] There was no turning back, however. African women's perception of themselves and their situation had changed dramatically during the years following independence. They had begun to question the status quo and to assert their right to have a say, not only in affairs that affected them directly but in every issue that impacted on society as a whole.

The ATRCW took those facts into account during the process of visualizing a positive scenario in the 1980s in which African women's aspirations could be met. The centre reviewed the policy premisses on which the Five Year Programme for Women and the ATRCW itself were grounded. It found that the 1970s illustrated the correctness of involving a wide range of concerns rather than maintaining a narrow focus, and that such an approach needed to be intensified. The centre also looked at macro influences. For example, government attempts to respond to the economic crisis by restructuring often cancelled out the gains made by their activities that addressed women's needs. The structural adjustment programmes (SAPs) had a similar negative impact on the situation of women. Thus, as the centre's work progressed, it became necessary to question the rationale for activities directed solely to women. The same held true at the Copenhagen World Conference when it became clear that women's lives should be viewed in the broadest context possible.

The ECA and decentralization

Since many of the problems faced by women in both domestic and public life were intricate and would require time to improve, African women leaders were anxious to see organizations or entities that would follow women's situations in a sustained manner and with a long-term perspective. Structures would have greater powers of persuasion and more impact than individual efforts. Although a number of countries in Africa had already established national institutions or machineries to improve the situation of women, in order to accelerate gender-related interventions action was now required at sub-regional and regional levels as well.

With the ECA's new decentralization policy in effect in the various sub-regions of Africa in the late 1970s, it finally became possible for the ATRCW to respond to the long-desired goal of women: that it establish its presence at sub-regional levels. This would ensure that the sub-regional system would become gender-sensitive and would revise its programmes accordingly.

The ECA's decentralization policy arose from its original mandate: to promote the economic development of Africa with the purpose of raising the standard of living of the population, while strengthening the economic relations between its countries as well as with the outside world.[2] To meet the socio-economic need of the whole region was a noble goal. In reality, however, as Africa is a region of diverse cultures and of people endowed with different resources, it was essential to address the problems of specific sub-groups. There was thus strong pressure on the ECA from member states to decentralize its activities into the sub-regions. Hence, in consultations with governments, the countries were grouped together in sub-regional entities in order to tackle their unique problems.

Among the efforts made by the ECA to focus on sub-regional matters was the setting up of the United Nations Development Advisory Teams (UNDATs) in 1971. Their purpose was 'to help member states in planning, implementing, public administration and management and to provide advisory services where they were needed'.[3] However, after the UNDATs had been in place for seven years it was determined that a machinery giving more than just 'advisory services' was needed to meet the severe conditions that were then prevalent in African countries. The major appeals to the ECA were actually for technical assistance.

To understand what lay behind this urgency it is only necessary to recall that when the new African countries emerged from the colonial era they found themselves economically dependent on the limited number of commodities they were able to produce. As a result, they were extremely vulnerable to any changes in the international market economy. By the early 1970s inflation was rampant, and oil prices especially were rocketing. Although many countries in the global community were affected by the oil crisis, the impact on fragile African economies was dramatic. At the same time the stability of the countries was also at risk due to internal disturbances, as different forces struggled to shape governmental structures.

In that negative environment a new formula was devised in 1977 to protect African countries. Based on the ECA's *Revised Framework of Principles for the Implementation of the New International Economic Order in Africa 1976–1981*, UNDATs were replaced by the Multinational Programming and Operational Centres (MULPOCs) in 1977.[4] The primary objective of the MULPOCs was the promotion of economic co-operation through creating sub-regional common markets, as a step towards establishing a regional common market.[5] The idea was to make Africa more self-reliant and less dependent on external economic forces. MULPOCs were meant to be the operating arm of the ECA and thus were poised to bring 'meaningful benefits to the African states in trade, agriculture, industry, transport, energy, tourism, manpower and social development'.[6]

The ECA's move to decentralize was seen at the ATRCW as a golden opportunity to initiate gender concerns at the sub-regional level. A review of MULPOC programmes revealed that women were rarely recruited to staff professional positions, so it was not surprising that little or no attention was given to gender issues. The ATRCW was also convinced that even though African women as a whole had similar problems to cope with, their world-view and day-to-day concerns differed significantly, depending on the area is which they lived. That reality had to be considered if development goals were to be attained. The ATRCW's new objective was to sensitize the MULPOC system to women's needs, as well as to assist women in articulating their desires and aspirations.

A three-tiered structure for women emerges

The opportunity for women to have their presence felt at sub-regional levels through the MULPOCs brought with it certain advantages. Staff from the ATRCW would be outposted at the MULPOCs offices and would thereby be able to influence the overall programme since they would be in close touch with the women they served. Intermediary advisory bodies would be created to link national machineries with the regional advisory body. Together, they would form an Africa regional co-ordinating committee.

The establishment of machineries at sub-regional level would create the final tier of a three-tiered structure to represent women's interests from national to sub-regional to regional levels. Each level would have both a policy body and a secretariat: the national commissions would relate to bureaux; the sub-regional intergovernmental bodies to MULPOC officers; and the regional co-ordinating committee would have the ATRCW. This system was based on the wishes of member states and was included in the ECA's Medium Term Plan for 1976–1981 which the UN General Assembly approved.

At the apex of that three-tiered system was the formal intergovernmental regional body (the regional co-ordinating committee) that had first been recommended at the Rabat conference in 1971 and again in the African Plan of Action of 1974. Composed primarily of heads of national machineries, it could become the advocate for the millions of African women who were invisible and voiceless, because it was in a position to influence the ECA's top governing group, the Council of Ministers. The ideas were clear, but a master plan was needed to resolve the procedural questions as to how the regional committee would relate to the sub-regional levels (the MULPOCs), to the ATRCW, and to the ECA Conference of Ministers. The plan would also have to include the needs of women locally so that their proposals for action could be brought to each level in the system.[7]

The Nouakchott Regional Conference on the Implementation of National, Regional and World Plans of Action in 1977 offered a good opportunity to bring the final plan together. The ECA was asked to report to the conference in the Mauritanian capital on the progress made in Africa since the World Conference of International Women's Year held in Mexico. Seventy-one official participants representing thirty-five governments attended the Nouakchott meeting, which was officially opened by the then President of Mauritania, H.E. Moktar Oulddaddah. The United Nations sent a top official from Headquarters, Ms Lusibu N'Kanza (Zaire) who was the Director of the Centre for Social Development and Humanitarian Affairs.

During the conference James Riby-Williams of the ECA worked round the clock to come up with an acceptable proposal for institutionalizing the structures. The final plan, based on the Rabat recommendations and the African Plan of Action, was endorsed by Adebayo Adedeji, the ECA's Executive Secretary. In the early hours of 1 October, the proposal containing two basic provisions was presented, discussed and finally endorsed by the Nouakchott conference.

The first proposal established the Africa Regional Co-ordinating Committee for the Integration of Women in Development (ARCC). The second provision set up committees within existing MULPOCs at the sub-regional level.

The task of the ARCC was to be, *inter alia*, to assist and advise all ECA activities directed towards the advancement of women, relative to similar activities in governments and other agencies in the region. The ARCC would also co-ordinate the activities of the sub-regional committees (see below). With the ATRCW as its technical arm, the ARCC was to initiate studies, design surveys, exchange information, 'for a proper understanding of the situation of women and the factors facilitating or limiting their advancement'.[8]

Finally, the Nouakchott plan proposed that a comprehensive regional conference be held every three years on the question of women so that progress made in the region as a whole could be assessed.

During the conference debates, many misgivings were expressed. Some delegates were uneasy about the supra-national structure of ARCC, fearing that national machineries would lose their autonomy. Pan-African organizations were concerned about possible competition and questioned whether the ARCC would simply duplicate the work of the ATRCW that the ECA had established. Senegal, Mali and Guinea were among the few who abstained from the discussions because the proposal appeared too political, while others, like Niger, questioned the need for sub-regional entities.[9]

In the end, the concerns were adequately addressed. The new system would allow for the affirmation of women's role in the whole agricultural cycle, from production to marketing. It would promote and enhance the view of women as agents of development rather than as recipients of benefits, and give credit to the influence women had on the younger generation. The majority of participants began to agree that the ARCC would provide the necessary 'platform' for women to spread their message.

The astute chairperson of the conference, Assaita Kane, President of the National Mauritania People's Party, had the difficult task of building consensus. Finally, the ECA Executive Secretary himself intervened in the debate. He made it clear to the conference that the rejection of a proposal which took so much effort and compromise, and which was reflective of so many resolutions, would constitute a setback to the progress being made in promoting the well-being of women in Africa. After several amendments, the meeting adopted the three-tiered machinery proposal, thus completing the process of integrating women's interests throughout the administrative system of the ECA.

To most governments the attractive feature of the plan was that it promised the decentralization of resources and activities in the ECA Women's Centre to the sub-regional and national levels. To the ATRCW it signified an opportunity to extend its work throughout the region. Stronger guidance from the member states through the Conference of Ministers would also be a positive outcome.

Implementing the plan

Though the conference in Mauritania approved the network of structures, several steps were needed before the plan became operational. The committees at both the sub-regional and regional levels had to be established officially, and then each sub-regional committee had to elect three government representatives to serve as members of the ARCC. The ARCC had to meet in an inaugural session and send its constitution to the Fourteenth Session of the ECA and to the fifth meeting of the Conference of Ministers which were meeting in Morocco in March 1979. Thus 1978–1979 was a most hectic period for the ATRCW.[10]

The ECA was acutely aware that, to make the sub-regional programme functional, human and material resources were both required. Therefore, in 1981 the ATRCW commissioned a study on the critical needs of women within the framework of the Gisenyi and Lusaka MULPOCs. The report noted that their national, sub-regional and regional organizations had all drawn impressive work plans and embarked on projects in behalf of women. Their potential to achieve their programme goal had been severely constrained by a variety of structural, manpower and financial problems.[11] Fortunately, the UNDP recovered from its liquidity crisis and, with its long-promised support, came to the rescue.

Marcel Dookingué, Assistant Administrator of the UNDP and Regional Director for Africa, had argued as early as 1979 that:

> The issue was not whether or not women would be involved in the development process, since they already were, but rather a matter of ensuring that their efforts were recognized and more equitably rewarded. That implied that men must resist the temptation to provide the leadership in women's activities and let women themselves plan their business.[12]

He thus agreed to give $2.6 million to make the ARCC and the MULPOC programme for women functional for the duration of the UNDP cycle (1982–86). As a result, the UNDP became a major donor to the Women's Centre of the ECA. Using these funds, and in consultation with the ARCC, the ECA started the process of recruiting programme officers in each MULPOC. The candidates were to be recruited from the sub-region concerned but not from the host countries of the MULPOCs, in order to avoid undue pressure from these countries.[13]

Soon after taking up their posts each co-ordinator paid individual visits to the ECA/ATRCW for briefing and discussion. In June 1980, a special five-day workshop was arranged at the ECA office in Addis Ababa to give co-ordinators an in-depth orientation on trends in the MULPOCS, ATRCW and ECA in general which would help them to harmonize their work programmes and their relationship with the ECA. ATRCW workshop director Sori Bangura had invited relevant ECA department heads to the workshop to address some of the issues raised by the coordinators.

A follow-up training workshop was organized in 1982 by the ECA in collaboration with the UNDP. The main aim this time was to introduce the co-ordinators to UNDP Country Programming Roundtables and NATCAPs.[14]

In 1979, the inaugural meeting of the ARCC was held in Rabat. The fifteen founding member states, nominated from each sub-region, were all present.[15] This first meeting turned out to be a stormy one. The participants, fresh from their sub-regional elections, saw the ARCC as being the highest co-ordinating body for women in Africa. Led by the committee-elected President, Delphine Tsanga, Minister of Social Affairs of the United Republic of Cameroun, they questioned the need to hold a regional conference every three years with all member states present. They were also impatient with the ATRCW's progress in decentralizing some of its resources and decision-making powers to the sub-regions. In short, they viewed the role of the ARCC as much more than 'to assist and advise ECA in its activities directed towards the integration of women in development ...' As a result, the draft terms of reference for the ARCC proposed in Nouakchott were revised and replaced by a more active role for the ARCC.

One of the ARCC's functions now became to 'evaluate and implement work programs bearing in mind the availability of resources'. Another was to 'organize the exchange of information and experiences'.[16] Despite the apprehension of the secretariat regarding these functions, which were clearly those of the ECA, they were adopted by the ECA Conference of Ministers in Resolution 365 (XIV) (see Annexe 10c). This event indicates the seriousness with which women leaders viewed their responsibilities as members of the ARCC.[17]

The inaugural meeting of the ARCC was a proud moment for African women. It was held in the presence of Helvi Sipila, United Nations Assistant Secretary-General for Social Development and Humanitarian Affairs. Sipila paid tribute to African men and women who she said were making great efforts towards a goal of the International Development Strategy for the Second Development Decade – the full integration of women in the development effort. Sipila thought that an important step had been taken with the establishment of regional and sub-regional committees to work in close collaboration with national governments and machineries to promote the advancement of women.[18]

Once established, the ARCC became the policy-making body and subsidiary organ of the ECA for the purpose of focusing on the advancement of women; its recommendations could now be directly submitted to the annual meetings of the ECA Conference of Ministers. In fact, the ARCC became the political arm of the women's programme.

Selina Taylor, a former President of the ARCC, says:

> The structure of the ARCC brought a number of changes ... the representatives brought reports detailing activities at national levels, new ideas on women's health, education, community development, poverty alleviation, etc. The reports were so rich in themselves, frank in their compilation, that the forum offered member participants the opportunity to learn, give and take from each other.[19]

With the exception of the year 1980, the committee has held its annual meetings religiously up to the present time. Using the reports it receives from the sub-regions, it presents in a concise manner the needs and wishes of African women to the highest organs of the ECA. These proposals, when endorsed, find their way to ECOSOC and eventually to the UN General Assembly.

As a major advocate for the women of Africa, the ARCC has strongly argued for more research, and for the gathering and dissemination of statistical data at national levels. Such information can be used as the basis for concrete activities and projects that meet the development needs of women. The ARCC has also continually urged the UN and other donor organizations to increase the allocation of material and human resources for the women's programme at all levels. This effort has included a sustained request for permanent posts for the ATRCW.

Additional advocacy on the part of the ARCC has been directed to encouraging African governments to ratify the UN Convention on the Elimination of All Forms of Discrimination against Women (CEDAW).[20] The committee strongly urged these same governments and other entities to endorse the 'Arusha Forward Looking Strategies for the Advancement of Women' (1984), as well as the 'Abuja Declaration on Participatory Development: the Role of Women in Africa in the 1990s'.

In all such efforts the ARCC has kept the advancement of African women as its major concern. Considering African women leaders as the central force for change, the ARCC has seen the building of consensus among them as one of its outstanding achievements. The ARCC was able to alert the leadership to the issues to be addressed at the Copenhagen World Conference in 1980 and, more important, at the Nairobi World Conference in 1985.

It was during the annual statutory meetings of the ECA that the ARCC

played its most important role, particularly at the Technical Preparatory
Committee Meetings of the Whole (TEPCOW). When ARCC reports
were presented, one could sense an uneasy feeling among the predominantly male members of TEPCOW. There were lengthy questions and
discussions on women's issues, especially in the meetings that took place
in Cameroun (1986), Addis Ababa (1987), Niger (1988) and Tripoli (1990).
The major apprehensions of TEPCOW seem to have centred around
their fears about the impact on African women of the worldwide movement for the emancipation of women. They did not yet understand the
African origins of the women and development movement. These fears
have been admirably reflected by the Nigerian poet Molara Ogundipe-
Leslie who said that:

> the male dominated society reacts in the usual sexist fashion by denying that
> there is any oppression of women in Africa; glorifying an unknown pre-colonial
> past where our African mothers were totally happy, accusing conscious women
> activists of being victims of Western ideas and copy cats of white women;
> claiming that the 'family' is more important than the fate of the individual;
> brushing aside women's concerns with hypocrisy that 'national development' is
> a greater priority now than women's liberation; asserting that women anyhow
> do not need to be liberated because they have never been in bondage. So you
> have a compounding of historical and sociological falsification. The most vocal
> and courageous who continue to talk socially and politically are stigmatized.[21]

At these meetings, presidents and members of ARCC such as Selina
Taylor (Ghana), Assaita Kane (Mauritania), and Mariama Sow (Guinea)
spoke at length and with courage to sensitize the members to the importance of African women. They also presented the legitimate demands
of African women for consideration so that TEPCOW would help to
ameliorate negative conditions. The ECA secretariat was fully conscious
of the role the ARCC was playing at these meetings. It soon became
unthinkable to present gender-related issues without taking into consideration the views of the ARCC. 'What would ARCC say?' was a frequent
question asked by ECA colleagues when organizing meetings and conferences that touched on gender.

Training at sub-regional level (MULPOCs)

Time and again it has been said that Africa does not lack human resources;
in fact it has a young, vibrant workforce. What it lacks is a skilled workforce
able to exploit Africa's potential in the war against poverty, ignorance and
disease. It is in this context that we need to view the importance of
imparting knowledge and know-how to women. It was the ECA Women's
Programme's major policy premiss: the most serious problems of development defy solution without women.

A basic evaluation of the ATRCW's work mentioned earlier was undertaken by major donors and prominent women from the region; they confirmed this view, and their 1978 report had a major impact on programme orientation.[22] The review mission's primary task was 'To assess the appropriateness of the Center's objective and program in response to national and regional priorities for increasing the participation of women in the development process.'[23] In line with their particular field of interest, members of the review mission travelled to Gambia, Cameroun, Ghana, Tanzania, Zambia, Kenya, Mauritania, and Senegal, where they held extensive discussions with women at all levels. Their report endorsed the emphasis that the ATRCW placed on training programmes, because they enabled African women to expedite rural development, to increase their efficiency in the cash sector, to manage and conserve their resources, and to market their products profitably.

As noted previously, the ATRCW also stressed the training of trainers in their specialized fields. The review mission now recommended that the centre's programme should include the training of trainers in the formulation and elaboration of projects and in leadership skills. The trainers could then more effectively mobilize and organize women in the development arena.[24]

It became increasingly clear to women that they needed skills in project writing if they were to tap domestic or external resources. Because the sub-regional committees of the MULPOCs agreed with the idea and with funds obtained from UNIFEM, the ATRCW organized a series devoted to writing skills in the MULPOCs immediately after the committees' inaugural meetings.[25] The exercises consisted of sub-groups drafting project proposals on selected topics under the supervision of the ATRCW workshop team. Field visits were organized to ongoing projects, and at the end the draft projects were presented and critiqued. The women leaders from Lusaka and Niamey, two of the largest MULPOCs, said they were being exposed to the subject for the first time.[26] The ATRCW continued to hold such training workshops in the region throughout the eighties, and in 1984 published a *Guide for the Preparation and Implementation of Project Proposals on Women in Development*.[27]

In its report, the review mission recommended that 'the role of the Center be primarily catalytic, leaving much of the actual implementation of the training to other agencies or to existing institutions'.[28] This policy had already been started by the ATRCW in Francophone countries (see Chapter 5). In the role of catalyst, the ATRCW worked with Jean Newman of the Population Council and with the Eastern and Southern Africa Management Institute (ESAMI) to initiate a course on 'Women Management and Development Planning' at ESAMI in the Lusaka MULPOC region. This course was the first of its kind, and elicited much interest. Nancy Hafkin from the ATRCW and Misrak Elias from ESAMI gradually developed the curriculum for the course which presented ways to consider the issue of gender in national and regional management planning. Participants were men and women in middle- and high-level positions in government planning organizations. At one time or another, the course has been funded by the UNDP, UNIFEM and the Netherlands Government. The programme has been institutionalized within ESAMI. It was the ATRCW's experience in this course that induced it to promote some related studies. One of these was *Women, Planning and Policy in Malawi* by Professor David Hirschmann of the University of Malawi.[29]

The training that African women leaders received from ATRCW not only helped them in formulating viable programmes for their constituencies but also stood them in good stead during regional and global meetings. They were articulate and able to hold their own in the often heated discussions. Although they came from countries of great diversity, the women spoke on behalf of their sisters throughout the region. They were also determined to keep the role of women in development in focus during meetings.

From Lusaka to Copenhagen

There were several reasons for the ATRCW and ARCC to organize a meeting of all the countries in Africa in Lusaka, Zambia, in 1979. The need to take stock of progress made since Nouakchott and since the Mexico World Conference adopted the World and African plans of action in 1975 was one of them. It was equally urgent for African governments to prepare for the World Conference of the United Nations Decade for Women – 'Equality, Development and Peace' – scheduled to take place in Copenhagen in 1980.

Opening the meeting in Lusaka, the Zambian President, Kenneth Kaunda, said that he believed that the Africa region had made great progress during the first half of the Decade, by establishing the tri-level machineries to implement the World and Africa plans of action. Nevertheless, he warned, many complicated tasks lay ahead because the emancipation of women was intricately intertwined with the political, educational and socio-cultural aspirations of the people. Furthermore, the quest for the equality of the sexes had definite similarities to the fight for racial equality being waged in Southern Africa.

With its philosophy of humanism, Zambia understood and supported the worthy cause to which conference participants were committed.[30] Lucille Mair, Secretary-General of the Copenhagen World Conference, had these complimentary words to say to the delegates in Lusaka:

> Africa was the first region to set up a Women's Programme in 1972, before the International Women's Year, and the first to establish a Training and Research

Centre for Women. It also was the first to discuss the meaning of the New International Economic Order for women at the Nouakchott Conference in 1977.

Mair also noted that the regional and sub-regional machinery set up as a result of that conference was a unique system for reaching down to the grassroots and emerged from Africa's tradition of independence and strength.[31]

A succinct report on the situation of women in the region since 1975 was presented to the Lusaka conference by Margaret Max-Forson, (Ghana) Consultant to the ECA. She found no direct correlation between the contribution of women to the economies of their countries and their status:

> Women were generally confined to traditional sectors of the economy where they had little access to the high or even low status jobs in the sectors that would expand through industrialization, and they were significantly less represented than men in all the non-traditional sectors.[32]

One of the agenda items of the Lusaka meeting was 'Apartheid and the Status of Women in Southern Africa'. This subject, close to the hearts of African women, was scheduled to be discussed in Copenhagen as well. The representatives of five liberation movements, namely the ANC, PAC, SWAPO, ZANU and ZAPU, were dissatisfied with the working paper on Southern Africa prepared by the OAU and ECA for the meeting. Consequently, they issued their own joint statement in Lusaka in which they described in vivid detail how life had deteriorated in that part of the world.

Lucille Mair reminded those in attendance that Southern Africa epitomized the antithesis to the Copenhagen conference theme of equality, development and peace. Women were considered superfluous appendages to their husbands and had lost half of their children by the age of five, she said. Yet these same women were in the forefront of the struggle, and it was a tribute to their spirit that the issue of apartheid had been included on the agenda of the world conference. In a strongly worded resolution the Lusaka meeting 'Called upon the women of Africa and the world to pressure their governments to sever all links, political, economic, diplomatic and military with the *Apartheid* regimes and to disseminate information on the effects of Apartheid as widely as possible'. Resolution 45 of the World Conference in Copenhagen reflected faithfully the Lusaka resolution.[33]

An important event took place at the Lusaka conference when, for the first time, African governments and women leaders took an official stand on female genital mutilation.[34] Though the topic was not on the official agenda for Copenhagen, it was felt that a meeting so representative of

African women was an appropriate forum to consolidate their unity in condemning such practices. This would be one of the most positive contributions African women could make during the UN Decade for Women. The practice of female mutilation was rampant in many African countries. Hence, the Somali representative introduced a comprehensive report on the subject and the representative of the Association of African Women for Research and Development (AAWORD) indicated the association's vital concern with the issue. The discussions culminated in a resolution which condemned infibulation and other female sexual mutilations. Included was a call to African governments to assist national women's organizations in their search for a solution to this problem and to promote studies on the causes and consequences of such sexual mutilations.[35]

The ATRCW had signed a co-operative agreement with AAWORD in 1978 to promote collaboration and co-ordination in matters of research. A similar agreement was signed in 1988 with the Inter-African Committee on Traditional Practices affecting the Health of Women and Children. This committee is still actively engaged in the eradication of female genital mutilation, and its secretariat headquarters is now housed within the ECA in order to work closely with the ATRCW. In 1989, African women again strongly condemned female genital mutilation, this time in the ECA's 'Abuja Declaration on Participatory Development: The Role of Women in Africa in the 1990s'.

The declaration appealed to religious leaders, traditional rulers, women's organizations, professional bodies and others to act as pressure groups by disseminating appropriate information against these harmful cultural practices.[36]

The valuable work done by Fran Hosken on female genital mutilation provides statistics that are staggering. This inhuman tradition is still practised in more than twenty countries in Africa in one form or another. Over 110 million women and girls are estimated to have been subject to mutilation, and it still continues.[37] The topic remains at the forefront of the African agenda.

The Lusaka conference, having reviewed the agenda and themes of the Copenhagen World Conference, found that they were of immense interest to women in the Africa region. Thanks to the recommendation of the Commission on the Status of Women at its Twenty-seventh Session, the sub-themes of the conference were to be Employment, Health, and Education. African women found that they could easily identify with those concerns. It was the Commission, also, that was responsible for placing on the Copenhagen agenda the item 'Effects of Apartheid on Women in Southern Africa' referred to above.

In Copenhagen, African delegates were unanimous in supporting the Programme of Action proposed by the conference, which demarcated priority areas such as food, rural women, child care, migrant women, unemployed women, and women who were solely responsible for their families. Delegates decided to channel assistance to Southern Africa through the liberation movements recognized by the OAU. With the ECA delegation, African delegates welcomed Resolution 21 which urged the regional commissions to make institutional arrangements for strengthening their offices by recruiting women for posts at the decision-making level. Of the 48 resolutions adopted by the conference, at least 17 were of direct relevance to African conditions.[38]

There was no unanimous agreement, however, on many of the issues raised in the course of the deliberations, in particular those relating to global politics and economics. Many delegates, including Africans, had come to discuss women-specific questions such as access to land, education, and employment, plus the establishment of national machineries. The broader, 'political' issues baffled them. Informal caucuses were called by the OAU to exchange views with delegates, the ARCC and the ECA on these and other issues, and to review the African position on which there had been earlier intergovernmental agreement.

For developing nations, the most important carry-over from the 1975 conference at Mexico City was the statement on the New International Economic Order that appears in paragraph 2 of the Copenhagen Programme of Action. Although the statement caused some controversy, its inclusion was considered necessary as a starting point for the integration of women in development.

Underlying some controversies was the wide divergence between the views held by women from the South and those held by women from the North on the relevance of global issues to women's issues. (This question had, of course, arisen at the Mexico conference five years earlier.) Many delegates from the North took the position that the condition, status, and roles of the world's women should be the primary function of a world conference; therefore 'political' issues should be avoided. Women from Non-Aligned and Developing Countries, in contrast, saw the larger economic and political issues as intrinsic to the kind of environment in which women lived, and thus as exerting a great influence on the quality of women's lives.

The Programme of Action adopted at the Copenhagen conference needed to be followed up by the ATRCW itself as well as by African governments. For that purpose the centre produced a study entitled 'The World Conference of the United Nations Decade for Women: Its Implication for the Africa Region', highlighting the areas and sections of the Programme of Action relevant to Africa. It stressed the recommendations of the conference on the women of South Africa and Namibia, on refugee women and on rural women. The resolutions on research and training as tools to promote the interests of women in those areas were also highlighted.[39] The study was presented to the Second Meeting of the ARCC and to the Seventh Meeting of the Conference of Ministers responsible for Economic Planning and Development. in April 1981.

Notes

1. *The Arusha Strategies for the Advancement of Women in Africa Beyond the End of the United Nations Decade for Women*, ECA, June 1985, p. 46.

2. 'Terms of Reference and Rules of Procedure of the Economic Commission for Africa', United Nations. E/CN.14/111/Rev. 8.

3. 'ECA: 21 Years of Service for Africa 1958–79', *Africa Target*. It explains: 'UNDATS were set up in Yaoundé, Cameroun in 1971, in Niamey, Niger in 1974, and in Lusaka, Zambia in 1974. As an example, in Niamey, the UNDATs studied among other things the development of Tourism and the production and trade of rice in 13 West African States in collaboration with the West African Rice Development Association (WARDA). In Lusaka UNDATs completed studies to integrate rural development, interstate cooperation and multinational industries in the subregion' (pp. 13, 14).

4. 'Revised Framework of Principles for the Implementation of the New International Economic Order in Africa, 1976–1981', Addis Ababa 27 June 1986. E/CN.14/ECO/Rev. 3.

5. 'Workshop for Co-ordinators of Women's Programmes in the Multinational Programming and Operational Centres of the Economic Commission for Africa,. Addis Ababa, 25–30 June 1980', p. 3. ST/ECA/ATRCW/82/14.

6. Ibid. MULPOCs are often misunderstood as duplicating the work of ECA headquarters. In fact, though they are somewhat autonomous administrative and operational entities, their work programme is an integral part of the ECA as a whole.

7. In due course, at several meetings of the ARCC, Mr Masemola, Deputy Legal Officer of the ECA, explained: 'By virtue of their membership and their functions the regional committee and sub-regional committees were both intergovernmental organizations and subsidiary organs of the ECA. The two statutes were not mutually exclusive. Many bodies, the ECA Conference of Ministers among them enjoyed both. ARCC was directed to report to the ECA Conference of Ministers and invited to attend its meetings; the bureau of the sub-regional committees attended the meeting of the MULPOC Council of Ministers. Both were thus part of the deliberative system of the commission at the regional and sub-regional level'. Report of the Fifth Meeting of the Africa Regional Co-ordinating Committee for the Integration of Women in Development, May 14–16 1984, p. 8, para. 33. E/ECA/CM.10/33.

8. *Report of the Regional Conference on the Implementation of National, Regional and World Plans of Action for the Integration of Women in Development*, Nouakchott, Mauritania, 27 September–2 October 1977. E/CN.14/ECO/128/Rev. 1; E/CN14/ATRCW/77/ Rpt., SOC/150/84, Annex, p. 3, (e), (i).

9. Ibid., p. 10.

10. The Great Lakes Countries MULPOC inaugurated the sub-regional committee in January 1978; the Eastern and Southern Africa MULPOC in June 1978;

the Central Africa MULPOC in July 1978. The West Africa MULPOC set up its sub-regional committee in 1979 and the North Africa MULPOC set up its in March 1981.

11. Laketch Daresse, ECA consultant 1981, *The Critical Needs of African Women and Appropriate Strategies in the Framework of the Gisenyi and Lusaka MULPOCs.* ST/ ECA/ATRCW/81/05, (ATRCW Research Series) p. 17.

12. Annual Report, United Nations, New York, 1979, p. 71. E/1979/50/CN.14/ 725.

13. Co-ordinators for women's programmes who were appointed at MULPOC level were: Mariama Aribot, Niamey MULPOC; Claire Siraninzi, Gisenyi MULPOC; Denise Gazania, Yaoundé MULPOC; and Victoria Mwamwaja, Lusaka MULPOC. Funding for the activities in the respective sub-regions was also provided by the UNDP.

14. National Technical Co-operation Assessments and Programmes.

15. The members were: Botswana, Cameroun, Congo, Central African Empire, Rwanda, Zaire, Burundi, Zambia, Mauritius, Côte d'Ivoire, Sierra Leone, Senegal, Morocco, Tunisia, Sudan and Mauritania (ex-officio).

16. *Economic Commission for Africa, Annual Report* (5 May 1978–28 March 1979). E/1979/50-E/CN.14/725. Resolution 365 (XIV): 'Structure and Terms of Reference of the Africa Regional Co-ordinating Committee for the Integration of Women in Development', p. 188.

17. In due course, agreement was reached between the secretariat and the ARCC that the ARCC's major role was to formulate policy and that the ECA would execute programmes. See *Report of the Second Regional Conference on the Integration of Women in Development, Lusaka, Zambia 3–7 December 1979,* E/CN.14/744, p. 15.

18. 'Report of the Inaugural Session of the Africa Regional Co-ordinating Committee for the Integration of Women in Development', Rabat, Morocco, 1979, p. 4. E/CN.14/716.

19. Interview with Selina Taylor by Margaret Snyder, Accra, November 1993.

20. Sixth meeting of the ARCC, 1985, Resolution 4.

21. Margaret Busby, 'Women Writers Speak Out', *Africa Forum*, Vol. 1, No. 1, London 1991.

22. Chaired by Hon. Lily Monze, MP, Minister of State in the Ministry of Economic and Technical Co-operation, Zambia, the review mission included member states, bilateral donors, and UN agencies. Members were: Ms Ursula Linnof (Germany), Ms Elletha Schoustra (Netherlands) , Ms Eva Forsherq (Sweden), Ms Margaret Bonner (USAID), Ms Susan Goodwillie (Ford Foundation), Dr. Jean Delaney (FAO), Ms Virginia Hazzard (UNICEF) and Ms Albastros (ILO). They were strengthened by prominent women from Africa who participated as regional advisers: Ms Saida Agrebi, Head Arab Women Workers, Arab Labour Organization (Tunis Office); Ms Kayissan Brenner, Ministry of Health, Social Affairs and Promotion of Women, Togo; Ms Martha Bulengo, Executive Director Community Development Trust Fund of Tanzania; Lettie Stuart, Planning Officer University Secretariat, University of Sierra Leone. *Report of the Review Mission,* 7–24 March 1978. E/CN.14/715E/CN.14/ECO/145, p.2.

23. Ibid., pp. 1, 2.

24. Ibid., p. 25.

25. 'Report of Two Workshops on the Preparation and Implementation of

Project Proposals – Lusaka, Zambia; Niamey Niger'. ECA/ATRCW/IYW/709/ 02-UNECA 1979.

26. Ibid., Annexe 111. Among the participants were: in Lusaka MULPOC, Hon. Julie Manning, Minister of Justice, Tanzania; Ms Christine Walubita, Executive Secretary Womens' Brigade, Zambia; Ms Terry Kantai, Head, Women's Bureau, Kenya; Ms Simone Mireille Arneppy and Ms Florence Mophosho, Head Women Section of the ANC. In Niamey MULPOC, Hon. Elizabeth K. Collings, National President Liberian Women Social and Political Movements; Ms Rosalind Ford, Chief Social Development Officer, Sierra Leone; Mme Djibo Fatou, Président du Bureau Départmental de L'NF, Niger; Ms Ladi Gobir, Assistant Chief Social Development Officer, Federal Ministry of Health and Social Welfare, Nigeria.

27. UNECA, ST/ECA/ATRCW/83/03.

28. *Report of the Review Mission, ATRCW*, p. 6, Programme (5).

29. Research Series – ATRCW, ST/ECA/ATRCW/82/27 and E/ECA/ATRCW/ 3.1 (ii) 89.

30. *Report of the Second Regional Conference on the Integration of Women in Development, Lusaka, Zambia, 3-7 December 1979.* E/CN.14/744, 15 February 1980, p. 3.

31. Ibid., p. 6.

32. Ibid. p. 10. The basis of this report was the reply to a questionnaire sent to all member states of ECA. Unfortunately, only eighteen countries provided data; however, the analysis and conclusions were not disputed by the participants of the meeting.

33. *Report of the World Conference of the United Nations Decade for Women, Equality, Development and Peace, Copenhagen, 14–30 July 1980.* A/Conf.94/35, p. 108.

34. *The Hosken Report on Genital and Sexual Mutilation of Females*, by F.P. Hosken (fourth revised edition published by Women's International Network News, 1993, p. 147) refers to a 'Seminar for Women in Public Life' held in Addis Ababa in 1960, which requested the WHO to make a study of the Health Effects of Female Circumcision.

35. *Report of the Second Regional Conference*, p. 26.

36. *Abuja Declaration*, pp. 22, 23.

37. *The Hosken Report*, op.cit, p. 44.

38. *The World Conference of the United Nations Decade for Women: Its Implications for the Africa Region.* E/CN.14/787-E/CN.14/TPCOW/11/3, pp. 17, 18.

39. Ibid.

A Ministry for Women: a conversation with Opika Opoka

Q: You are Permanent Secretary of Uganda's Ministry of Women in Development, Culture and Youth. When was it set up, and what are its priorities?

OO: Back in 1988, the Ministry of State was established in the Office of the President of Uganda, to promote women's issues. We had no previous experience. The ministry has to chart its course in carrying out the mandate given by the President of this nation.

Our first priority is land. Women legally don't own land. No, no. Although the law of our nation does not discriminate against women, it also does not make specific reference to women's concerns in terms of inheritance or ownership. Lacking ownership, a woman does not have collateral to secure loans or embark on business.

What is your next priority?

It is to sensitize everybody about women's concerns. Women's issues are not understood by most people in this country, including women themselves. Some women think that women must remain perpetually in the condition in which they find themselves. So we must tell them, 'No, you deserve better treatment than that.'

To complicate matters, even we men take it for granted that women are always submissive, that they have to follow whatever we want. Women labour from morning to evening continuously, with no time to recreate. They have no time to attend meetings where major decisions are taken on their behalf.

Is there one event, one activity, one group that has had a special impact?

There are quite a number of projects being spearheaded by women. We've got the Association of Women Lawyers. They assist women when they get entangled in domestic problems. We've got the Women's Credit and Finance Trust, where women form themselves into co-operatives, and the trust helps them get a loan that does not require the normal collateral – a title deed, a building, or such. There are women entrepreneurs, women who are engaged in business. They've got an association.

How do you discuss women and development?

Men and women are partners in development. That's how we handle the question in Uganda. We would like men and women to realize that they have a common role to play, for the good of the society.

If you had limited funds for women and development, where would you put them?

The very fact that funds are limited also limits my ability to assist. Anyway, I would look to the grassroots women, the women in the villages who do not have access to anything, who have benefited from nothing. That is the target group I would focus on. Try to help them out of their quagmire.

Uganda has come up with a plan. The women are now organized in a structure that begins from the grassroots. We have got the women council bill, which has become law. You start with the grassroots, and you work yourself up to the apex, up to here. This is the structure through which we can get the feel of what goes on in the grassroots.

Susan Muwanga, Women and Development Officer at the ministry, what is your comment?

For women, it will be a long road. But we have started in Uganda by having a ministry that has done a lot. And we even have a Women's Day. Children ask: Why don't we go to school on such a day?' So it has even sensitized the children.

Kampala
June 1993

CHAPTER 10

A DUAL APPROACH: WORKING WITH WOMEN BOTH DIRECTLY AND THROUGH THE ECA PROGRAMME

Agencies that conduct programmes for women often have to make a choice between whether to give direct or indirect assistance to their target group. Early in its history the African Training and Research Centre for Women was faced with such a dilemma. On the one hand the 1978 Review Mission referred to earlier had recommended that the centre become a 'co-ordinating and a catalytic agent rather than an executing one, drawing on the expertise of other United Nations agencies for research, training, and other programme activities'.[1] On the other hand, African governments' requests to the ECA for direct assistance continued unabated. These included: the upgrading of management skills; the establishment of small businesses and access to credit; strengthening of national machineries; and pilot projects that addressed the needs of rural women who were now suffering the brunt of famine and drought.

In order to meet these diverse requests the centre began to map out a dual strategy. One effort would address women's needs directly, especially through the MULPOCs mechanism; another would attempt to ensure that gender concerns permeated the entire programme of the ECA. By using both approaches at the regional and sub-regional levels, the ATRCW remained a forceful advocate for the women of Africa.

Beating the drum

Since the United Nation Decade for Women there has been much 'Beating of the Drums';[2] women have been directed to a variety of sources to obtain assistance for their activities. The ATRCW, for example, conducted a cluster of operational projects addressed to women in the business sector of African economies because African governments advocated efforts to strengthen indigenous entrepreneurial capacity to achieve economic re-covery and development. The rationale for this was based on the fact that domestic trade had not been keeping pace with demand in the region, causing shortages of food and commodities. Recognizing the considerable role women play in this sector, governments urged that they should be trained in all aspects of running businesses: management, marketing and co-operatives. Self-employment of women could also be increased by the provision of guarantees or loan funds.[3] ATRCW activities in this sector were parallel to the task force project mentioned previously.

In mid-1982 the ATRCW project manager Jasleen Dhamija and Danielle Bazin completed the ECA/ILO/SIDA Handicrafts and Small Scale Industries project. Among the activities undertaken under its aegis were: skill training for women at the Suba Centre, Khartoum, Sudan; research for an integrated rural development project in Seyoum Governate, Egypt; skill training at the Somalia Women's Democratic Organization in Mogadishu; upgrading of the Menaguesha pottery project in Ethiopia, and a similar project in Côte d'Ivoire. Diversification of skills to produce marketable commodities was the major focus; to use the experience women gained, Karen Himmelstrand of SIDA, a long-time supporter of the ATRCW, approved a related project entitled Training Women Entrepreneurs (TRAWE) which provided women with management skills in conducting their businesses. Basic to every activity was the centre's determination to examine the needs of entrepreneurs in small-scale enterprises. In a study tour to Ghana organized for women from Eastern and Southern Africa, conditions were studied at first hand. Organized by ATRCW staff members Françoise Wege and Mekdes Gebremedhin, the tour enabled participants to appreciate both the business acumen of Ghanaian women and the fact that women could undertake large-scale enterprises with considerable success.[4]

At a session held in Niger in 1988, ARCC members heard at first hand the views of women traders who had been invited by the Trade Division of ECA to attend the Regional Seminar on the Integration of Women in Trade and Commerce. Their dual objective was to identify problems which affected African businesswomen in the sphere of commerce, and to discuss practical ways of improving their skills. Pragmatic as women are, they turned the meeting into a 'small market', with women showing their samples of clothing and other items for immediate sale or for future orders! Their recommendations were just as practical. Government financial institutions and agencies of the United Nation system were called upon to improve market infrastructures, training, and provisions for loans and credit facilities. A request was also made for an inter-agency programme for training businesswomen traders in technical and managerial skills, all in consultation with member states. These recommendations were eventually endorsed by the ECA Conference of Ministers in Resolution 627 (XXXIII).

Unfortunately, much of the economic activity carried out by large numbers of women is unrecorded in official statistics because they operate in the so-called informal sector. In 1988, an inter-agency group (ECA, OAU, INSTRAW, ILO and UNSO) received funding from the UNDP for an important project which would measure women's contribution to the informal sector and examine the policy environment in which women operated. The group was aware of the phenomenal increase in the number of men and women entering that sector of the economy in recent years. In fact, by 1989, there was evidence to prove that the trend towards the informal sector was beyond doubt. Not only was the size of the female labour force engaged in agriculture decreasing in sub-Saharan Africa, but the same was true in developing countries elsewhere.[5]

This change in work habits caused the migration of many people to urban areas where, unfortunately, the modern sector of wage employment was unable to absorb them, especially the women. As a result of the rapid demographic growth of the cities, newcomers, who were often school leavers, had to enter the informal sector to earn a living. The inter-agency group's aim was to offer credit facilities and training, and to propose an appropriate policy on behalf of this sector. It was an important endeavour because 'women are not usually more numerous than men in the informal sector. However, female participation rates are much higher in the informal than in the formal sector.'[6]

The ILO has reported that in 1990, in sub-Saharan Africa alone, 16 million women were estimated to be engaged in the informal sector.[7] Women cluster around selected activities such as trade, commerce, construction, manufacturing etc. Although official statistics often ignore the activities of women who are engaged as street vendors, hawkers, or in personal services etc., the informal sector is increasingly the path women choose since they have no training, little or no capital, and it does not require the bureaucratic hurdle of obtaining a licence.[8] Supportive services for this sector have been slow in coming in Africa due to the notion that it can only provide a meagre existence, and is in fact a hallmark of underdevelopment. On the positive side, however, the sector, if nothing else, can be for some people a useful training ground for business and sometimes a stepping stone for higher levels of investment.

An overall view of the UNDP-funded inter-agency project led by the ECA indicates that the OAU sensitized labour ministers, who in turn began to recognize the importance of the informal sector by taking it into account in national development plans. Technical handbooks were produced by the Statistics component of the project for wide distribution. Training received by women in the pilot countries resulted in the upgrading of their skills and in some cases altered their activities to more profitable ones.[9]

In order to improve the policy environment and adequately target the appropriate group, research is still required to determine the exact size of the sector and the percentage of women operating in the system. The profile of the women also needs to be sharpened in terms of their background, earnings, variety of jobs, age group, etc. This is an ongoing concern of the ATRCW.

It has been said of women in the informal sector that 'perhaps the key issue is the difficulty women have in obtaining credit to expand business'.[10] Jennifer Kargbo and Dorothy Iwugi of the ATRCW produced a draft handbook and a guide on credit and entrepreneurship. In May 1990, an expert group meeting was organized by the ATRCW to look at the drafts. The participants came from chambers of commerce, universities, management institutes and development banks. They were able to give valuable insight and advice on increasing women's access to credit, suggesting that the African philosophy of borrowing needs to be taken into account because it influences borrowing habits. The group also noted that women need to be more active in seeking information, and that they should not be overly dependent on women's organizations or national machineries. The ATRCW's package approach, which included information, training, confidence building and resource support, was a step in the right direction, the experts concluded.[11]

With its accumulated experience, the ATRCW felt it was necessary to create an umbrella organization for women entrepreneurs in order to forge linkages and a system of mutual support. In October 1991, a group reviewed the general situation of women entrepreneurs and recommended that a viable solution might be to set up a federation composed of the national associations of women in business. Such a federation would reinforce women's entrepreneurial capabilities and enable full utilization of their potential in this sector.[12] As an NGO, the primary task of the federation would be to 'promote legal provisions as well as appropriate economic and financial policies towards women entrepreneurs'.[13] It would become a resource centre providing information and giving various levels of support to women for successful ventures in the trade sector.

In June 1993, the Federation of African Women Entrepreneurs was officially established as an ECA-sponsored institution. This was the culmination of a concerted effort on the part of member states and the ATRCW in recognition of women's role in this important sector. (See Annexe 20.)

National machineries: a continuing concern

Despite the diversity of its activities, the ATRCW's focus on national machineries remained permanent. As pressure groups, they performed invaluable service to women. In addition to the seminars, the regional survey and the booklet on national machineries in the 1970s, other activities were undertaken by the ATRCW on their behalf. Early in 1982 the ATRCW began a study in Ghana, Kenya, Senegal, the United Republic of Cameroun and the United Republic of Tanzania. Its purpose was to consider the situation of these organizations in depth with a view to producing a film. Outstanding items to be explored included the organizational form of the machinery, financial and personnel problems, and the extent of co-operation among women. This documentary film, produced by Decade Media Inc., was called *Widening the Circle*. It shows activities in Zimbabwe, Cameroun, Ethiopia and Senegal and excerpts from the regional seminar on national machineries (see below).[14] The film was shown at every opportunity and was widely distributed.

The ATRCW organized the Regional Seminar on National Machineries for the Integration of Women in Development, the first of its kind, in 1982, when a number of countries had seven or more years of experience. When the representatives of forty-two governments met to share their experiences, they reviewed several types of organizations in order to assess which could best serve the largest number of rural and urban women. Due to the diversity of models, however, there was no consensus on what constituted the most effective model for a national machinery, nor on where it should be located in the government structure. Some countries had established ministries or ministerial departments. Others had national councils or commissions funded by their governments, while the women's wing of political parties served as machineries in thirteen countries.

During the seminar, the ECA's effort in promoting these structures was well recognized and appreciated. CSDHA representative Chafika Sellami-Messlem, Director of the Branch for the Advancement of Women (BAW), considered national machineries to be the key for the implementation of the World Plan of Action, and pointed out that the Africa region had been regarded as a pioneer in establishing these structures.[15] The participants at the seminar defined them as entities that ensured the participation of women in the political, economic, social and cultural development of society, and recommended that governments work with them to ensure that national statistical offices collect adequate data on all aspects of women's economic activities, including and especially those of poor women. At the same time they encouraged the national machineries to undertake research on women's needs before drafting action programmes, and to strengthen their research capabilities. In view of the limited material and human resources in the organizations, the seminar urged that greater use of the national media should be seen as imperative if attitudinal changes towards women were to become a reality.

While recognizing the success of women's political associations for mobilizing the masses, the seminar cautioned the delegates about the fragility and temporary nature of national machineries that were closely affiliated with political parties. The need for technical and administrative competence was also emphasized.

Two years later, African women took a firmer position in the Arusha conference and the delegates endorsed this statement:

> In view of the pivotal role which national machineries could play in the

enhancement of women's position and opportunities it is imperative that these bodies be placed in strategic locations where they can monitor national trends, seize all relevant occasions to advance women's interest and work to implement the Forward-looking Strategies.[16]

Phoebe Asiyo, a Kenyan Member of Parliament, reiterated this view recently: 'If women's bureaux are in low positions in Government they have no impact whatsoever. But if they are at a higher level ... they can bring positive changes. And that is where we want to see them.'[17]

One concern of national machineries has been the slow flow of information. Through the ARCC, the members of ARCC passed a series of resolutions requesting the centre to intensify its effort in disseminating information on developments taking place in the region. After the ECA established the Pan-African Development Information System (PADIS), the ATRCW quickly took advantage of new technology and in 1982 made available to PADIS its entire publications list. The contents were abstracted and entered into the Devis Index, which is circulated throughout the Africa region and beyond. Thus, subscribers to the PADIS terminal are now able to obtain instant copies of any ATRCW manuscripts they desire.

The ATRCW mailing list was computerized by categories of recipients, countries and languages so that the most appropriate target group to receive a particular publication could easily be identified.[18] The ATRCW publications and the Reference Unit of the centre were built up, much credit for which belongs to ATRCW staff members Nancy Hafkin and her assistant Tadesse Alemu. Hafkin became PADIS's Acting Director in 1987.

It was not sufficient just to provide literature and statistics to national machineries, however. The ATRCW soon realized that it was also important to train their key personnel in the use of research as a tool in policy development and programme planning. Contrary to common belief, much data was already available for users. Thus, in collaboration with the UN Statistical Office (UNSO) the first Sub-regional Seminar on the Utilization of Research was organized in Zimbabwe in 1982. Its purpose was to sensitize national machineries to the importance of research, to promote awareness of the existing body of literature and data on the topic of women and development, and to train them in interpreting, using and disseminating this data. The goal was to institutionalize research into the daily work of women's organizations.

Interestingly, among the recommendations of the participants was the suggestion that women's projects move from isolated, fragmented approaches to the national development mainstream, and that literature on this approach should be collected and disseminated. It was also suggested that delegations to regional conferences should realize their responsibility to provide systematic feedback to their constituencies upon return.[19]

Considerable effort was made by the ATRCW to go on with its pioneering work of the early 1970s towards gathering the baseline data and statistics on the role of women in development vitally required by national machineries. The call for such information by development agencies increased throughout the decade; the agencies urged that more attention be given to improving data on the situation of women and making it available to interested individuals or entities. In 1985, therefore, the ATRCW conducted a seminar on training both users and producers in the compilation of statistics and indicators for governments and national statistical offices. This was done in collaboration with the International Research and Training Institute for the Advancement of Women (INSTRAW), which had done considerable work with UNSO in this field. In addition, after undertaking studies on information gaps on women and development in Botswana, Egypt, Burkina Fasso, Côte d'Ivoire and Senegal, the ATRCW and PADIS convened an expert group meeting in May 1989 to consider a model for a data bank: Women's Information Network for Africa (AFRIFEM).

The on-going crisis in Africa

Constantly impinging on the activities of the centre has been the environmental crisis in the region. The first half of the 1980s was a particularly severe period for Africa. Vast areas were affected by drought and desertification, including the Sahel region, Sudan, Ethiopia, Somalia, Mozambique, Botswana and Lesotho.[20] The Horn had the largest percentages of refugees and displaced persons in the region; drought and famine were at their height in 1983–85. In 1982, concerned by these conditions, and particularly by the plight of women and children, the ARCC adopted Resolution 5 at its Third Meeting in Douala, Cameroun. It urged African states, agencies, and women's organizations to donate material and technical assistance to refugees so that they could become self-reliant contributors to their countries of asylum. Furthermore, it requested the ECA and governments to carry out studies aimed at determining qualitatively and quantitatively the role of women in alleviating the food crisis in Africa.

Collaborating with the OAU, the ATRCW has remained concerned with the situation of refugees and displaced persons. Women who had suffered from the effects of apartheid and those who were fighting within national liberation movements have received assistance from the centre since 1978. The centre also offered training workshops in critical areas during 1978–80, as well as scholarships to African institutions.[21]

In a larger context the ATRCW participated actively with the inter-agency meeting on refugees in Somalia (held in Geneva in March 1980), as well as in the fact-finding mission to Somalia. Agnes Aidoo, an ATRCW staff member, participated in the United Nations inter-agency group (of

ECA, UNESCO, UNICEF and UNHCR experts) which studied the educational and social development needs of refugees. She led the group in studying 14 major settlements in the Blue Nile, Kassala and Red Sea provinces in eastern Sudan. The group recommended assistance to 21 camps and settlements in the Sudan. In October 1981 the refugee population in the Sudan was estimated to be 550,000 by the office of the Commissioner for Refugees, Sudan. The majority were women and children. The ATRCW played a principal role in writing the report, thereby ensuring coverage of the needs of refugee women. It was submitted to the United Nations Secretary-General and was issued by ECOSOC to the General Assembly.

The most significant aspect of the ATRCW's involvement in refugee issues in Africa has been its ability to draw attention to the special needs of those who are often overlooked, namely women refugees and displaced persons. In transit to and during settlement in the countries of asylum, African women refugees have suffered untold dangers, hardships, abuse and exploitation. The appalling sight of thousands of men, women, and children uprooted from their habitat, helpless and hungry, was an immense challenge to the inter-agency group. No easy solutions could be seen without first tackling the root causes of involuntary human displacement.

Because of the desperate situation, the region was receiving considerable international and humanitarian assistance in the form of food during this period. In examining that aid, the ATRCW realized that the recipients did not gain the maximum benefit from the precious gift of food because of a lack of nutrition education. Hence, the ATRCW developed a pilot project entitled 'Study and Training in Optimal Nutrition Use of Food Donated for Relief and Food for Work Activities in Ethiopia'. Collaborating with the Ethiopian Nutrition Institute, the project had a threefold objective: to provide information and analysis to facilitate the country's decision makers in selecting programmes which offered the food most suitable for the population's health and also acceptable to the people; to train the drought-stricken population in basic aspects of health and nutrition; and to promote self-reliance when the programmes were terminated. There were eighteen settlement areas targeted within Bale, Illubabor, Gemu Goffa, Wollega and Gojam provinces.[22]

The project was developed by Jocelyn Mackomic of the ATRCW/FAO and was funded by UNIFEM for a number of years. The needs of the local community and their eating habits were identified in order to facilitate the residents' adaptation to the food introduced by the aid agencies. Rural women were taught certain elements of health, nutrition and agriculture. The activities were carried out by seventeen Ethiopian extension workers trained for this purpose by the Nutrition Institute of Ethiopia in collaboration with the ATRCW. The Ethiopian Government took over the project after it was favourably evaluated, and the activities continued well into 1992.

Incorporating women's concerns

The efforts the ATRCW made to ensure that gender became a concern of the system as a whole, and permeated the entire programme of the ECA, were strengthened by two events in its evolution: the new status given to ATRCW and two resolutions of the United Nations General Assembly.

As the demand for the ATRCW's assistance increased, it became clear that to continue successfully the centre required a strategic position in the ECA bureaucracy. With a decade of accomplishments behind it, the ATRCW was poised by 1980 to demand both autonomy and representation at the divisional level of the ECA. The centre argued that being placed under the Social Development Division, while initially useful and appreciated, could be interpreted to mean that women's concerns had only a social dimension. In reality African women's needs could only be adequately met by a multidisciplinary and multisectoral programme. Another strong argument made was the need to reduce the layers of bureaucracy under which the ATRCW operated so that it could respond efficiently to requests being received both from the regions and from interested international institutions.

The Review Mission of 1978, mentioned earlier, had recommended that steps be taken:

> To elevate ATRCW to divisional status within the organizational structure of ECA, based on the significance of its past work and potential impact in the region. ... ATRCW meanwhile to give priority to the establishment of closer working relationships between the Centre and other Divisions and sections in order to integrate programme concerns for women into the plans, projects and activities of other units of the secretariat; and to the Chief Technical Co-ordinator of ATRCW having a voice in top-level decision making.[23]

In 1981 the Administrative Management Service of the United Nations (AMS) commented that the centre was the 'most successful of all organizational elements at ECA which had operational responsibilities'. It proposed that the Centre should be separated from the remainder of the Social Development Division and given two budget posts, in addition to the two already assigned to it. Its chief should report to the Deputy Executive Secretary of the ECA as 'the Unit for the Integration of Women in Development'.

At the second ARCC meeting in Sierra Leone in March 1981, Resolution 5 supported the review mission recommendation:

> Noting the commendable efforts on the part of the African Training and Research Centre for Women ... *Urges* the Executive Secretary of the Economic Commission for Africa to take appropriate steps to provide permanent posts for the professional staff of the African Training and Research Center for Women and to elevate the Center to Divisional status.[24]

The ECA hierarchy needed to be convinced by this resolution which, fortunately, could not simply be ignored. Thus an internal evaluation group was set up by the Executive Secretary to examine the ATRCW's scope of work as an operational unit in relation to its staffing situation, and the organization and management of its work in terms of effectiveness.[25]

After reviewing different recommendations, the evaluation team rejected the idea of relocating the centre. It said that the AMS proposal would have little advantage because if the centre was under the Deputy Executive Secretary it would be out of touch with other divisions which had no direct communications with that officer. The evaluation group also said that the ATRCW would lose the support it received from the Social Development Division.[26] The ATRCW responded to these views arguing that, with its present status, it could not effectively interact with other divisions/offices. Since the centre's focus was multidisciplinary and multisectoral and not simply social, it should have direct access to other divisions and participate as an equal partner in policy meetings of the ECA. Only in that way could the ATRCW integrate itself into the activities of other divisions and vice versa. Eventually it was evident to all that the volume and scope of work of the ATRCW qualified it to be a division. The ATRCW suspected that what was really missing was a willingness on the part of the ECA to give the centre the necessary resources to support its new status.[27]

In April 1983 the ATRCW was finally moved to the Cabinet Office of the Executive Secretary as an autonomous unit. While this was a major breakthrough for the centre, it must be acknowledged that the initial stance of the review mission, the worldwide women's movement, the pressures exerted by the ARCC and by the donors strengthened the ATRCW position.

The second support for making gender a concern of other divisions came with General Assembly resolutions 40/105 and 40/108, which called upon regional commissions to incorporate women's concerns at all levels in their overall work programme for the biennium 1988–89 and subsequent years. They were 'To take the necessary measures to ensure that all projects and programmes take into account the need for complete integration of women and women's concerns'. In this effort regional commissions were also asked to take into account the System-Wide Medium-Term Plan for Women and Development, and the Nairobi Forward-looking Strategies for the Advancement of Women. The ECA Commission as a whole had to report on the implementation of these resolutions to the Secretary-General.

These directives made the question of women a concern of all departments in the ECA, not just the ATRCW; as such, the major responsibility fell to the ECA Policy and Programme Co-ordination Office (PPCO). Its director at the time, J. Aighebussi, saw some difficulties because many programme managers would not know how to incorporate women's concerns into their programmes. He indicated that for these resolutions to be implemented it would be necessary to produce some guidelines to assist the staff.

The guidelines were soon produced by the ATRCW. Two ideas were discussed, which were implicit in the resolutions. One sought to ensure that women were included in the projects and programmes of the ECA: a question of participation. The other guaranteed that, substantively, the programmes and projects would deal with women's concerns in those areas that affect women in their multiple roles.[28]

Gradually the guidelines began to be used by the various divisions. Staff in many divisions were assigned to work closely with the ATRCW However, it was not all smooth sailing; many of the staff of the commission questioned the necessity of integrating women into their programme. Was not the ATRCW sufficient to address women's needs? Indeed, this same reaction is often put forward at national levels, when government departments are asked to be gender-sensitive. Was there not a national machinery for women? why should we deal with this question?, they often ask.

At an inter-agency meeting organized in New York by DIESA, various United Nations agencies, including regional commissions, met to consider the implementation of the Nairobi Forward-looking Strategies in their total programme. The ATRCW, representing the ECA at the meeting, reported on the efforts made to reflect the Nairobi Forward-looking Strategies in the entire 1988–89 Work Programme. In terms of planning at least, the ECA was found to be one of the few organizations which had made adequate provisions for the Nairobi strategies in its 1988–89 Programme of Work.[29] A wide range of items favouring women were included in the Programme and sub-programmes of Work:

— the expansion of food production
— food product marketing policies and programmes
— the development of an agricultural statistical database
— internal trade and finance
— inter-African trade
— the promotion of integrated rural development
— employment in the rural environment
— the development of agro-industries
— the improvement of the capabilities of small-scale entrepreneurs
— the Pan-African Documentation and Information System (PADIS)
— manpower training for African roads, road transport and railways
— the development of hotel management
— a population programme in Africa related to demography, fertility and training
— demography and social statistics.

However, it is at the 'output' level of programmes that activities related to women can be seen most clearly. Outputs in UN terms are the specific kind of results that can be expected from good management of the project input. They are the projected final outcome of activities and invested resources.[30]

The activities were developed by the divisions concerned as part and parcel of their core programmes. It is clear that the surge of activities on behalf of women that resulted from the General Assembly directives required co-ordination and joint planning by all concerned. Thus, the 1990–91 ECA Programme of Work for the Integration of Women in Development was shared among the various divisions, with the ATRCW remaining the focal point for the programme. In Annexe 12, the entire gender-related outputs for 1990–91 can be seen. It was estimated that almost 50% of outputs on the subject of women were being implemented by divisions other than the ATRCW.

The ATRCW simultaneously helped African women leaders to address the question of national development plans. In fact, the centre had had the reviewing of national development plans in the curricula of its training programmes during the 1970s. Such plans determined the allocation of national resources in most African countries. As late as 1986, an ECA study on the subject found that only ten African states made specific references to women in their development plans, and fewer than five made specific budgetary allocation for the promotion of women.[31]

At the Seventh Meeting of the ARCC in Cameroun in 1986, several women leaders revealed that they had not participated in the formulation of their countries' plans; they had not even been invited by the planning authorities to join in the exercise. Given this information, it became evident that an in-depth look at planning in relation to gender had to be taken: in particular, how women's concerns could be incorporated into the planning stages of the development process had to be examined.

Traditionally, and unfortunately, women were still viewed by planners as recipients or passive observers of the decision-making process that determined national priorities and the allocation of resources. What was constantly overlooked was the fact that women's concerns transcended the welfare-type activities planned on a sectoral basis, such as health, education, and trade. Their exclusion from both political and technical aspects of the development planning process meant that women had no voice in decisions that affected both sexes.[32] In 1988 the Expert Group Meeting on Women and Development Planning came to the same conclusion after reviewing various plans. The outline for an ATRCW guideline on the subject was also discussed. The need for such a publication was unanimously supported. Eventually, the ECA published the *Guideline for the Incorporation of Women's Concerns in National Development Plans*,[33] as a reference tool for planners. It discussed the role of development planning in the transformation of African economies and why and how women should be included in development planning. This publication has been very popular among the member states.

Women and the ECA

Human and material resources for the ECA sub-regional and regional programmes for women has been a continuous concern of the ATRCW. At sub-regional levels some funding has been available from the United Nations Trust Fund for African Development (UNTFAD). This fund replenishes its resources every two years by pledges from the region or elsewhere and the money is used for specific projects or put into a general fund at the ECA. This has been a wholesome development because it denotes some effort at self-reliance in the region. In 1981 for instance, there were pledges specifically earmarked for ATRCW programmes. Contributors have been Lesotho, Botswana, Congo, Nigeria, Gabon and Zaire. Such support indicates the successful efforts made by the ARCC for pledges for women. The funds were modest but affirmed governments' commitment to women's programmes, especially in MULPOCs. These resources were particularly appreciated after UNDP assistance to women's programmes in the MULPOCs came to an abrupt end in 1987, after a period of five years.

It became apparent during the Eighth Meeting of the ARCC in April 1987 that a financial crisis was imminent, due to this decision of the UNDP not to include in its Fourth Programming Cycle the activities related to women at MULPOC level, nor to continue with grants for the functioning of the ARCC.[34] That decision evoked deep concerns among African women. Up to that moment women leaders in the various sub-regions had enthusiastically embraced these programmes as their very own, and a healthy competition was developing among the sub-regions. The Women Co-ordinators in the MULPOCs had undertaken missions, organized workshops, and carried out studies and training programmes tailored to the particular needs of the sub-regions. The UNDP decision sent shock waves throughout the system.

Of necessity, the Eighth Meeting of the ARCC was totally preoccupied with the crisis. The difficult session, led by its president, Selina Taylor of Ghana, and the veteran Assaita Khane of Mauritania, worked round the clock and immediately submitted a resolution (subsequently adopted) to the Thirteenth ECA Conference of Ministers. This resolution appealed to the UNDP to continue its support for these programmes and urged the Executive Secretary of the ECA to mobilize and diversify the resources.[35]

In addition, a memorandum justifying the need for maintaining these regional and sub-regional structures was sent to the Administrator of the UNDP and the ECA Executive Secretary directly. As a result of this effort, the UNDP extended the duration of the projects for a few months.

At the same time the UNDP set up an evaluation mission composed of UNDP/ECA/ARCC representatives; Ingrid Palmer (UK), Gladys Mutukwa (Zambia) and Assaita Khane (Mauritania) represented these organizations respectively. The mission's objective was:

> To re-evaluate the WID components of the MULPOCs in order to determine their achievements, impact and constraints ... and capabilities to respond to the future orientation of the WID activities and possible UNDP assistance during the Fourth Cycle. To examine and assess the appropriateness of alternative or complementary structures at the regional and sub-regional levels.[36]

The evaluation mission visited the MULPOCs, the Economic Community of West African States (ECOWAS), the Preferential Trade Area (PTA) for Eastern and Southern Africa, and the Southern African Development Co-ordinating Committee (SADCC) because these organizations' mandates were similar to those of the MULPOCs. Upon completion of its work, in August 1987, the evaluation mission reported its major conclusions:

a. Analysing in detail the ATRCW MULPOC programme for 1986, the mission scored the performance of the ATRCW programme co-ordinators as 'very good'. Table 10.1 shows the activities they planned and carried out in each MULPOC for 1986.

Table 10.1 Planned and actual MULPOC activities, 1986[37]

	Workplan for 1986		Actual activities	
	Workshops/ Seminars	No. of Studies	Workshops/ Seminars	No. of Studies
Niamey	4	1	3	1
Yaoundé	4	4	2	1
Lusaka	4	2	4	2
Gisenyi	2	2	3	1
TOTAL	14	9	12	5

b. MULPOC women in development co-ordinators were also involved in UNDP Country Programming, Donors' Roundtables, NATCAPs, and World Bank Consultative Group Meetings; hence they were working under great pressure. The mission criticized both the ECA and the UNDP for having added this assignment to the duties of the Co-ordinators because 'ECA's mandate does not extend to Country Programming, NATCAPs and Roundtables. The ECA staff should not have been used to implement what is a UNDP mandate. UNDP country offices have the responsibility of implementing UNDP mandates at country level.'[38]

c. There was no alternative to replace the present structures of the ECA sub-regional programme for women, and the sub-regional focal point of the programme should remain in the MULPOCs.

d. A new project should be drawn up covering activities, taking into account the priorities defined in the Arusha Strategies.

e. The ATRCW should be strengthened in order to fulfil more effectively the role of catalyst, co-ordinator and source of information while at the same time lending the necessary support to the sub-regional programmes.

The UNDP did not go along with the recommendations. Its position was that it would not consider a new project unless the cost of the sub-regional meetings and the women and development officers was borne by the ECA. The ECA on the other hand stated that it was unable to provide regular or permanent posts to the MULPOCs ATRCW officers, though such a request had been made to UN headquarters. A further complicating factor was the fact that the entire MULPOC programmes were currently undergoing scrutiny at UNDP headquarters in New York. The UNDP did agree, however, to extend the posts of the MULPOC co-ordinators to 31 December 1987.

Despite these developments there was no doubt that the primary objective of sensitizing the sub-regional system to women's needs had been achieved. Since the above events, several MULPOCs, notably Gisenyi, by mobilizing extra-budgetary resources, utilizing UNTFAD funds, have continued to organize meetings, carry out research, and publish bulletins on women in development. One MULPOC director indicated: 'We do not necessarily need female staff for these programmes, we need only gender-sensitive staff.'[39] Some governments, like Egypt, even deployed a Woman Programme Officer to their MULPOC (North Africa). The commitment women leaders continue to display to these programmes through resolutions at sub-regional and ARCC meetings is a testimony to the role they perform in meeting the needs of women in the sub-regions.

Turning to the question of resources at regional level, it must be said that one cannot write the history of the ATRCW by only enumerating what it did and did not do within its mandate without considering the environment in which it operated, namely the ECA itself and the United Nations, as well as the human and material resources it had at its disposal. Chapter 8 discussed the staffing of the centre in the context of its relationship to financial resource mobilization, of the ECA's own staffing and of the centre's changing perceptions of the type and extent of its institutional commitment to women and development. Here, we update that information to 1992, and add the larger context, the United Nations

Secretariat, of which the ECA is one part. Three aspects of this overview are: the situation of women assigned to the ATRCW; women working in the ECA as a whole; and African women as a percentage of all women working in the United Nations system.

Equality between men and women is a guiding principle of the United Nations as embodied in Article 8 of its charter, both in the Universal Declaration of Human Rights and in the Convention on the Elimination of All Forms of Discrimination against Women. The General Assembly has also adopted a number of resolutions establishing the increased employment of women as an objective. Secretaries-general of the UN have issued directives time and again stating that men and women must be given equal opportunity and treated equally; gender should not be an inhibiting factor in any decision affecting conditions of employment or opportunity for career development, they said. In short, the appointment, placement, assignment and promotion of staff members are to be made on merit, in accordance with Article 101 of the Charter, without regard to the sex of the staff member.[40]

In recent years three additional measures have been taken for women working in the United Nations. In mid-1980, a Steering Committee for the Improvement of the Status of Women in the Secretariat, with Mercedes Pulido de Briceno as Assistant Secretary-General and Co-ordinator was created. Targets were set up so that women in posts subject to geographical distribution (permanent posts) would reach 30% in 1990 and 35% in 1995.[41] Emergency measures were initiated in 1990 which introduced flexible administrative procedures to facilitate the attainment of the targets, such as earmarking a certain percentage of vacant posts for women, and converting women project posts into permanent ones.

The ATRCW staff reached a peak of seventeen professionals including the MULPOC officers in the early 1980s. Two of the staff occupied permanent United Nations posts and the rest were financed by a donor coalition. The number dropped to seven in 1992, with four in permanent posts. While the increase in permanent posts may prove to be positive, the actual number was too small for a viable programme. The political will to maintain a strong centre was lacking and resources were short. There was a growing sense in the ECA administration that the centre now served mainly as a catalyst and therefore did not require additional permanent posts.

These attitudes created a dilemma for the ATRCW. Despite the fact that its staff was doing substantive work, individuals were kept for many years as project personnel on fixed and often short-term contracts. The Chief of the ATRCW, for example, occupied a project post for twelve years while other staff remained in such posts for sixteen years. An effort was made to achieve the conversion of ATRCW project posts to permanent ones. Credit must be given in this attempt to major donors of the programme, especially UNIFEM, UNICEF, SIDA and FAO, who insisted that unless the ECA increased regular budget posts in the ATRCW, they would withhold their assistance. UNIFEM's Intergovernmental Consultative Committee, chaired by Ava Mignott of Jamaica, and later by Rose Arungu Olende of Kenya, for several years kept a great deal of pressure on the General Assembly. The committee sought to influence the UN Secretary-General and the Executive Secretaries of the regional commissions to appoint women to regular posts at senior level. Credit must also be given to the ARCC; its resolutions in 1981, 1982, 1986, 1987 and 1988 kept pressure on the ECA to give the ATRCW additional permanent posts at high levels. The Steering Committee for the Improvement of the Status of Women in the Secretariat, mentioned above, also gave sustained support for the acquisition of permanent posts. The ECA Staff Council through its President, Mbaye Diouf, played an important role. At the time of writing, however, the number of regular permanent posts at the centre remains four.

The centre has also been concerned with the employment of women in the ECA as a whole. Despite the many resolutions and directives mentioned above, the number of women professionals and the level at which they served remained stagnant. Though the ATRCW had published a series of 'Rosters of African Women Experts', it was often alleged that there was an insufficient number of qualified African women for consideration for the various vacant posts. Another allegation made was that qualified but married women often declined posts unless their husbands were able to obtain jobs in the new location. Finally, women themselves were reluctant to move their dependants to countries that were affected by civil unrest. Thus, women professionals were few in the ECA, only 12.7% of the total in 1989. (See Annexe 8.)

A series of directives from UN headquarters in January 1990 spurred action in the ECA.[42] Aware that the 30% target by 1990 was not being attained, the UN Secretariat allowed a number of measures to increase the number of women professionals, including those in higher-level posts. It proposed, among other things, that 50% of vacant posts that were subject to geographical distribution could be earmarked for women; it also allowed for more rapid promotions under certain conditions.

In these circumstances, it was deemed necessary to establish some mechanism to monitor the situation in the ECA with a view to improving the status of women. The centre proposed the idea of setting up a task force to look into the question of women in the ECA in order to advise the Executive Secretary on measures that should be taken. This proposal was accepted in February 1990 and the Task Force on Women in the ECA (TAFWE) was established. The final list of members approved was twelve, four women and eight men.[43]

The number of women professionals, subject to geographical distribution, rose to 17.4% of the total by February 1991. (The figure in 1988 was only 7%.)[44] By 1992, women occupied 20% of regular posts, and 9% of extra-budgetary ones. Thus things began to move, and credit must be given to TAFWE members, especially to the supportive attitude of the ECA Chief of Personnel, H.Y. Kabore. A sub-committee established by TAFWE proposed a long-term plan for women in the ECA, which involved a 3% annual increase in female staff so that the target of 35% could be reached in 1997. The sub-committee noted that although the ATRCW itself is evidence of the ECA's efforts to integrate women into development activities, the overall progress made within the ECA to promote equality between men and women left much to be desired.[45]

With regard to the number of women in the UN Secretariat as a whole, as of June 1990 the percentage of women in the UN Secretariat was 28.13%. The number of women was 725 out of total staff of 2,561. In 1990, women from the Africa region were 14.6% of the total number; the lowest percentage of women were from Eastern Europe (9.2%); the highest came from Western Europe (33.1%).[46] It is not always realized that women's position in African countries and the status of female staff working in international organizations such as the ECA reinforce one another. The strength of one is the strength of the other and vice versa. In these circumstances, monitoring each other's situations should be a continuous exercise that will result in mutual benefit.

Notes

1. *Report of the Review Mission, 7–24 March 1978.* E/CN.14/715, E/CN.14/ECO/145, p. 6.

2. This expression comes from the 'Report of the Expert Group Meeting on Project to Increase Women's Access to Credit' held in April 1990, in Ethiopia. It really means initiating action to direct women to entities where they can get resources and technical help.

3. *The Lagos Plan of Action for the Economic Development of Africa 1980-2000*, OAU, Addis Ababa, paras 313, 318.

4. *Report of the Activities of the African Training and Research Centre for Women, April 1986–1987.* E/ECA/ATRCW/ARCC.IX/88/3, pp. 7, 8.

5. *1989 World Survey on the Role of Women in Development,* United Nations Office at Vienna Centre for Social Development and Humanitarian Affairs. United Nations Publications Sales No. E.89.IV.2 ST/CSDHA/6, p. 213.

6. Ingrid Palmer, *Gender and Population in the Adjustment of African Economies: Planning for Change*, ILO Publication, 1991, p. 109.

7. *ILO Africa Employment Report 1990*, JASPA, Addis Ababa, p. 69, quoted in E/ECA/ATRCW/ARCC.XIV/93/5, 20 March 1993.

8. Karanja Wambui, *Study on the Status of Women Entrepreneurs in the Informal Sector*, ATRCW, Addis Ababa, 1988.

9. Fama Bangura, 'Improving African Women's Role in the Informal Sector, Production and Management'. Progress Report (RAF/87/042), 1992.

10. *1989 World Survey on the Role of Women in Development*, United Nations, sales no. E.89.IV.2 ST/CSDHA/6, p. 223.

11. 'Report of the Expert Group Meeting to Review ATRCW Documents (a) Handbook on "Accessing Women to Credit" (b) Guide for the "Promotion and Development of African Women Entrepreneurs and Their Access to Credit"', April 1990, E/ECA/ATRCW/ARCC.XI/90/7, pp. 5–7.

12. See Report of the Ad Hoc Expert Meeting on Modalities for the Creation of a Regional Association of Women Entrepreneurs, E/ECA/ATRCW/ARCC.XIII/92/5, 1992, p. 3.

13. *The Federation of African Women Entrepreneurs (FAWE)*, ECA, Addis Ababa, 1993.

14. The Producer of the film was Bettina Corke; it was financed by the VFDW (UNIFEM).

15. *Report of the Regional Seminar on National Machineries for the Integration of Women in Development*. St/ECA/ATRCW/NM/82/01, February 1983.

16. *The Arusha Strategies for the Advancement of Women in Africa – Beyond the End of the United Nation Decade for Women*, ECA/OAU, 1984, p. 48.

17. Interview with Phoebe Asiyo by Margaret Snyder, Nairobi, June 1993.

18. In the 1982–83 period alone, using the computerized mailing list ATRCW distributed 18,000 copies of newly published or reprinted materials. 16 of the publications were in English, 17 in French and 1 in Arabic. These publications included some valuable material such as the *Manuel d'informations pour femme en Afrique* (available in English as well), which included a guide to developing project proposals, a list of potential sources of funding, and details of the structure and publications of the ATRCW. (This publication was produced in collaboration with the International Womens' Tribune Center of New York.) In the same period (1982–83) the ATRCW satisfied 1,025 individual requests for publications from Africa and other parts of the world. See *Activities of the African Training and Research Centre for Women – April 1982–1983*. ATRCW/ARCC/83/WD.1.

19. *Activities, 1982–1983*. ATRCW/ARCC/83/WD.1, p. 15.

20. 'Africa's Submission to the Special Session of the United Nations General Assembly on Africa's Economic and Social Crisis'. OAU/ECM/Rev2-E/ECA/ECM.1Rev.2, p. 17.

21. These activities were financed by UNIFEM.

22. *ATRCW UPDATE*, No. 9, 1987, published by UNECA, p. 18.

23. *Report of the Review Mission*, op. cit., p. 6.

24. *Report of the Second Meeting of the Regional Co-ordinating Committee for the Integration of Women in Development*. E/CN.14/809, E/CN.14/ATRCW.11/26-25 March 1981.

25. 'Submission of the Interim Report on the African Training and Research Centre for Women (ATRCW)' dated November 1981.

26. Ibid.

27. From a memo addressed to J. Riby-Williams from the Chief of the ATRCW dated 10 December 1981, on the 'Interim' Report on the African Training and Research Centre for Women. 26 November 1981.

28. See *Guidelines for the Incorporation of Women's Concerns at All Levels in the 1988–1989 Work Programme*, ATRCW, 1986.

29. Progress Report of the African Training and Research Centre for Women, 1986–1987.

30. *Project Evaluation Perspective and Methodology*, Canadian International Development Agency, Evaluation Division, October 1977. For example, two outputs of the joint ECA/FAO Division during that period were the following:

(a) *Subregional Cooperation in the Area of Cereal and Tuber Production in West Africa, with Special Emphasis on the Role of Women*, a study that covered five West African countries namely, Burkina Faso, Benin, Senegal, Mali and the Gambia. It indicates that cereals account for more than 50% of the total energy intake in the diet of the people, while more than 50% of the world production of roots and tubers originated from Africa. It highlighted the importance of these crops and the role of women in their production. Because of disparity in production it draws attention to the need of cooperation among the countries concerned.

(b) *Measures for the Improvement of Womens' Holdings and Land Rights*, a publication that addresses the fundamental problem of the dependency of agricultural production, a mainly female activity, on constantly deteriorating lands. It highlights the restrictions imposed on women in terms of land ownership and their repercussions on the exploitation of these lands, the access of women to other factors of production and the employment of rural women. The study further highlights how the double standards inherent in land legislation often provoke confusion in regard to the rights of women to land and to other factors of production.

31. *Planning for Women in the United Nations*. E/ECA/ATRCW/ARCC.VII/4. 1987.

32. *Women and Development Planning: An Africa Regional Perspective*, ATRCW, Addis Ababa, 1983.

33. By Abosse Demekssa, ATRCW consultant.

34. The UNDP warned as early as 1979 that funds were becoming scarce. The UNDP would continue to give as much support as possible to the MULPCOs, but was not in a position to provide all the resources required for the various programmes. See *Report of the Inaugural Session of the Africa Regional Co-ordinating Committee for the Integration of Women in Development*. E/CN.14/716, March 1979, p. 9.

35. *Report of the ATRCW Activities*, 1986–1987.

36. See *Programme for the Integration of Women in Development Through the MULPOCs RAF/82/011-RAF/82/012-RA/82/013-RAF/82/014, Report of the Evaluation Mission* (August 1987) p. 21.

37. Ibid., p. 21.

38. Ibid., p. 18.

39. Observation made by the Lusaka MULPOC director Muzumura, at the Sub-regional Committee Meeting in Lusaka, Zambia, in March 1992.

40. 'Secretary-General's Bulletin, Equality of Men and Women in the Secretariat'. ST/SGB/154, 8 March 1977.

41. UN General Assembly Resolutions 44/75 and 44/185 of December 1989.

42. Kofi Annan, circular dated 23 January 1990 on 'Special Measures to Attain the Target of 30% for Women on Posts Subject to Geographical Distribution and Measures to Increase the Number of Women in the Secretariat at Higher Level'.

43. The TAFWE committee chairman was Tchouta Moussa, Deputy Executive Secretary; members were: W.N. Wamalwa, Jeggar Senghor, A.H. Gholo, Martha Schmelszer, Nana-Sinkham, H.Y. Kabore, S. Rweyemamu, Crispin Grey Johnson, Christine Kronaure, Mary Tadesse and Mbaye Diuouf.

44. See the record of the Ninth Meeting of TAFWE, 1 February 1991.

45. Report to TAFWE on Drafting a Comprehensive Plan including targets, for

the approval of the Executive Secretary for Improving the Situation of Women in
ECA – prepared by TAFWE Sub-Committee, Chaired by Martha Schmelzer, April
1991.
46. 'Report of the Secretary-General to the Forty-fifth Session of the General
Assembly "Improvement of the Status of Women in the Secretariat"'. A/45/548/
dated 1 October 1990.

A conversation with Mabel Milimo

*Q: Has there been any special event that moved forward the concept of
women and development in Zambia?*
MM: The women's movement has been growing quite gradually
from the time of our independence, the struggle for independence,
although in those days the struggle was just known as nationalism.
Gender was not an issue. In 1971–72, we began to make our voices
heard, and from time to time the government reacted. Laws have
been changed, and new laws passed. A good example is the law on
inheritance. It is still insufficient, but is a beginning. There are still
hundreds of laws that need to be revised.
*Is Zambia feeling the trend towards female-headed households that is sweeping
over the world?*
About a third of the households, especially in the rural areas, are
headed by women. In some provinces it is much higher, as much as
50%. This is quite an issue. We talk and write about it; we need to
explore it more.
*What are some of the problems young women face today, that you did not
have to face?*
In our days I didn't have to struggle for a place in school. During
the colonial period they literally thanked me for enrolling. That
situation has changed dramatically. Now children have got to fight
to be able to go to school. And the dropout rate among females is
very high these days. Very few girls and women go to secondary
school, and fewer still to university. I think women are only some
20% of students here at the University of Zambia.
If you had limited funds, where would you put them?
I would put them into a project that would fight hard to change
the attitudes of men and women, probably through the education
system. As long as attitudes remain as they are, as long as people,
including a lot of women, don't realize there is a problem, then we
are fighting to no avail.

Lusaka
November 1993

A conversation with Kebkabe Tafesse

Q: How did the Ministry of Women's Affairs get its start?

KT: The Transitional Government of Ethiopia chose to democrat-
ize all activities of the nation, and within that to treat men and
women equally. Their first move was to create the Ministry of
Women's Affairs in the Prime Minister's Office.

A task force then drafted a national policy, and women from all
regions of the country reviewed it before it was forwarded to the
government's Council of Ministers. With some argument and improvement, it became national policy.

Our job at the ministry is to implement the policy. One of our
strategies is organizing a women's department in each of the regions.
We have started training women who will return to their regions
and organize those departments.

Are there women at high levels in other Ministries?

The Transitional Government has appointed women as Ministers
of Health, of Labour and Social Affairs, and of Education, in
addition to vice-Ministers. These women are actually as competent
as men.

If there were one or two things you could do for women, what would they be?

First of all, alleviate their arduous household chores by giving
them some improved technologies. Also, give them training in skills
for both home and farm activities, because women do so much
work on the farm.

Because of the immense problems we face, it will take more than
five or even ten years to put women on equal footing with men. We
don't want to be over men, to be dictators. We want equality for
men and women in all aspects: education, health, employment,
appointment and circumstance.

Addis Ababa
November 1993

INFLUENCING POLICY

In the 1980s Africa's deteriorating situation was the subject of several regional strategies which were policy-oriented; these included the Lagos Plan of Action (LPA), and the Africa Priority Programme for Economic Recovery (APPER). During the same period African women drafted their own region-wide strategies at conferences held in Arusha (1984) and Abuja (1989). When they attended the World Conference in Nairobi, in 1985, women found that their issues harmonized with global concerns.

R.H. Green succinctly described the African situation: 'The economic record of Africa in the 1980s has been dismal in respect to growth, external balance, poverty and food security.'[1] From the outset of the decade there were alarming signs. According to an ECA study of 1980, the average per capita income of the African region was only $741 as compared with a per capita income of $9,684 in the industrialized countries. (For the low-income sub-Saharan African countries the figure was $239!) There was high unemployment and mass poverty. Out of the 33 million people that were added to the African labour force in the 1970s, as many as 15 million found no access to remunerative employment. To make matters worse, even the prevalent low income was unequally distributed among the population. The young dominated the figures; 44% of the estimated total population were under 15 years of age.[2]

In that same year, 1980, each African had around 12% less home-grown food than in 1960; the food self-sufficiency ratio had dropped. There were more mouths to feed and the population growth rate was high – around 2.9% – mainly due to high fertility levels and declining infant mortality. The average family size was six to seven children. Internally, the African economy was over-dependent on agriculture, while the industrial base remained small. Above all, according to the ECA, 'The African economy remained the most exposed in the world. External trade constituted the single major stimulus to Africa's internal socio-economic progress.'[3] In these circumstances women struggled to survive. As a consultant for the ATRCW described:

> The life of an African woman in the 1980s was characterized by hard manual work, using traditional and inefficient implements and methods, frequent births, high mortality rates, rampant malnutrition coupled with poor health, low literacy

rates, lack of professional and technical skills, widespread and entrenched anim-
istic beliefs and subservience to men.[4]

Of economically active women, 80% were in agriculture, where a working
day of sixteen hours was common. Maternal mortality rates were among
the highest in the world, and two thirds of pregnant women were suffering
from anaemia due primarily to inadequate nutrition. Illiteracy in rural area
was almost 80% among the 15–24 age group.[5] These statistics indicated
that actions taken during the first half of the Women's Decade were not
enough, despite all the efforts made within the region.

The Lagos Plan of Action and women

Reflecting on the situation, the ATRCW concluded that in a continent
where governments controlled resources and had enormous influence in
shaping the lives of their people, and in which the private sector was still
relatively undeveloped, influencing government policy was one of the most
effective strategies to adopt for the advancement of African women. Any
effort was worthwhile if it convinced decision makers of the following
statement:

> Concern about gender division of labor, women's exclusion from decision
> making and unequal access to land/skill is not simply egalitarian, humanitarian,
> nor in a narrow sense feminist. It is central to the reduction of national
> household poverty and in a number of cases to substantial increases in the rate
> of growth of production.[6]

The First Extraordinary Session of the Assembly of Heads of State
and Government of the Organization of African Unity, which was devoted
entirely to economic problems, met in Lagos in April 1980. African
governments began with the determination and enthusiasm to redirect the
course of events by adopting an ambitious development strategy: this was
The Lagos Plan of Action for the Economic Development of Africa (1980–2000). The
strategy provided a widely accepted framework for initiatives to reorient
Africa's development towards more autonomous and self-sustaining approaches. In adopting the Lagos Plan of Action (LPA) the African heads
of state and governments made a solemn promise:

> We commit ourselves individually and collectively, on behalf of our Governments
> and people, to promote the economic and social development and integration
> of our economies with a view to achieving an increasing measure of self
> sufficiency and self sustainment.[7]

In that historic document it was gratifying to note that the LPA devoted
an entire section to women and development. The ATRCW draft proposals,
based on the strategies defined by women leaders at the Lusaka regional

conference, were merged within the LPA; for the first time in a combined OAU and ECA regional policy document, the question of women became an integral part of overall strategy. Among the priorities of the LPA that needed particular attention were two interdependent issues: optimum use of all human resources and the integration of women in development.

In designing the Lagos Plan of Action the heads of states and governments acknowledged that women were the critical factor for accelerating economic development. At last 'the primordial role of women in socio-economic life was being increasingly recognized'.[8] As Salim Ahmed Salim, Secretary-General of the OAU, said: 'The Lagos Plan of Action and the Arusha Strategies do emphasize the imperative need to move the African women from the periphery of our decision making process to the main stream of our socio-economic planning.'[9] The LPA also played an important role in promoting gender concerns in Africa; this was acknowledged by government delegations which came to Arusha in 1984.

Agriculture and industrialization: the Arusha conference

Two subjects that featured highly in the Lagos Plan of Action were agriculture and industrialization. These topics, of vital concern to women, also dominated the ECA/OAU regional conference in Arusha in 1984, which was organized to prepare the region for the Nairobi World Conference of 1985. Arusha reached consensus on the necessity to increase women's contribution to these sectors of the economy.

As documented earlier in this text, over 80% of the active population is engaged in agriculture; in most countries it makes up more that 50% of Gross National Product. The production rate declined, however, between 1970 and 1980 to less than 2%. As a result the Gross National Product per head became one of the lowest in the world.[10] Meanwhile, even though women still produced over 80% of the continent's food, their interests as farmers went unheeded and many needs remained unmet. The actual situation in which the woman farmer existed was seldom identified as a factor in plunging per capita productivity.

The Arusha conference filled this knowledge gap by identifying the major obstacles that still persisted. Of utmost importance was the differential access women had to the means of production such as land, agricultural finance, credit, subsidies and other inputs, as well as their inability to access training and technology. The delegates also noted that a thriving agricultural sector in which women were the principal producers was a *sine qua non* for industrial development.

Agriculture impacts on the industrial base in Africa, since it is both the major supplier of raw materials and the principal market for industrial output. Because Africa sought to diversify the industrial sector into more of its countries, and to raise industry's contribution to GDP above the prevailing 10% (1980), governments declared an Industrial Development Decade (IDDA), 1980–90, as a major policy. The purpose was to promote industrialization of African economies to achieve 'internally self-generating economic development'. The IDDA strategy was different from earlier plans which had focused their programme on large-scale enterprises. Governments now realized that the small-scale enterprise sector had grown in its contribution to GDP and in generating employment. The IDDA 'recognized that such industries are also important for meeting the basic needs of the population, for developing a semi-skilled manufacturing labour force and stimulating indigenous entrepreneurial activities'.[11]

Because the Arusha conference would place huge expectations in the Lagos Plan of Action, the ATRCW prepared four case studies in 1984 to look at the question of industrialization *vis-à-vis* women, and to examine the place women would have in the IDDA. The studies revealed that women were concentrated in light industries such as food processing, pharmaceuticals and electronics, but that men were replacing women in other industries, such as textiles. The high unemployment rate, combined with the lack of economic diversity, now forced men and women to compete with each other for jobs in the industrial sector.

The ATRCW's studies laid out the benefits and limitations of various options. One option was to strengthen the status quo by having planners assign additional resources through directives and incentives to women employed in the sub-sectors of industry. Unfortunately, this tactic would lead to 'the clustering of women in low-skill low-income jobs with limited promotional possibilities. It would also make them vulnerable if techno-logical changes take place.'[12]

A more viable option appeared to be a strategy for non-traditional employment. With media support, governments would campaign to recruit women into new areas of industry. At the same time, prospective employers would be encouraged to provide the women with appropriate training. Such a campaign, however, would have to extend over a long period of time because it would involve a radical change in the perceptions not only of employers about women, but of women about themselves. The studies went on to discuss G.E.A. Lardner's proposal in which he states: 'With vision, energy and determination, women can steal a considerable march on men by going in for specialization in areas in which lots of Africans will be required in about 10 to 15 years, or in which only a relatively small number will be required but will be for critical positions in the socio-economic system.'[13] Here the problem seems to be the insignificant number of women who would be integrated within the industrialized system. Would the token few have enough power to alter the general condition of other women?

The studies raised an important overall question. If and when African economies are restructured, what guarantee is there that women will participate equitably in the industrial order? A tentative answer is given: 'Perhaps in the last analysis the answer is not one of economics or social processes but rather, as in the past, an issue of collective awareness and the political mobilization of women.'[14]

With the ATRCW's research available as a resource, Tanzanian president Julius Nyerere opened the Arusha conference by reminding delegations of the African position on women and development:

> The history of the world shows that the oppressed can get allies – and need to get allies – from the dominant group as they wage their struggle for equality, and progress. But no one, and no group, can be liberated by others. The struggle for women's development has to be conducted by women, not in opposition to men, but as part of the social development of the whole people.[15]

Financing for the conference was obtained from the Ford Foundation, which enabled the ATRCW to commission a number of papers. The World Conference Secretariat (Vienna) met the cost of the expert group meeting on 'Forward-looking Strategies for African Women to the Year 2000' which preceded the Arusha conference. Chaired by Mary Chinery Hesse of Ghana, the experts addressed the questions of agriculture and food production, industrial development, human resource development, apartheid in South Africa and Namibia, and refugee and displaced women. The Southern Africa problem made peace the most elusive goal of the Decade for Women. A parallel meeting of African NGOs was also held in Arusha to prepare for Nairobi.

The conference itself was chaired by Gertrude Mongella, Minister of State of the United Republic of Tanzania, now Secretary-General of the World Conference in Beijing, 1995. It adopted 'The Arusha Strategies for the Advancement of Women in Africa Beyond the UN Decade for Women'. The strategies were policy-oriented and were meant to be guidelines for planning the full integration of women in development by sector and at every level to the end of the twentieth century. The thirty-nine member governments of the OAU and ECA present in Arusha requested all African governments to take appropriate steps to harmonize their national development plans with the objectives and integrated approach of the Arusha Strategies, which later became part of the women's brief presented to the world conference in Nairobi, Kenya.

Nairobi: women of the world meet on African soil

The period between the 1984 Arusha conference and the World Conference to Review and Appraise the Achievements of the United Nations Decade for Women: Equality, Development and Peace in Nairobi, in July 1985, was a time of concern for African women leaders. The Third Meeting of the Commission on the Status of Women, acting as the preparatory body for the Nairobi conference, took place in Vienna in March 1985; it ended inconclusively. There was no consensus on the documentation related to the review and appraisal of the achievements of the decade and to the 'Forward-looking Strategies', nor was there agreement on the rules of procedure for the world conference. Five African member states attended the meeting.

Though the summaries and recommendations of the regional meetings (such as the Arusha conference) were presented at that time, it was felt by almost everyone that the World Conference Secretariat strategies had not reflected the regional strategy documents. The Africa group that constituted itself in Vienna had worked with the Group of 77 to write substantial amendments to the strategies. Since there was no agreement at the preparatory meeting, either on the acceptance of the documents or on proposed alternatives, it was decided that the documents as written would be submitted at Nairobi, together with a report of the preparatory meeting. In addition, since there was to be a fourth preparatory meeting as well as a meeting of ECOSOC prior to the Nairobi conference, member governments could still amend some of the provisions within the documents.[16]

The ATRCW brought these decisions to the attention of the ARCC, which met in Addis Ababa in April 1985. The ARCC recommended not only that Africa send high-level delegations to the Nairobi meeting but requested 'African women to adopt and maintain a firm, united stand in order to ensure that the political, economic, social and cultural interests of the continent are taken into consideration and safeguarded'.[17]

The fact that the world conference was taking place in the Africa region gave rise to a sense of special responsibility, which was shared by all Africans. Full support was given to the Government of Kenya for the efforts it was making to host such a huge gathering. The ATRCW chief accompanied Leticia Shahani, Secretary-General of the world conference, to Kenya for preliminary discussions and to review preparatory activities. Meetings were held with all concerned, including the Foreign Minister. Kenya's commitment to the success of the conference was evident to everyone. The Secretary-General emphasized that, while the 1975 International Women's Year meeting had been an enthusiastic first statement of concern on women's situation, and the 1980 Copenhagen conference had been an opportunity for closer examination of the issues involved, the Nairobi conference was expected to bring a sober assessment of what had been achieved and what strategies were needed to build a better future.[18] This message was uppermost in the minds of African women *en route* to Nairobi.

When the Nairobi conference finally took place, all fifty African member states were represented. World opinion was impressed by the nearly 16,000 participants who flocked to Kenya. Some 14,000 were attending the non-governmental Forum; it was an impressive gathering. The Secretary-General of the United Nations, Javier Pérez de Cuéllar, was right when he referred back to the beginning of the Decade for Women: 'International Women's Year 1975 had been an important event in that it directed the world community's attention not only to the needs but also to the strength of women.'[19]

African member states, assisted by the OAU and ECA, held meetings throughout the conference to seek common positions on issues. Chaired by Mali, the Africa group drafted and sponsored at least six resolutions based on the recommendations of the Arusha conference. These dealt with Namibia, refugee and displaced women, front-line states, apartheid, the programme for women up to the year 2000, improved conditions, and opportunities for women.

Nearly eighty resolutions presented by member states, however, including those of the Africa group, were not considered by the world conference because there was no time. At the closing session the President, Margaret Kenyatta, assured the conference that the draft resolutions and a draft declaration would be reproduced in an annexe to the conference report and brought to the attention of the UN General Assembly for consideration and action as appropriate.[20] (The fact that these draft resolutions were not considered may have facilitated the success of Nairobi since many of them could have been contentious.)

The most important outcome of the conference from the point of view of Africa was the unanimous adoption of 'The Forward-looking Strategies for the Advancement of Women', (FLS), a very comprehensive document. 'Its aim is to express women's view on world affairs … issues of peace, war, development, human rights, natural resources and environment, culture, politics, and economics, relationships between men and women, family and children – everything!'[21] The women of the world had reached an extraordinary consensus. To understand just how extraordinary, we have only to recall the confrontations at Copenhagen and the diverse positions of North and South that were evidenced at the Mexico conference, where the Declaration of Mexico had to be created to contain controversial issues.

At Nairobi, there was a new and deeper understanding that both broad economic and social factors – many of which are outside women's control – and issues of sex/gender impacted strongly on women's potential to contribute to their own progress and to the well-being of their families and nations. Paragraph 24 of the FLS is telling:

> If current trends continue, the prospects for the developing world, particularly the low-income and least developed countries, will be somber. … In order to redress this outlook and thereby promote the advancement of women, policies should be re-oriented and reinforced to promote world trade, in particular so as to promote market access for the exports of developing countries.[22]

The global women's movement had reached a new maturity at Nairobi. For the achieved unanimity at the conference, the efforts made by the Secretary-General of the United Nations and the Government of Kenya must be commended.

What many official delegates regretted was that they were unable to attend the equally stimulating meeting that was taking place in Nairobi, in the Forum of NGOs. Unhampered by government directives, the women of the world were coming up with many bold ideas. They were raising fundamental questions. 'Stop asking for women what has not worked for men ... we are looking for participatory processes for our full share in the direction of larger development policies.'[23] African women at the Forum were pointing out 'that the externally oriented development model adopted by several African countries in the 60s is now recognized as having depleted human and material resources, undermined local knowledge and skills, and contributed substantially to the critical shortages of food, water and energy on their continent'.[24] It is said that while the Forum revealed the common experiences of women from all over the world, it also exposed how differently the problems women faced were perceived by women from the developing countries and by those who came from more advanced industrialized countries.

Nairobi, which brought together such an impressive number of women from the four corners of the world, was a historical event for Africa. More than ever before, the women of Africa realized that their aspirations and struggles were not isolated efforts but part of the human quest for dignity and recognition. Their immediate preoccupation was how the lofty aims of the Nairobi FLS could be implemented in the context of the continuous decline in African economies.

The search for a solution to the African crisis

The ATRCW began to study the implications of the Nairobi FLS for its programme. The socio-economic situation in Africa continued to deteriorate, which made it difficult to advocate that adequate national resources be directed to gender concerns. By this time Africa's total debt had reached $144.2 billion (sub-Saharan Africa was in debt to the tune of $81.7 billion). Many were questioning the reasons for these debts. It has been suggested that their origin goes back to the 1970s with the commodities boom, when African governments were encouraged to indulge in large-scale borrowing. When the boom collapsed it was difficult for countries to reduce the level of spending already in place, so they had to get additional financing by borrowing. The escalation of the price of oil, policy errors, overvaluation of currencies, weak incentives and structures: all combined with other circumstances to aggravate the situation further.[25]

It is in that context that structural and sector adjustment lending by the World Bank began early in the 1980s. These loans were primarily intended to improve economic allocation efficiency through appropriate pricing, trade policies, expenditures and production activities. Very often these adjustment programmes (SAPs) either mirrored or complemented traditional IMF policies whose objective was to restrain domestic demand as a means of achieving quick improvement in the current account.[26]

There are those who contend that with the major focus being predominantly on adjustment in a country's overall internal and external balance, SAPs are not in themselves development objectives, such as measures designed to meet the basic needs of the population or to relieve poverty. SAPs are introduced to redress glaring imbalances in countries' economies. Though lack of data makes it impossible to assert that their impact on African women was totally negative, it is a fact that women's situation was made worse by these measures. There is after all a direct relation between reductions in subsidies and services and lower standards of health, education and food consumption. Under the impact of these measures, women had to take up the slack by providing services such as health and education to their dependants, thus increasing their workload. When public sector employment is cut back, women are disproportionally squeezed out.[27]

The Economic Commission for Africa in 1986 asserted that external resources to support adjustment efforts often have to be recycled to pay outstanding debts. African countries are not able to raise domestic resources or generate foreign exchange to support the adjustment programmes because of the continuing slump in the price of commodity exports. In addition, high rates of interest and volatile exchange rates often result in African countries paying more than the actual benefits they get from adjustment programmes are worth.[28]

In an effort to find some other formula to stem the crisis faced by the continent, the ECA and OAU produced the Africa Priority Programme for Economic Recovery (APPER) for the period 1986–90, which included input from the ATRCW. From the perspective of women, the primary importance of this document lies in the fact that African governments resolved to undertake immediate joint, urgent actions to ensure harmonious economic and social development for their countries. Second, APPER assigned great importance to the food and agricultural sector: governments pledged to raise the level of investment to 20–25% of total expenditures. This was of direct relevance to women. The programme also asserted that efficient use of Africa's human resources was imperative if progress was to be made in the region. Specifically as a result of the input of the ATRCW, the document does admit to the important role women play in the food sector, though it did not make them central to the arguments as one would have wished.

At the Seventh Meeting of the ARCC in Yaoundé, Cameroun, in April

1986, the news that APPER was to be presented to the Special Session of the General Assembly on the Africa Crisis was welcomed by the women gathered there. In a three-part resolution they affirmed the key role that women play in African development, asked that a specific percentage of funds for economic recovery be allotted to women food producers and appealed for women's inclusion in any machinery set up to implement the recovery programme.

During the Special Session, held in May 1986, the UN General Assembly transformed APPER into UNPAAERD: the United Nations Programme of Action for African Economic Recovery and Development. This approach by the UN, R.G. Green states, 'Sought to strike a bargain: increased African efficiency in resource use ... in return for a substantial increase in soft resource debt service relief.'[29]

As a result of UNPAAERD, African countries began to pay particular attention to assistance programmes for small farmers and to ways of strengthening the self-help efforts of the rural population through participatory organizations and co-operatives. According to an ECA survey, four fifths of African countries took specific measures to enhance the role of women in agricultural production and other development processes.[30]

The Abuja Scale

At the end of the 1980s, research was done to discover what progress African women had made since the Arusha and Nairobi conferences. The findings were to be the subject of the ECA Fourth Regional Conference in Abuja, Nigeria, during November 1989. The ATRCW initiated studies on the 'changing socio-economic conditions of women in Africa in the context of the Nairobi forward-looking strategies'.[31] The research included various sectors such as Law and Legislation; Agriculture; Education and Training; Health and Nutrition; and Employment. Measures taken by governments, the ECA and other United Nations units, plus various agencies, to translate the recommendations of Nairobi into concrete actions were reviewed.

The ATRCW reported to the ARCC and the Conference of Ministers that within the framework of the FLS, and despite financial and human resource constraints, changes in favour of women were now apparent in various sectors of most countries. For instance, in the employment sector there was an undeniable trend showing that women were moving into professional categories which were previously the exclusive domain of men. In education and training there was an increase in girls' enrolment at all levels of the educational ladder; the setback was in the low enrolment of girls in science-based training programmes. Unfortunately, women's illiteracy rates remained unacceptably high, over 90% for some countries in 1988.

At the decision-making level, countries like Gabon, Mauritius, Senegal, the United Republic of Tanzania, and Uganda had introduced measures to increase the number of women in key positions in both public and private sectors. (More recently, women in Burundi, Cameroun, Côte d'Ivoire, Ethiopia, Mali and Kenya have attained ministerial, ambassadorial, and parliamentary positions.)[32] A survey of the economically active population by sector and by sex for 1988 showed that 77.7% of women were in agriculture, 6.1% in industry and 16.3% were in services.[33]

The ATRCW's series of studies on law and the status of women in Africa gave valuable insight on the situation in nine countries. 'A Comparative Study of National Laws on the Rights and Status of Women in Africa' was produced in 1989.[34] It concluded that most countries provide for sexual equality in their constitutions; however, these rights are often abrogated by customary and/or religious laws and practices.

Although there are many differences between countries in Africa, they share a similarity in the areas that need reform. These relate mainly to family law, marriage, the minimum age of marriage, inheritance, the acquisition and administration of property, access to education, employment, credit facilities, provision for family planning, equal pension benefits and insurance.

African women in general did not face a long struggle to obtain political rights as women did in many Western countries. Since independence there has been universal suffrage in most African countries, and the age of eligibility to vote varies between 18 and 21. Though women have the right to vote and to be elected, their participation in the political arena has been minimal. At the time of the study, women constituted over 50% of the electorate yet they amounted only 6% in national legislatures. Besides the traditional obstacles, there were other impediments to women's participation in the political field that related to electoral laws. Many candidates for electoral office are required to have skills in several languages, a certain level of education, and to deposit a certain sum of money.[35] Such provisions are discriminatory since women are usually the least educated and the poorest segment of the population. On the whole, women have to confront a complicated legal system and difficult access to the courts. Many countries are now setting up legal reform committees and legal aid clinics, while associations of women lawyers and jurists are attempting to do away with discriminatory laws.

Adherence to the Convention on the Elimination of All Forms of Discrimination against Women has been slow (see Annexe 5). In 1987 the ATRCW conducted an in-depth study on the convention in a number of countries to assess what was being done to implement it. (A country that ratifies the convention is obliged to adhere to its provisions, and revising its domestic laws.) The ATRCW found that, even at the highest level, officials who were familiar with United Nations activities relating to women were not familiar with the convention.[36] It was clear that if women are to exercise their rights, they must first know what rights they have. The picture seemed to improve by 1990. Reports to the Committee on the Elimination of Discrimination against Women (CEDAW) indicate that several African countries are reviewing civil codes, administrative laws, and penal and communal codes that discriminate against women.[37]

After all of the above studies were assembled, Assaita Kane, representing the ARCC, was sent to selected countries to sensitize them and to discuss the ECA's plan to hold the Fourth Regional Conference, in Abuja, on the Integration of Women in Development and on the Implementation of the Arusha Strategies for the Advancement of Women. The aim of the conference, in addition to examining the extent to which the Arusha recommendations had been implemented, was to consider the emerging socio-economic problems that were already affecting the lives of African women, with a view towards proposing changes and/or new policies for the future.

Funding for the Abuja conference was obtained from SIDA. ARCC President Selina Taylor and colleague Assaita Kane personally appealed to William Draper III, Administrator of the UNDP, who agreed to help. The Government of Nigeria, the host country, generously met the bulk of the expenditures and the ECA mobilized its resources on an inter-divisional basis. As the conference coincided with the tenth anniversary of the ARCC, special programmes (which included an exhibition, folk dancing, and panel discussions) were woven into the conference. The ATRCW took several missions to Nigeria to finalize the arrangements with Dr Ndidi Chibogu, Federal Director of Social Development, and J.O. Lijadu Oyemade, of the Office of Planning and Budget, who devoted themselves fully to the task.

Maryam Babangida, First Lady of the Federal Republic of Nigeria, took a personal interest in the conference, even though she was pregnant. Selina Taylor, Assaita Kane and the ATRCW worked together to put the final touches to the preparations. Nevertheless, when the conference actually took place in November 1989, its size was overwhelming in terms of logistics. There were approximately 1,187 participants attending the meeting; most came from the host country, Nigeria: 41 governments sent representatives, 30 organizations sent observers, and over 20 papers were presented to the meeting. The conference was described thus: 'In the largest such gathering ever of African women ... the set of goals they came up with was remarkable for its pragmatism.'[38]

The tone for this pragmatism was set by the opening speech of General Ibrahim B. Babangida, President of the Federal Republic of Nigeria.

> I want you to arrive at a declaration through what I would call the *Abuja scale*. You are to weigh the Arusha strategies and subject them to in-depth scrutiny. ... Despite the adverse effects of the world economic system on the developing countries, our economies are beginning to show signs of growth once more.

Nigeria has made giant strides with regard to the advancement of women. Women were being highly placed both in the public and private sectors. Nigeria has both signed and ratified the UN Convention on the Elimination of All Forms of Discrimination against Women, a Women Commission and the Better Life Programme for Women have all been established.[39]

In line with the concept of the 'Abuja Scale', a regional assessment, based on the ATRCW's studies, was discussed by the conference. There were indications that an increasing number of women were participating in family planning services, pre-natal and post-natal programmes; their nutritional status had also improved. Nevertheless, the conference classified health in general as an area in which little progress had been made. While overall mortality rates had declined, maternal mortality rates were still among the highest in the world; 1 out of 21 African women died as a result of pregnancy or childbirth. Fertility levels were above six children per woman. Furthermore, hazardous practices were current in the region such as early marriage and pregnancy, female circumcision and food taboos. The importance of education was re- emphasized by Susan Mubarak, First Lady of the Arab Republic of Egypt:

> Education is a basic tool which equips women to fulfil their duties as wives, mothers, and partners in development. Education mobilizes the untapped resourcefulness of women in order for them to contribute most effectively to their surroundings. Schooling imparts knowledge and skills and brings about new, positive attitudes towards the welfare of the society.[40]

Although the increase in literature about women's role in agriculture was significant, the subject of land scarcely surfaced at the conference (nor at recent ECA meetings) as being decisive for women, despite the fact that many writers and scholars had already alluded to the land problem as crucial to women's empowerment (see Chapter 2).[41]

J. Maud Kordyias, in her paper at the Abuja conference, supported the view that the agrarian crisis in Africa was due to a lack of historical perspective and to a blatant disregard for local knowledge. She argued that successful maintenance of a high population density depends on a production system in which environmental management, social institutions and agrarian practices are intimately linked. African traditional agriculture had once included all these elements, but that fact had been ignored.

The delegates in Abuja noted that numerous non-governmental organizations, UN agencies, and regional institutions were making invaluable contributions towards realizing the Arusha and Nairobi objectives. To further accelerate progress towards the socio-economic transformation and recovery of Africa, a major shift in policy was required. With that in mind, the Abuja conference put together a declaration entitled the 'Abuja Declaration on Participatory Development: the Role of Women in Africa in the 1990s'. The Drafting Committee chaired by Elise Therese Gamassa of Congo used a pragmatic approach and substantially revised the draft written by the secretariat. As a result the Abuja Declaration is unique; its objectives touch upon all pertinent issues and are clearly defined. Targets for the year 2000 are listed numerically (see Annexe 21).

On a broader scale the Abuja Declaration deplored Africa's internal strife and urged governments to put an end to civil wars and the abuse of human rights. It also appealed for greater co-operation between government-sponsored organizations on the one hand and NGOs on the other. The follow-up to the declaration was to be a concerted effort by member governments, the ATRCW and the international community. After the declaration was endorsed by the ECA Conference of Ministers, the ATRCW publicized it widely and held sub-regional workshops to sensitize participants.

Two important subsequent documents issued by African leaders endorsed the Abuja Declaration.

(a) The African Charter for Popular Participation in Development and Transformation (Arusha 1990). It stated that in monitoring popular participation: 'We proclaim the urgent necessity to involve the people in Africa on the basis of agreed indicators.' One of the indicators would be the 'extent of implementation of the Abuja Declaration on Women (1989) in each country'.[42]

(b) The Kampala Document Towards a Conference on Security, Stability, Development and Co-operation in Africa (May 1991):

> Africa's development in all aspects cannot be assured without the full involvement of women in decision-making processes at all levels and their full access to all factors of production (land, labour, capital). This calls for appropriate policies and implementation of strategies at the national institutional and regional levels. Specifically, we call for the early implementation of the African Declarations on the Advancement of African Women, notably the Abuja Declaration, and the Arusha and Nairobi Forward-looking Strategies.[43]

The ATRCW realized that the adoption of declarations and strategies was only the first step in creating an environment wherein women would be free to develop their potential and equally free to contribute towards the advancement of their societies. The burden of translating their aims into action lies on the shoulders of each country and especially on its women. African women have succeeded in highlighting their concerns in the global, regional, and national agendas. What remains are hard, tedious, but rewarding tasks of initiating and sustaining practical action for the fulfilment of their aspirations. As the Abuja Declaration argued, 'In the best of times, there is no automatic link between economic growth and improvement in the situation of women.'[44] The history of the ATRCW shows that efforts were made to provide that missing link.

Notes

1. Reginald Green, *Africa, 1975–95: The Political Economy of Boom, Decline, Conflict, Survival and Revival*, United Nations Non-Governmental Liaison Service, Occasional Paper, August 1991, p. 23.

2. *ECA and Africa's Development 1983–2008 – A Preliminary Perspective Study*, ECA, April 1983, pp. 7–8.

3. Ibid., p. 15.

4. Magdalena Abrokwa, 'Participation of Women in Development both as Agents and Beneficiaries'. ECA, Addis Ababa, 1987.

5. *World's Women Trends and Statistics 1970–1990*, United Nations, Sales No. E.90 XVII 3, pp. 89, 47.

6. Green, pp. 14, 15.

7. *The Lagos Plan of Action for the Economic Development of Africa 1980–2000*, p. 5.

8. *The African Training and Research Centre for Women and Assistance to Member States in Implementing the Lagos Plan of Action and the Copenhagen Programme of Action*, ATRCW/ARCC/82/Wd/2- 1982.

9. From a speech delivered at the *Regional Conference on the Integration of Women in Development and on the Implementation of the Arusha Strategies*, November 1989, Abuja, Nigeria.

10. *Measures to be Taken to Improve Basic Statistics on Women in Agriculture in Africa*. E/ECA/CM.15/11, March 1989.

11. *Women and the Industrial Development Decade in Africa*. ATRCW Research Series, E/ECA/ATRCW/86/05, pp. 7, 8. The study was co-ordinated and compiled by Eleanor T. Fapahunda with contributions from Etmad Mohammed Allam, Sion Solomon and Laeticia Theresa Mukurasi.

12. Ibid., p. 9.

13. Ibid., p. 15.

14. Ibid., p. 17.

15. See *The Arusha Strategies for the Advancement of Women Beyond the End of the United Nations Decade for Women*, ECA, Addis Ababa, pp 4, 5.

16. *Report of the Sixth Meeting of the Africa Regional Co-ordinating Committee for the Integration of Women in Development*, April 1985, p. 15.

17. Ibid., Resolution 2.

18. *Report of the Intergovernmental Preparatory Meeting for the World to Review and Appraise the Achievements of the United Nations Decade for Women: Equality, Development and Peace/Third Regional Conference on the Integration of Women in Development, 8–12 October 1984*. E/ECA/RCIWD/OAU/14, para. 105.

19. UN, *Report of the World Conference to Review and Appraise the Achievements of the United Nations Decade for Women: Equality, Development and Peace, Nairobi, 15–26 July 1985*. A/CONF.116/28/Rev. 1, p. 98.

20. Ibid., p. 90.

21. Hilkka Pietila, and Jeanne Vickers, *Making Women Matter: the Role of the United Nations*, Zed Books, London, 1990, p. 45.

22. *The Nairobi Forward-looking Strategies for the Advancement of Women*, United Nations Department of Public Information, Division for Economic and Social Information, April 1986, p. 11, para. 24.

23. Attributed to an Indian woman. Taken from Caroline Pezzulo, *For the Record*

... *Forum' 85*. Written for the NGO Planning Committee, 777 UN Plaza, 12th Floor, New York, NY 10017, September 1986, p. 6.

24. Ibid., p. 7.

25. Tony Killik and Martin Mathew, *African Debt: the Search for Solutions*, UN Africa Recovery Programme Briefing Paper No. 1, June 1989, p. 3.

26. Ellen Johnson Sirleaf, *Some Observations on Structural Adjustment and the African Woman*, UNIFEM, September 1988.

27. *The World's Women 1970–1990*, p. 95.

28. *Africa's Submission to the Special Session of the United Nations General Assembly on Africa's Economic and Social Crisis*. OAU/ECM/.1/1Rev.2,-E/ECA/ECM.1/1Rev.2, p. 29. In 1988 the well-known *ECA Africa Alternative Framework to Structural Adjustment Programmes* (AAFSAP) argued that long-term measures, structural in nature and people-centred, need to be simultaneously pursued if SAPs are to succeed.

29. Green, p. 2.

30. 'The Impact of the Economic Crisis on the Vulnerable Groups in African Societies: Women'. Submission of ATRCW staff member Mebo Mwaniki to the International Conference on the Human Dimension on Africa's Recovery and Development, Khartoum, Sudan, 1988.

31. Mebo Mwaniki defined 'changing' as the creation of conditions under which women can be involved in social and economic transformation on better terms. It also meant, she said, concerted efforts to achieve reforms at every level and sector.

32. *Changing Socio-economic Conditions of Women in Africa in the Context of the Nairobi Forward-looking Strategies*. E/ECA/ATRCW/ARCC, March 1989.

33. Sources: ECA Statistical Division.

34. 'A Comparative Study of National Laws on the Rights and Status of Women in Africa', E/ECA/ATRCW/ARCC/X1/90/6. Based on case studies of Nigeria, Ghana, Ethiopia, Tanzania, Zaire, Morocco, Burundi, Central African Republic and Mozambique, the study was compiled by ATRCW staff member Maria Magdalena Kenig.

35. Ibid., p. 5.

36. 'Implementation in Africa of the Convention on the Elimination of All Forms of Discrimination against Women'. E/ECA/CM.13, February 1987.

37. *Progress Report on the Appraisal and Assessment on the Implementation of the Abuja Declaration on Participatory Development: the Role of Women in Africa in the 1990s – A Regional Perspective*, E/ECA/ATRCW/ARCC. XIV/93/5, March 1993.

38. *Africa Recovery*, 1990. Published by the United Nations Department of Public Information.

39. *Advancement of Women: Forging a Strategy for the 1990s*, UNECA, 1990, p. 2.

40. Ibid., p. 3.

41. One member state does give land ownership the highest priority in its efforts to emancipate women and bring them into the economic mainstream. 'Legally, women don't own land,' the Permanent Secretary of the Ministry of Women, Culture and Youth of Uganda has said. 'Although the law of our nation does not discriminate against women, it also does not make specific reference to ... inheritance or land ownership. Lacking ownership, a woman does not have collateral to secure loans or embark on business.' (Interview with Mr Opika Opoka by Margaret Snyder, Kampala, June 1993.)

There is no doubt that 'Gender-sensitive allocation of land rights can increase smallholders' productivity.' Land ownership as an important collateral opens the door to many other privileges. (Margaret Snyder, 'Farmers and Merchants: Some Observations on Gender and the State in Africa', *Africa Contemporary Record*, forthcoming.)

42. *African Charter for Popular Participation in Development and Transformation*. E/ECA/CM.16/11. UNECA, Addis Ababa, March, 1990, p. 32.

43. *Africa Leadership Forum*. Post Office Box 2286, Abeokuta, Ogun State, Nigeria/821 UN Plaza, 7th Floor, New York, NY 10017, USA, p. 30.

44. 'Abuja Declaration on Participatory Development: the Role of Women in Africa in the 1990s'. ECA, Addis Ababa, p. 14.

New horizons for women: a conversation with Minister Ndioro Ndiaye

Q: How did the women and development movement arise in Senegal?

NN: The role of women in development was clear long before the official independence of our countries.

The women and development movement arose from the independence movements. In some countries women were engaged with men in liberation wars. In others, where there were no wars, women were still conscious of the major roles they must play in the economic and social construction of our young states.

Here in Dakar, for example, our teacher training institute for girls has played a fundamental role in the formation of African women leaders. At the time of independence, the women who had worked with men in gaining independence became our first teachers.

By 1985, when we evaluated the work of the UN Decade for Women, we found that African women had contributed to their political parties, and some had risen to responsible posts in their new governments, in their parliaments, in local government – areas that were previously male preserves.

Here in Senegal, we have seen how women have benefited from investments in education. Now, they engage in commerce, and create wealth. They are in all sectors where financial capacity is evolving.

As Minister for Women, Children and the Family, what are your hopes for women?

Today, we want more, in order to achieve near-equality with men in the twenty-first century. To achieve that, it is absolutely necessary for women to have more education. We must invest material, financial, and human resources to eliminate illiteracy. This is a necessary condition for women to play their roles in the next century.

Another necessary condition is that women rise to professional positions, not only in the primary sector – agriculture, fisheries and rural life – where we most often think that women must rise, but in all sectors. Doors must be opened to women.

It is urgent that women have scientific and technological education, and improved access to material and financial resources such as credit.

We have a schedule for each year, for lifting certain constraints on women. Listen, we say, we have 72% illiteracy now. Next year it will be 70%, then 65% and so forth. We want appropriate technical and professional training, opening of markets, in order to create wealth from which the family, and the nation, will benefit.

This is what I wish for women. These are the horizons that we want to open to women. The year 2000 must be a year when all targets are met. The year 2000 must be the beginning of the explosion of women's talents.

Dakar
December 1993
(English summary)

CHAPTER 12

WOMEN ON THE MOVE:
THE FUTURE

Women are on the move in Africa in the 1990s. As we have seen in this book, they follow proud traditions. Historically, African women proved themselves to be astute managers of local economies, capable of playing important roles in war and peace. They were skilled in diplomacy and when necessary in public protest. They carried out their responsibilities with tenacity and determination. History proves beyond doubt that African women built their own strong foundations for the women and development concept and movement.

In the waning days of colonialism, women were eager to share in building their new nations as they saw independence approaching. Then, the creation of the United Nations Economic Commission for Africa in the late 1950s brought with it a unique opportunity for women to strengthen their positions. As evidence mounted to prove women's economic as well as family contributions, the ECA asserted that women's needs were inextricably bound up with the priority needs and aspirations of the region. The commission's fundamental concept was that the most serious problems of development defied solution without the active participation of women. This concept – the basic tenet of the 'women and development' approach – led the commission to seek advice directly from African women themselves. Jaqueline Ki-Zerbo summed up the ECA's early function:

> ECA was the very good entry point for African women to development, because at the time, ECA was a strong focus of communication and co-ordination of ministries of planning and it was very important to have women's issues discussed in this forum.[1]

Having heard women's views, the challenge to the ECA was to initiate and implement a viable Africa regional programme that met their needs. Charting unfamiliar territory and undertaking unconventional activities, the ECA created first its Women's Programme and then the ATRCW. The comprehensive plan and genuine inter-agency partnership programme that resulted soon became the model for other regions of the world.

Playing pioneering roles, the Women's Programme and ATRCW broke new ground by assembling a regional knowledge base and providing activities targeted to human resource development and institution-building for both governments and civic groups. The ATRCW made major contributions to raising men's and women's consciousness about women's roles in the region, and to building both confidence and consensus among women. Justice Annie Jiaggie described that process:

> The main work was done by Africans meeting Africans and African conditions as well. The Women's Centre spearheaded that sort of education. It was most useful.[2]

The centre's activities also took into account that women exist not in isolation but amidst external political, economic and cultural environments, and helped others to see those areas as integral to the women and development concept and movement. All three became correctly identified as 'women's issues'. For the centre, neglecting development issues when speaking of women was just as misguided as neglecting women when speaking of development.

Such perceptions informed the centre's outreach to the ECA's other divisions. The aim was that every programme of the commission would incorporate the active participation of and benefits for women. Outreach was then extended to sub-regional level in Africa, making possible the truly representative, region-wide ARCC which, in turn, was able to influence the perceptions and decisions of the ECA's highest advisers, the ministers of planning of member states. Ki-Zerbo found the regular meetings at each of these levels very important, enabling women to 'see from one point to another what are the priorities, what has been done, and what is left to do'.[3]

Women today

The economic environment for women and for Africa today is more threatening than it has ever been since independence. Gloomy forecasts are everywhere. They are based on combinations of civil unrest, military coups, drought and disease – all exacerbated by the steady decline in national income earned from exports, and by foreign debts that amount to more than 90% of gross domestic product. Also, the very adjustment measures that are taken to cure some of these ills in African economies have had at best mixed results for economic growth. Such measures are proved to have negative social impacts, pushing people – predominantly women – into poverty. The World Bank's chief economist for Africa has said that the poor are often women, and that they take the brunt of adjustment.[4]

The paradox for Africa is that while many of its countries have taken impressive steps towards keeping the promises of reform made to their own people and to the United Nations in UNPAAERD, since the drought emergency of the mid-1980s the industrial OECD countries have taken few steps toward keeping their part of the agreement. The result has been a disastrous drop in public and private investment in and loans to the continent. Official development assistance plunged 33%, and overall financial flows to Africa fell by 43% in 1992 alone.

During the years when the social and economic crisis deepened and the conditions of women deteriorated accordingly, African women were catalysed into action to ensure the survival of their households and communities. Their response explains why, despite a very hostile environment, and despite their fewer opportunities as compared to men, women today are still on the move.

There has been an avalanche of activities, studies and new organizations at all levels – many of them led by young African women. These have been enhanced by empowering factors such as the expansion of education, the momentum of women's aspirations for independence, the experience of Africa's women and development pioneers, and the global women's movement. The increased family and household dependence on women's earnings is an additional factor that has led more women than ever to move rapidly into market-oriented activities, especially in the informal sector of their economies.

What is obvious from the new surge of activity is that women remain aware of what was said at the Nairobi and Abuja conferences: even when the external environment is favourable, an improvement in women's conditions does not follow automatically. Women must take the future into their own hands, and they do just that. As Karetsa Adagala expressed it: 'Women now know that you have to take action ... no one is going to hand you things on a platter.'[5]

One is left to imagine how the fruits of women's efforts could be multiplied if conditions were different – if there were no burdens of debt, and if the residue of inappropriate governance were lifted. Professing democracy is not enough when there is no independent judicial system or free press, and when ethnic conflicts continue. A terrible increase of poverty accompanies war, economic downturn and some adjustment prescriptions. Yet the environment for development can be created. Specially targeted reforms in policy and actions can be put in place to induce fundamental change.

Perhaps that change will occur in the 1990s: there are glimmers of hope. In some countries, wars are subsiding and in others they are concluding. Apartheid has collapsed in South Africa. Military and one-party dictatorial regimes are giving way to governments that are accountable to their citizens. Several countries have adopted democratic systems as the way to 'create a more favourable environment for achieving good governance and for sustaining economic development'.[6]

At the Abuja conference, Ndioro Ndiaye, Senegal's Minister for Women, Children and the Family, added the final, necessary dimension to the description of change in Africa. 'What is new today,' she said, 'is that women are in full agreement.' She explained that the success of development rests essentially on the quality of women's work. Women should participate at the conception, the initiation, and the execution of national and regional development programmes.[7]

Our experience with the region and the advice that African women gave us during the course of writing this book lead us to identify four potential areas for focusing action on in the future: two are the subjects of change, namely educational opportunity and economic empowerment, and two are the instruments of change, namely coalitions among women, and transformed institutions. We complete this volume with a brief discussion of each of these areas.

Subjects of change

Educational opportunity

A very positive gain over the last two decades that promised better lives for women and families is girls' attendance at school in greater numbers and to higher levels. (See Annexe 1.) Yet several challenges remain. First, the momentum of that gain is endangered by the economic downturn and by adjustment programmes. The imposition of school fees when government budgets are slashed has the predictable result that thousands upon thousands of peasant and other low-income families simply cannot keep their children in school.

Statistics lag, but evidence is increasing. Phoebe Asiyo gave us an example: 'I know of a school where two years ago there were 45 students: 22 girls and the rest were boys. I went back to that school this last month and there were only 11 girls. The headmaster said: "Look, their parents cannot afford to cost-share education. They can't afford to buy textbooks for the girls. So now they are only educating the breadwinners who are boys."' Asiyo added: 'The fundamental thing is education. And when girls don't go to school, in their motherhood they will not have the knowledge they need to bring up their children.'[8] Their chances of having incomes are also slim indeed.

But even when girls are educated, in hard times jobs are not guaranteed. Christabel Motsa told us that the formal education system prepares girls for academic and office life, for which employment is nearly nonexistent. 'So the number of girls who are out of school and staying at home and not doing anything has increased.'[9]

It is clear that more specific evidence and more political pressure is called for if the gains made in formal education and its relation to employment are not to be reversed. Some positive evidence of a specific long-term value of educating girls comes from a multi-country study. It was found that countries that achieved near-universal primary education for boys in 1965, but in which enrolment rates for girls lagged far behind, had about double the infant mortality and fertility rates twenty years later, of countries with a smaller gender gap.[10]

Second, while progress in the enrolment of girls is visible from primary to tertiary levels, girls still lag far behind boys in the critical contemporary fields of science and technology – the fields of the future. Recognizing this very very low enrolment of girls, the Abuja conference stated categorically:

The participation of women in scientific and technical professions in Africa is critical to the future technological development of the continent.[11]

Girls need to be encouraged to enter such fields, so that they will gain access to the scientific professions. (See Annexe 6.)

Third, adult education which includes areas such as legal literacy can be intensified. Some countries are ensuring women legal rights through inheritance and other types of ownership and/or usufruct rights to land that were lost when consolidation projects and settlement schemes were introduced during and after the colonial period. Other inheritance legislation affects widows and children. Experience with these changes – such as recent inheritance legislation in Ghana, Kenya and Zambia – should be widely shared. Violence against women is another area for legal literacy in a number of African countries. The impetus has come from women lawyers.

Economic empowerment

Maude Mugisha of Uganda is one of the many women we interviewed who said that if there was just one thing they could give to their fellow women, it would be economic independence. She spoke especially of young women who are threatened by the AIDS crisis. The hardships of civil strife and a fragile economy have taken a toll on girls' education, she said. 'They are faced with AIDS ... and when they are illiterate ... they are still very dependent on men – older men.' The result of that dependence is that girls are four times more likely to be affected by AIDS than boys of the same age. The poverty of adult women pushes many of them into sexual activity and keeps them from seeking medical attention when it is needed. Clearly, economic empowerment would make it possible for girls and women to have a choice of ways in which to support themselves and their families.[12]

In an interview, Lucia Quachey praised women's economic autonomy uncompromisingly: 'Women don't have to shout for their rights or their empowerment when they are able to be economically independent; then these come automatically.'[13] Karetsa Adagala explained that 'women have tried this and have tried that, and what it has come down to is economic empowerment. What the democratization process has brought out is how to operationalize empowerment and how to operationalize autonomy. There is more urgency now'.[14]

Can women earn better incomes? At present, the prospects for waged employment are not bright. (See Annexe 3.) The few formal-sector jobs that remain after economic retrenchment usually go to men. But the shrinkage in the formal sector leaves few options for either women or men to increase their incomes. Some women find seasonal labour in agriculture, while others enter the informal sector – micro-enterprise and trade – where they eke out meagre incomes that may or not meet subsistence requirements. Women in the informal sector tend to have less education and to earn far less than men do.

A persistent obstacle to women's earnings in Africa as elsewhere is the myth of the male breadwinner. The belief that all families are supported solely by men suppresses the truth about who is actually responsible for the family. It is women, more than men, whose lives are most shaped by family obligations. In an increasing number of African families – one third of all households, on average – a woman is the sole breadwinner. (See Annexe 7.) Furthermore, men and women often keep separate accounts. Because women are known to spend more of their earnings on family needs under dire economic circumstances than men do, their incomes are more critical than ever to family survival.

Thus, economic empowerment means not just increasing labour productivity or earning money, but controlling the products and income from that labour. Without this power, women's status and the well-being of their families seldom improves. A widely recognized dimension of the potential improvement in women's status is the increased respect women receive from their husbands when women have incomes and use them to benefit the family.

Even those women who supplement family income through micro-enterprise at home, such as selling vegetables or sewing clothes, are affected by factors beyond their control. The lowering of tariffs on textiles, as part of SAPs, has allowed imported secondhand clothing to flood into many countries, forcing national textile mills to close, and leaving many persons unemployed. It happened in Zambia. 'You know, some of the used clothing is very pretty and colourful and stylish,' said Joyce Mapome, 'but it really has killed the business those women were in.'[15] The conclusion is that, if women are to be economically empowered, international trade has to become a women's issue.

Exchange of experience and promotion of supportive policies for agriculture, agro-industry, other micro-enterprise and internal trade are called for, to enable women and men to support their families even at the level of necessities. Enhancing women's access to other work-related resources, such as credit, technologies, marketing and management advice, and training is making some progress, but more is needed. Under-secretary Isabella Katamzi and Catherine Mwanamwambwa agreed that support should go to women who are 'already moving' – who initiated their own entrepreneurial activities. 'More women are happy to go into businesses of their own', Katamzi said.[16] Mwanamwambwa added:

> We should go to where the women are, for example, in agribusiness. Go to a village woman who is cultivating sunflower, and get an oilpress to her to process her sunflower so that she can sell it. She can use the sunflower cake and feed it to the chickens with the maize she has. Don't tell her to form a club and sew.[17]

The ATRCW has already sponsored the African Federation of Women Entrepreneurs and houses its headquarters at the ECA's Africa Hall in Addis Ababa. More can be done. Listen to Mebo Mwaniki, the newly appointed Chief of the ATRCW:

> One thing that is very crucial to the women of Africa is economic empowerment. We will give more attention to entrepreneurship, and promote women's intra-Africa trade. We would like women to move away from the informal sector, to get into larger production and marketing. Women are moving into private business: consulting firms, legal firms, import-export, construction. They can go into electronics and engineering. They can make it.[18]

Educational opportunity and economic empowerment have not come about automatically. They have been promoted through professional and political action by women and men in civil society and by institutions that we describe as the instruments of change.

Instruments of change

Coalitions among women

Women's savings, production, marketing and mutual aid groups typified African societies for generations. These groups offered solidarity between women even when their projects failed to produce the expected incomes. Women also formed national branches of international women's organizations over many years. Since the 1970s there has been a surge in specialized groups formed by lawyers, businesswomen, bankers, home economists and other professionals. Their members, described by some as 'very aggressive', are most often young, educated women in the towns.

Many of these groups, such as the credit trusts and environmental movements, have outreach in the countryside, but most rural village mutual aid groups are the result of local initiatives. The members produce and market, perform community self-help tasks, plant trees and build roads. (A recent census initiated by the Women's Bureau in Kenya counted an astonishing 30,000 such groups.) Groups are able to have economic goals because custom allows women to keep the money they earn communally.

New co-ordinating organizations have also been created for the purpose of coalescing support from among women's groups, on behalf of efforts such as inheritance legislation, educational programmes, and the celebration of International Women's Day. Heightened gender consciousness has made a number of groups considerably more vocal than in previous times. An example is the new groups that counter violence against women – a subject that was not previously discussed publicly but one that is recognized worldwide as often interrelated with deteriorating economies and increased poverty.

The democracy movements have occasioned the birth of politically oriented groups to educate voters and/or train women candidates at this time in which, despite some progress, women have captured relatively few elected or appointed decision-making posts. (See Annexe 5.) Terry Kantai explained:

> Democracy is about choice. In Africa, women are bogged down by the amount of work they have to do. They have not had chances to be educated about democracy. Neither governments, opposition groups nor NGOs have had time or resources to educate the people. Civic education is a must.[19]

It is a task that is only starting to be done. Yet, women have themselves sustained the democratic ideal through their solidarity groups, says Karetsa Adagala.

> During the times when we were talking about lack of democracy at the national level, the women's groups kept democracy going in their micro way. They had their elections, then they sat democratically and decided what they wanted to do. They put their money together and shared it equally. The participation was there. They kept an alternative development perspective. They kept democracy going.[20]

The moment of independence was opportune for women to put down the roots of the women and development concept and movement. Similarly, the moment of democratic change may offer opportunity to harvest its fruits.

The multiplication of women's voluntary groups is a departure from the recent, almost exclusive international emphasis on gender-integrated activities. Women organize themselves in groups separate from men for solidarity purposes, even while they work with men in many ventures. They certainly do not hold men accountable for all the ills in the region. Having fought side by side with men, they argue that the fight against adverse environmental conditions, hunger, disease and ignorance can be won by women and men working together.

Women's unity is actually fostered by the diversity of their special interest groups, and it enables them to work with men from a position of strength. Co-operative inputs add to the persuasiveness of their arguments and give credibility to their logic. Christabel Motsa told us how a combination of women from NGOs, the university, and the private sector, including banks, approached the Minister of Home Affairs to press for a national celebration of International Women's Day. Having succeeded, the group worked towards the formulation of a national policy on women.

Joyce Mapoma told us how women co-ordinated their pressure tactics on the Development Bank to set up a credit guarantee scheme. 'It took two or three years to set it up. But eventually government gave in.'[21] Joyce Mangvatt explained that FEMNET, which she directs, promotes networking for the exchange of experiences among African women and groups, across national borders. FEMNET works closely with ATRCW.

Coalitions between grassroots women and educated women are still infrequent despite the great potential they hold for exerting pressure on governments to meet the immediate needs of rural women and to enact national policies that place human development and food security first. Since many educated women were born in the cities, they may experience themselves as distanced from the concerns of the rural areas that are home to the vast majority of African women and the wellspring of self-reliant development. Coalitions between grassroots and educated women would lessen that sense of separation and would be mutually educational.

Another type of coalition could produce profound change in Africa and even globally: namely, greater unity between women of the South and the North; such unity has been found to demand a hard-to-achieve mutuality of giving and receiving. Recall that the Nairobi conference of 1985 produced a new convergence of views between women of industrial and developing countries on the dual sources of women's disadvantaged position. Women at Nairobi began to accept macro political and economic issues as women's issues, and to see the interrelationship of these with human rights and equity issues.

Women of industrial countries are uniquely positioned to influence international economic systems that originate either in their own countries or in institutions over which their countries have power, such as the United Nations Conference on Trade and Development and its proposed successor the World Trade Organization, and the Bretton Woods organizations.

Transformed institutions

Women's concerns and needs must be on the agenda of governments, not just voluntary groups. Even though women have strong and vital NGOs, in a region such as Africa, where the private sector is not significant, it is essential to establish women's influence within the government and political party structures. Florence Abena Dolphyne has described the results of that strategy:

> The creation of women's bureaux and councils in various African countries has meant a focus on women's issues at the national level to a degree not known in any of these countries before 1975.[22]

The continuing need for those and other governmental instruments was vividly illustrated by Senegalese researchers Sira Som Sy Seck and Aboubachy Dembe Lom, who produced a study on the integration of women in development plans and programmes sponsored by government and international agencies. They found a 'nearly total absence of consideration of women, except in the social sector'.[23]

Christabel Motsa looked to a next step: 'Unless there is someone at economic planning constantly, keeping the machinery reminded that there are women out there who have to benefit, women who have to participate, it just doesn't happen automatically. We need to have people who are consciences in all agencies of government, in addition to having a government co-ordinating office.'[24]

With experience as their guide, women's bureaux have sharpened the focus of their work. Ruth Oeri expressed the views of many when she said that bureaux have experienced and overcome a lot of problems. Some national machineries have been restructured in order to limit their major tasks to policy formation and the communication of data and information. They leave operational projects to NGOs and sectoral ministries of governments. Reservations that some professional groups have held as regards the national machineries are subsiding, since there are fewer politically allied machineries. This evolution promises greater effectiveness for both civil society and government, as mutual goals are pursued from the two perspectives.

Some women's offices are computerizing their information systems, with technical advice from the ECA. Others are reconsidering their administrative location in the government structure, with a view to heightening their influence. For example, a national machinery that is a ministry with portfolio has more clout than a cabinet office without a budget. One ECA staffer illustrated that point: 'If the other ministries are disposing of budgets of 200 million and you are talking about two professional staff and three secretaries, it just doesn't compare at all in terms of policy weight.'[25]

We would add a further point, that when national machineries are placed in strategic positions, their officials must be well prepared to participate on national budget committees, in SAP meetings, national planning exercises and the like. The doors are being opened to women, and women need to enter them well prepared. Technical data, facts and information should be priority concerns of each machinery, on a continuous basis.

What is the key to ATRCW's effectiveness? Nancy Hafkin said:

> I think the greatest strength of the ATRCW is its position at the heart of the United Nations Regional Economic Commission for Africa. So it can speak with a tremendous amount of authority. It is not simply an NGO, not simply a women's study group. The ATRCW can cite the backing, the support of member states. It can speak in the name of the United Nations, and from both of those bases it has a tremendous amount of access and tremendous amount of credibility.[26]

Recall Ruth Oeri's commonly heard sentiment that the ATRCW helped with the development of a database and information centre, and gave the Women's Bureau a lot of encouragement. A former President of the ARCC, Selina Taylor, identified the ATRCW as 'the only, most important institution on the continent that has the technical know-how, the capacity to advise national machineries'. She added that that capacity of the centre needs to be strengthened.[27]

Clearly, there continues to be a regional institutional role for the ATRCW to facilitate the sharing of experience between national machineries and to open up the ECA's technical resources to their search for greater effectiveness. The centre's experience also points out the continuing need to refine, distinguish and make complementary the roles of women's power centres at all levels: NGO co-ordinating groups, political party branches and governments. As political pluralism emerges, women may need to design different entities to ensure their presence in the political arena. Jaqueline Ki-Zerbo finds that the case. 'We have a new generation of young women, to whom the centre must be responsive,' she said.[28]

The ATRCW's function as an information centre has been universally recommended by women we interviewed. Using past research and work related to women, ATRCW can continue its search for and presentation of data on the importance of gender to development in Africa. It can make the work of national research institutions, workshops and seminars widely available. It can expand its capacity to collect the astonishing output of literature on African women, subject it to rigorous analysis, and sponsor research to fill in gaps in knowledge.

The old international discussions between women as to whether to establish separate women's institutions or just to integrate women's interests in 'the mainstream' are no longer relevant. African women and the ATRCW have proved that both are essential. Strong women-specific groups, centres and funds give women solidarity and clout with which to envision and act upon concepts and strategies for transforming mainstream institutions and changing society.

The effectiveness of the national and regional machineries depends on three key factors: one, the political will of the head of state or international organization; two, the strength of the institution's human and material resources; and three, the time frame in which goals can be achieved, including the task of transforming the parent bureaucracies.

The head of state or organization can evince political will when making appointments so that those appointments are not just isolated and token, but are actually building up a critical mass of women. Designation of women to high posts, such as permanent secretaries and chairs of boards of directors, and to middle levels, sends a message to women throughout a country. The assignment of posts to women and the appointment and promotion of women throughout the UN system also sends a message to women. The ATRCW's loss of human resource strength in the 1980s has been traced directly to the reluctance of some ECA officials to give it the support that it merited. That weakness discouraged several donors who would have continued to underwrite posts and operations had the ECA shown the political will to assign core posts to the ATRCW.

The road ahead

It is easier to speak and dream of institutional transformation than to achieve it. The cost of the necessary resources is high and often underestimated. Women everywhere, not just in Africa, have been reluctant to demand a fair share, opting instead to spend their meagre resources as wisely as possible. That is what we call the 'micro-resource mentality'; it has been a big part of the basis and excuse for the inequitable distribution of assets.

Transformation requires that women operate from positions of strength in both gender-specific and integrated institutions. It is our hope that the young women coming along will make realistic calculations as to the cost and the length of time the process of change will take. They can then assert their demands accordingly. And they can go beyond national borders to transform multi- and transnational institutions.

For example, now that the gender aspects of international and transnational relations are grasped as women's issues, organizations like the World Bank and the IMF can be transformed from institutions that pursue economic growth singlemindedly to institutions that look at development in terms of the quality of life of everyone, and so put priority on human development – on eliminating hunger and poverty – and on sustaining the environment, and see those issues through gender-conscious eyes. In other words, economic growth will become a means, and human development the overall purpose. ECA Executive Secretary Layashi Yaker spoke succinctly: African countries must make 'a concerted drive to enhance both their human development capacity and the diversification of their economies'. [29]

The enormity of the task before us brings to mind the statement of Helvi Sipila at the IWY Conference in 1975 in Mexico City: 'We have only two weeks to devise an appropriate strategy to overcome centuries of oppression and discrimination.'[30] Ingrid Palmer also spoke with urgency about the future for women: 'In no other region of the world are gender issues more critical to economic and social development than in sub-Saharan Africa.'[31]

The ATRCW's director, Mebo Mwaniki, spoke to us about her three priorities – areas where the centre's work can be strengthened. Economic empowerment is the first, engendered by promoting women entrepreneurs and the linkages between them, within and outside Africa. Second, she will concentrate more on the legal status of women, including the area of violence against women. Third, she will return to basic considerations, namely education and training, to see where the gaps are and to fill those gaps.[32] Mwaniki also described the centre's two-way communication network, which will build an effective link between the centre and member states, with national machineries, with research and funding institutions, and with the media.

To accomplish those tasks while maintaining current operations, and to strengthen its contacts with the increasingly important and empowering civil sector – NGOs and the private sector – the ATRCW must grow. Growth will enable the centre to effectively seize this moment of change and with it the opportunity to implement its dual strategy of directly addressing women's needs while also ensuring that gender equity permeates the entire programme of the commission. The centre must continue to draw the attention of women to emerging problems and come up with innovative ways to tackle them.

We asked Margaret Kenyatta, creator of the 1962 and 1963 national seminars and Chair of the 1985 Nairobi World Conference to Review and Appraise the Achievements of the UN Decade for Women, what was her hope for women. She replied:

> The one thing I could wish is peace for the women of the world. Then, after that, peace will enable us to do other things; we want development. And especially in the developing world we need more education and training for our women, so that they can get better opportunities to work, to be economically independent, to bring up better families, and to be of use to their countries.[33]

For women of the region to achieve Kenyatta's vision, experience proves that there is no alternative to women's solidarity. African women have an advantage over women from other regions in that they have the most effective solidarity groups in the world. The team spirit can be enhanced, the common experience can prevail over differences. Then the aspirations for equality, dignity and fulfilment will become realities for Africa's people.

Notes

1. Interview with Jacqueline Ki-Zerbo by Margaret Snyder, Ouagadougou, November 1993.

2. Interview with Justice Annie Jiaggie by Margaret Snyder, November 1993.

3. Ki-Zerbo.

4. *Economist*, London, 1 May 1993, p. 44. The *New York Times*, in an article entitled 'Investors Who Discovered Africa', 3 April 1994, p. 4F, calls Africa south of the Sahara 'a hot new target for international investing'. The actual size of these financial flows and their impact on overall flows to Africa is as yet unclear.

5. Interview with Karetsa Adagala by Margaret Snyder, Nairobi, November 1993.

6. The Global Coalition, 'Governance and democracy in Sub-Saharan Africa'. First Advisory Meeting of the Global Coalition on Africa, Paris, September 1991. The coalition asserts that 'there is considerable evidence that democratic processes have greater success in lowering infant mortality, raising literacy rates, mounting environmental safeguards and providing for certain societal groups more equitably, particularly women'.

7. Marie-Roger Biloa, *Jeune Afrique*, 8 January 1990. An interview with Nioro Ndiaye at Abuja.

8. Interview with Phoebe Asiyo by Margaret Snyder, Nairobi, June 1993.

9. Interview with Christabel Motsa by Margaret Snyder, Mbabane, November 1993.

10. The World Bank. *World Development Report, 1991*, OUP, New York, 1991.

11. *Abuja Declaration*. See Annexe 24.

12. Interview with Maude Mugisha by Margaret Snyder, Kampala, June 1993.

13. Interview with Lucia Quachey by Margaret Snyder, Accra, November 1993.

14. Adagala.

15. Interview with Joyce Mapoma by Margaret Snyder, Lusaka, November 1993.

16. Interview with Undersecretary Katamzi by Margaret Snyder, Mbabane, November 1993.

17. Interview with Catherine Mwanamwambwa by Margaret Snyder, Lusaka, November 1993.

18. Interview with Mebo Mwaniki by Margaret Snyder, Addis Ababa, November 1993.

19. Interview with Terry Kantai and Kathy Larin, Nairobi, December 1992.

20. Adagala.

21. Mapoma.

22. Florence Abena Dolphyne, *The Emancipation of Women: an African Perspective*, Ghana Universities Press, Accra, 1991.

23. Interview with Sira Som Sy Seck and Aboubachy Dembe Lom by Margaret Snyder, Dakar, December 1993. The study was sponsored by UNIFEM.

24. Motsa.

25. Interview with Nancy Hafkin by Margaret Snyder, Addis Ababa, November 1993.

26. Hafkin.

27. Interview with Selina Taylor by Margaret Snyder, Accra, November 1993.

28. Ki-Zerbo.

29. *Africa Recovery*, Vol. 6, No. 4, UN, New York, 1992–93.

30. Helvi Sipila, 'Opening Statement to the World Conference of the International Women's Year, Mexico City', 1975.

31. Ingrid Palmer.

32. Mwaniki.

33. Interview with Margaret Kenyatta by Margaret Snyder, Nairobi, November 1993.

ANNEXES

I. Data on women in Africa

Annexe 1 Education: estimated female enrolment in Africa (%)

	Primary	Secondary	University
1970	40	31	23
1980	43	37	27
1990	45	42	30

Source: Statistical Yearbook: 1980, 1985, 1993, UNESCO, Paris.

Annexe 2 Health

2a Maternal mortality rate (MMR) per 100,000 live births

Country	Year	MMR
Algeria	1980–88	140
Angola	1988–90	665
Benin	1980–90	160
Botswana	1980	200–300
Burkina Faso	1980–90	810
Burundi	1988	850
Cameroun	1980–90	430
Cape Verde	1988–90	44
Central African Republic	1980–88	600
Chad	1980–88	960
Congo	1980–88	900
Djibouti	1988–90	740
Egypt	1980–88	318
Ethiopia	1980–90	560+
Gabon	1980–90	190
Gambia	1988–90	1,050
Ghana	1980–88	1,000
Guinea	1980–90	800
Guinea-Bissau	1988	400

Annexe 2a (continued)

Country	Year	MMR
Kenya	1977	170+
Lesotho	1988–90	220
Liberia	1980	173
Libian Arab		
Jamahiriya	1988–90	60
Madagascar	1980–90	570
Malawi	1980–88	400
Mali	1980–90	2,000
Mauritania	1990	554
Mauritius	1980–90	99
Morocco	1974	300
Mozambique	1980–88	300
Namibia	1988–90	225
Niger	1988–90	700
Nigeria	1980–90	420
Rwanda	1980–88	210–12
São Tomé & Príncipe	1987	77
Senegal	1980–88	600
Sierra Leone	1986	450
Somalia	1981	1,100
South Africa	1980–82	84+
Sudan	1983–89	552
Swaziland	1988–90	107
Togo	1980–90	420
Tunisia	1988–90	70
Uganda	1980–90	300
United Rep. Tanzania	1980–88	340
Zaire	1988	800
Zambia	1980–88	150
Zimbabwe	1979	480

Note: + Data refer to periods other than 1980–1990, or differ from the standard definition, or refer to only one part of a country.

Sources: *Maternal Mortality rates: a tabulation of available information*, 2nd edition, WHO, Geneva; *The State of the World's Children*, 1994, UNICEF, New York; *World Development Report 1991*, World Bank, Washington.

2b Female genital mutilation

Country	Mutilated women %	Estimated total (millions)
East Africa		
Egypt	50	13.7
Sudan	80	10.0
Somalia	98	4.1
Djibouti	98	0.2
Ethiopia	90	23.2
Kenya	50	6.2
Total		57.4
West and Central Africa		
Nigeria	50	29.7
Mali	75	3.0
Burkina Faso	70	3.2
Senegal	50	1.9
Côte d'Ivoire	60	3.8
Sierra Leone	80	1.7
Guinea	60	2.2
Liberia	60	0.8
Togo	50	0.9
Benin	50	1.2
Chad	60	1.5
Gambia	60	0.3
Central Africa	50	0.7
Ghana	30	2.3
Total		53.2

Source: The Hosken Report – Genital and Sexual Mutilation of Females, Fourth Revised Edition, 1993, by Fran P. Hosken.

Annexe 3 Economic participation

3a Women as a percentage of total labour force

	1980	1990
Sub-Saharan Africa	39.3	37.6
North Africa	11.8	13.7
All of Africa	35.7	34.3

3b Percentage of population of all ages in the labour force

	Total			Female		
	1980	1985	1990	1980	1985	1990
Sub-Saharan Africa	43	42	40	34	32	30
North Africa	27	27	28	6	7	8
All of Africa	40	39	38	28	27	26

3c Percentage of females working, by sector

	Agriculture		Industry		Services	
	1980	1987	1980	1987	1980	1987
Sub-Saharan Africa	82	79	4	5	14	15
North Africa	24	19	22	26	54	56
All of Africa	71	67	8	9	21	23

Sources: African Development Indicators; United Nations Development Programme; New York; World Bank; Washington, DC, 1992.

Annexe 4 National machineries

Country	Title of machinery	Nature of machinery
Botswana	Women's Affairs Division	Governmental
Burkina Faso	Secrétariat d'Etat à l'Action Sociale	Non-governmental
Cameroun	a. National Advisory Board for Advancement of Cameroun Women	Mixed
	b. Ministère des Affaires Sociales et de la Condition Féminine	
Central African Republic	Direction de la Promotion Féminine	Governmental
Chad	Ministère des Affaires Sociales et de la Promotion Féminine	Governmental
Côte d'Ivoire	Ministère de la Promotion de la Femme	Governmental
Egypt	The General Department of Women's Affairs	Governmental
Ethiopia	Ministry of Women's Affairs	Governmental
Gabon	a. Secrétariat d'Etat à la Promotion Feminine et aux Droits	Governmental
	b. Union des Femmes du Parti Démocratique Gabonais	Governmental
	c. Association Gabonaise des Femmes d'Affaires	Mixed
	d. Association des Femmes Juristes Gabonaise	Non-governmental
Gambia	The Women's Bureau	Governmental
Ghana	National Council on Women and Development	Governmental
Guinea	Direction Nationale de la Promotion Féminine	Governmental
Guinea-Bissau	Ministerio de Promoção Feminina (UDEMU)	Non-governmental
Kenya	Women's Bureau	Governmental
Lesotho	Department of Youth and Women's Affairs	Governmental
Liberia	Women's Development Association of Liberia	Non-governmental
Malawi	National Commission on Women and Development	Mixed
Madagascar	Direction of the Condition of Women and Children	Governmental

Country	Organization	Type
Mali	Bureau Exécutif National de l'UNFM	Non-governmental
Mauritius	Ministry of Women's Rights, Child Development and Family Welfare	Governmental
Morocco	Direction des Affaires Sociales	Governmental
Mozambique	Organização da Mulher Mocambicana	Non-governmental
Namibia	a. Department of Women's Affairs	Governmental
	b. Sister Namibia Collective	Non-governmental
	c. YWCA of Namibia	Non-governmental
	d. Women's Solidarity	Non-governmental
	e. Namibian National Women's Organization	Non-governmental
Niger	Ministère du Développement Social, de la Population et de la Promotion de la Femme	Governmental
Nigeria	National Commission for Women	Governmental
Senegal	Ministère de la Femme, de l'Enfant et de la Famille	Governmental
Seychelles	Seychelles Women's Council	Governmental
Sierra Leone	Sierra Leone Women's Bureau	Governmental
South Africa	Women's Bureau of South Africa	Non-governmental
Sudan	General Directorate for Women	Governmental
United Republic of Tanzania	Women and Children Department	Governmental
Togo	Direction de la Promotion Féminine	Governmental
Uganda	Ministry of Women in Development, Youth and Culture	Governmental
Zaire	Ministère de la Condition Féminine et de la Famille	Governmental
Zambia	Women's Affairs Committee	Governmental
Zimbabwe	Department of Women's Affairs	Governmental

Source: Directory of National Machinery for the Advancement of Women, DAWN, Vienna, Austria, 1993.

Annexe 5 Political and legal data

Country	Date of independence	Date of women's vote	Parliamentary seats occupied by women 1991 (%)	CEDAW[1] Signed	Ratified
Algeria	1962	1962	10.0		1986
Angola	1975	1975	9.5		1992
Benin	1960	1956	6.3	1981	
Botswana	1966	1965	5.0		
Burkina Faso	1960	1965	5.6		1987
Burundi	1962	1961	9.9	1980	
Cameroun	1960	1946	12.2	1983	
Cape Verde	1975	1975	7.6		1980
Central African Republic	1960	1986	4.0		1991
Chad	1960		1.0		
Comoros	1975	1956			
Congo	1960	1963		1980	1982
Côte d'Ivoire	1960	1956	4.6	1980	
Djibouti	1977	1946	0.0		
Egypt	1952	1956	2.2	1980	1981
Equatorial Guinea	1968	1963			1984
Ethiopia		1958		1980	1981
Gabon	1960	1956	5.8	1980	1983
Gambia	1965	1960	7.8	1980	
Ghana	1956		7.5	1980	1986
Guinea	1958			1980	1982
Guinea-Bissau	1974	1977	12.7	1980	1985
Kenya	1963	1963	3.0		1984
Lesotho	1966		1.5	1980	
Liberia		1946	6.1		1984
Libyan Arab Jamahiriya	1969	1969			1989
Madagascar	1960	1959		1980	1989
Malawi	1964	1964	11.6		1987
Mali	1960	1956	2.3	1985	1985
Mauritania			0.0		
Mauritius	1968	1956	3.0		1984
Morocco	1956	1963	0.7		1993
Mozambique	1975	1975	15.7		
Namibia	1990	1989	6.9		1992

Annexe 5 (continued)

Country	Date of independence	Date of women's vote	Parliamentary seats occupied by women 1991 (%)	CEDAW[1] Signed	Ratified
Niger	1960	1948	6.0		
Nigeria	1960		2.2	1984	1985
Rwanda	1962	1961	17.1	1980	1981
São Tomé and Príncipe	1975	1975	10.9		
Senegal	1960	1945	11.7	1980	1985
Seychelles	1976	1948	45.8		1992
Sierra Leone	1961	1951		1988	1988
Somalia	1960	1956		1956	
South Africa		1994[2]	2.8	1993	
Sudan	1956	1953	4.6		
Swaziland	1968	1968			
Togo	1960	1956	6.3		1983
Tunisia	1956	1956	4.3	1980	1985
Uganda	1962	1962	12.6	1980	1985
United Republic of Tanzania	1961	1959	11.2	1980	1985
Western Sahara	1976				
Zaire	1960	1967		1980	1986
Zambia	1964	1962	6.7	1980	1985
Zimbabwe	1980	1957[3]	12.0		1991

Notes: 1. Convention on the Elimination of Discrimination against Women.
2. 1994 for all women.
3. 1957 only British women voted.

Sources: *Women and Political Power*, Interparliamentary Union survey carried out among the 150 national parliaments existing as of 1993; *Modern Africa*, Basil Davidson, Longman, 1989; *Africa South of the Sahara 1992*, Europa Publications, 1991.

Annexe 6 Tertiary-level science and engineering enrolment among women, 1987–88

Country	%
Algeria	16
Benin	10
Burundi	13
Burkina Faso	10
Comoros	10
Congo	8
Ethiopia	11
Equatorial Guinea	8
Ghana	9
Guinea	10
Guinea-Bissau	8
Kenya	14
Lesotho	20
Liberia	10
Madagascar	30
Malawi	16
Mali	9
Mauritania	15
Mauritius	24
Mozambique	17
Niger	6
Rwanda	10
Senegal	11
Somalia	10
Sudan	27
Tanzania	8
Togo	3
Tunisia	24
Uganda	11
Zambia	5
Sub-Saharan Africa	12

Source: *Human Development Report 1993*, UNDP, New York.

Annexe 7 Households headed by women

Country	Year	% (all ages)
Algeria	1987	11.0
Benin	1979	21.0
Botswana	1988	45.9
Burkina Faso	1985	9.7
Burundi	1990	24.7
Cameroun	1987	18.5
Central African Republic	1988	18.7
Comoros	1980	16.3
Congo	1984	21.1
Côte d'Ivoire	1988	15.6
Djibouti	1991	18.4
Egypt	1988	12.0
Ethiopia	1984	15.5
Ghana	1988	32.2
Guinea	1983	12.7
Kenya	1989	22.0
Liberia	1986	19.1
Madagascar	1975	15.5
Malawi	1970/72	28.8
Mali	1987	14.0
Mauritius	1983	18.5
Morocco	1987	17.3
Niger	1988	9.7
Réunion	1982	24.6
Rwanda	1978	25.2
Sierra Leone	1988/89	10.8
Sudan	1990	13.3
Swaziland	1986	40.3
Togo	1988	26.4
Tunisia	1988	11.3
Uganda	1989	20.6
United Republic of Tanzania	1991/92	18.6
Zaire	1984	16.1
Zambia	1992	16.2
Zimbabwe	1989	32.6

Sources: *Demographic Yearbook* 1987, UN, New York; *Women of the World*, Washington, DC; UN Statistical Office, NY.

II. Economic Commission for Africa and the ATRCW

Annexe 8 Staffing at the ECA

8a Staff in regular posts: professional and higher categories

Grade	1973			1980			1992		
	Total	Men	Women	Total	Men	Women	Total	Men	Women
ASG/USG	1	1	0	1	1	0	1	1	0
D2	1	1	0	1	1	0	0	0	0
D1	10	10	0	12	12	0	15	14	1
P5	18	18	0	25	24	1	35	34	1
P4	37	36	1	41	41	0	50	40	10
P3	46	42	4	57	51	6	64	50	14
P2/1	30	24	6	32	29	3	27	16	11
Total	143	132	11	169	159	10	192	155	37

8b Staff in extra-budgetary posts: professional and higher categories

Grade	1980			1992		
	Total	Men	Women[1]	Total	Men	Women
L7	2	2	0	0		
L6	10	10	0	14	7	7
L5	26	26	0	25	24	1
L4	29	26	3	14	13	1
L3	21	15	6	8	8	0
L2	3	2	1	11	7	4
L1	2	1	1			
Total	93	82	11	72	59	13

Note: 1. Of whom 8 were ATRCW staff.

Annexe 9 Finance

9a Extra-budgetary financing for the women's programme and the ATRCW,
1973–78: summary of grants for ECA women's programme and ATRCW

Donors	Grant I	Grant II	Grant III	Total
USAID	92,300	165,000	125,000	382,300
Federal Republic of Germany	104,524	15,600	150,822	270,946
Belgium	75,581	56,652	171,000	303,233
IPPF	19,168			19,168
Finnish UN Association	17,668			17,668
UNICEF	400,000			400,000
ZONTA International	87,395			87,395
SIDA	256,428	1,154,639		1,411,067
FAO/UNFPA	98,700[1]	454,041	222,000	774,741
ITDG	37,427			37,427
Ford Foundation	60,000			60,000
Netherlands	45,400[2]	116,850		162,250
OTC, UN	28,000			28,000
Rockefeller Foundation	21,318			21,318
VFDW (UNIFEM)	337,730[3]			337,730
Total	1,681,639	1,962,782	668,882	4,313,243

Notes: 1. Estimate: handled by FAO, Rome. 2. ECA training grant. This is an estimate 3. Does not include support for 2 senior staff.
Source: *Review Mission/ATRCW*, 7–24 March, 1978.

9b Financing for the ATRCW, 1987–92

	Grant I	Grant II	Total
Extra-budgetary donors			
SIDA	891,686	192,279	1,083,965
UNTFAD	199,579		199,579
Italy	548,698		548,698
Netherlands	120,000		120,000
Ford Foundation	275,063	10,000	285,063
UNDP	2,645,100	80,058	2,725,158
UNIFEM	80,000[1]	18,000	98,000
IDRC	10,500[1]		10,500
Total	4,770,626	300,338	5,070,964
UN regular budget (biennial)			
1988–89			396,300
1990–91			568,500
1992–93			500,400
Total			1,465,200

Note: 1. Estimates.
Source: ECA.

Annexe 10 Resolutions of the ECA Conference of Ministers and an ECA Women's Conference

10a Resolution Endorsing the Establishment of the ATCRW

269 (XII) Integration of African Women in National Development

The Conference of Ministers:

Recalling General Assembly resolutions 3010 (XXVII) of 18 December 1972 and 3342 (XXIX) of 17 December 1974, the recommendations[1] of the Regional Conference on Education, Vocational Training and Work Opportunities for Girls and Women in African countries held at Rabat in May 1971 and those[2] of the Regional Seminar for Africa on the Integration of Women in Development, with Special Reference to Population Factors held at Addis Ababa in June 1974

1. *Endorses* General Assembly resolution 3275 (XXIX) of 10 December 1974 on International Women's Year;

2. *Invites* member States to observe the Year by intensifying their efforts to achieve the full integration of women in the total development effort of African countries;

3. *Urges* the Government of member States to pay special attention, in their national development plans, to the potential of women as essential human resources for the development effort by providing them, especially in rural areas, with appropriate education and training with emphasis on labour-saving technologies and income-generating activities; by appointing women to positions at the policy-making level; by increasing the number of women in the wage-employment sector; and by encouraging the participation of women in all sectors of national life;

4. *Invites* member States which have not already done so to establish national commissions or women's bureaus, or similar Government machinery, to assure the integration of women in national development, as recommended by the Regional Conference on Education, Vocational Training and Work Opportunities for Girls and Women in Africa;

5. *Endorses* the commission's plan for the establishment of an African Training and Research Centre for Women to be inaugurated during International Women's Year as one of the Commission's major activities for the Year;

6. *Recommends* that the Governments of member States should extend their full cooperation and support to the work of the Centre;

7. *Urges* the Executive Secretary to show his concern for the progress and advancement of women by making a special effort to increase significantly the number of women among the professional staff of the Commission's secretariat.

ECA Conference of Ministers
183rd meeting
28 February 1975

Notes

1. See document DOK 565 A/a+b III-S 5/71 (ex.) Vol. I published by the German Foundation for Developing Countries.
2. See ST/ESA/SER.B/6 and Add.1.

10b Resolution on the Structure and Terms of Reference
of the ARCC

365 (XIV). Structure and term of reference of the Africa Regional Co-ordinating Committee for the Integration of Women in Development

The Conference of Ministers,

Bearing in mind the recommendations of the Nouakchott Regional Conference on the Implementation of the National, Regional and World Plan of Action for the Integration of Women in Development,

Having considered the report of the Africa Regional Co-ordinating Committee for the Integration of Women in Development,

Aware of the need to integrate the Africa Regional Co-ordinating Committee within the system of the deliberative Organs of the Commission:

1. *Takes note* of the report and recommendations of the Africa Regional Co-ordinating Committee on the desirability of amending the constitution and terms of reference of the Africa Regional Co-ordinating Committee;

2. *Decides* to amend the constitution and terms of reference of the Africa Regional Co-ordinating Committee;

(A) By replacing the provisions relating to the composition of the Africa Regional Co-ordinating Committee and its officers with the following:

I. The Africa Regional Co-ordinating Committee shall be constituted as follows:

(a) Three members designated by each sub-regional committee (with the right to vote);

(b) The Executive Secretary of ECA (without the right to vote), and the Administrative Secretary-General of the Organization of Africa Unity (without the right to vote);

(c) (i) The Pan-African Women's Organization;
(ii) United Nations agencies;
(iii) The representatives of donor Agencies

(the above being invited as observers if a particular subject under consideration is of interest to them.)

II. The Africa Regional Co-ordinating shall elect a bureau composed of:
— A Chairman,
— A first and second Vice-Chairman, and
— Two Rapporteurs.

III. The terms of office of the bureau will be two years. The Africa Regional Co-ordinating Committee will meet once a year when convened by the Executive Secretary after consultation with the bureau.

(B) The African Training and Research Centre for Women will act as secretariat of the Regional Co-ordinating Committee.

(C) The rules of procedure of the Committee shall be the same as those of the Economic Commission for Africa.

(D) By replacing the terms of reference of the Regional Co-ordinating Committee with the following:

1. To harmonize and co-ordinate the sub-regional programmes approved within the Multinational Programming and Operational Centres;

2. To evaluate and implement work programmes, bearing in mind the availability of resources and to oversee the implementation of the work programme;

3. To organize the exchange of information and experience;

4. To participate in the activities and meetings of the United Nations and other relevant organizations;

5. To mobilize resources for the implementation of programmes agreed at the regional and sub-regional levels;

6. To review and evaluate activities carried out in the region in the framework of programmes for the advancement of women;

7. To convene every three years, the Africa Regional Conference on Women and Development;

8. To report to the deliberative organs of the Economic Commission for Africa on the activities and programmes carried out in the sub-regions (Committee of Officials and Council of Ministers of the Multinational Programming and Operational Centres).

207 meeting
27 March 1979

Annexe 11 ECA Programme of Work for the ATRCW, 1976–77

Project aim

The long-range objective is to promote the full use of the combined human resources, male and female, for development within the countries of the Region, by
enabling women to play a full role within the new international economic order,
especially within integrated rural development

Specific aims of the Centre are:

— To assist member States in establishing national and regional machineries for
the integration of women in development
— To assist member States in developing skills and increasing job opportunities
for girls and women
— To assist member States in mobilizing the services of skilled individual women
to assist other women in their own countries, and in other member countries of
ECA as requested
— To work within a global UN network of co-operation on women and
development

Work content

(a) Assistance to countries and territories (1976–77)

1. Advisory services to assist in the formulation and evolution of projects and
programmes (FAO, UNICEF, CSDHA, ILO)
2. Team visits to conduct 3-day seminars and to advise on the establishment or
strengthening of national machineries
3. Advisory services to newly established commissions and bureaus on research,
planning and implementation of projects on request
4. Advisory services in integration of women in national development plans and
country programmes (with CSDHA, UN and regional agencies)
5. Advisory services for curriculum development, project planning, production of
handbooks for trainers and trainees
6. Pilot projects on village technologies for farm and home, small business, rural
day care
7. Internships at the Centre for selected trainers and trainees
8. Organization and operation of the African Women's Volunteer Task Force between countries

(b) Studies

National bibliographies and research on indicators of women's integration in de-
velopment programmes (in cooperation with UNRISD, CSDHA)
Study of the legal position of women in Africa (in cooperation with CSDHA)
Study of the needs, suitability, acceptability and adaptation of village technologies
(in cooperation with UNICEF, FAO, ITDG, ECA Science and Technology
Section and Joint ECA/UNIDO Industry Division)
Study on rural women as food producers: the impact of modernization and develop-
ment programmes (in cooperation with FAO, and UNFPA)
Updating country reports on opportunities for women in development
Study on women's participation in cooperatives and loan associations and relation-
ship to family size, in cooperation with FAO, UNFPA, ILO, and ECA Population
Division)

Study of demand for and availability of Task Force Volunteers (in cooperation with UNICEF and ZONTA International)

(c) Collection and dissemination of information

'African Women' Newsletter (issued three times a year)

Manuals for rural trainers, including child health and family size, home management, social planning and research, village technologies for farm and home

(d) Conferences, meetings, seminars and expert working groups

Itinerant national training workshops for trainers and planners in programmes to improve the quality of rural life (in cooperation with FAO, UNICEF, UNFPA, UNDP, bilateral donors and non-governmental agencies; ECA Public Administration, Management and Manpower Division and Population Division)

National training workshops and study tours on specific needs, i.e., food storage and preservation, small business, organization of cooperatives, communication and programme planning , marketing, family life and health and child spacing, and other relevant subjects, on request (in cooperation with FAO, UNICEF, ILO, and ECA Divisions concerned)

Sub-regional seminars, training courses or workshops on specific needs of women who are members of African liberation movements (in cooperation with OAU, UN agencies and bilateral donors)

Sub-regional workshop on research needs and techniques in relation to women and development (in cooperation with NGOs, African women's research group and UN agencies)

Regional Conference on Plans of Action for the Integration of Women in Development, followed by regional inter-agency meeting and donors meeting (in cooperation with OAU, CSDHA, Bilateral and UN agencies and NGOs)

Regional seminar for heads of national commissions on women and development to set up an inter-governmental standing committee to exchange experiences in relation to these agencies (in cooperation with UN agencies)

Sub-regional workshops on women's participation in cooperatives and crafts (ICA, FAO, ILO)

Inter-agency workshop on village technology (in cooperation with FAO, UNICEF, UNDP, ILO, NGOs ECA Science and Technology Section and joint ECA/ UNIDO Industry Division)

Related programmes

Collaboration with national commissions on women and development and other national groups as appropriate, OAU, UN and specialized and operating agencies, voluntary organizations, donor agencies, governments, ECA divisions concerned, etc.

Annexe 12 ECA Programme of Work for the Integration of Women in Development, 1990–91

(Pursuant to resolution 40/105 of the General Assembly, the approved 1990–1991 Programme of Work for the Integration of Women in Development was shared among the various Divisions of the ECA, with the ATRCW remaining the focal point of the Programme.)

Activities of other ECA Divisions

Final Outputs

1. Report to the follow-up committee of the Gisenyi based MULPOC on the promotion of institutional and support services for strengthening women farmers' capabilities for increased food production and productivity (first quarter 1990)
2. Technical publication. Guidelines, policies, strategies and measures for improving support services geared to the needs of women farmers (fourth quarter 1991)
3. Support to the following projects:

    (a) Training Seminar on the promotion of small-scale food industries
    (b) Training Seminar on statistical survey techniques for women
    (c) Training Seminar on the management of cooperatives

4. Report to the Council of Ministers of the Niamey-based MULPOC on the role of women in the production, processing and marketing of foodstuffs in West Africa (first quarter 1991)
5. Workshop on the development of entrepreneurial capability for cottage and small scale industries with particular emphasis on the role of women in the promotion of industrial development (second quarter 1990 and first quarter 1991)
6. Report to the Conference of African Ministers of Trade on the integration of women in the formal and informal modern trade sector
7. Report to the sixth session of the joint conference of African Planners, Statisticians and Demographers on the relative role of maternal and child health and family planning programmes, proximate determinants and socio-economic correlates influencing fertility (first quarter 1990)
8. Technical publication

    (a) Statistical compendium on contraceptive prevalence and practice in African countries (fourth quarter 1990) and
    (b) guideline on improving the delivery and evaluation of population and family planning programmes in African countries (fourth quarter 1991)

9. Technical publications

    (a) Life-table analysis of birth intervals with illustrative application in selected African countries for government demographers (third quarter 1990)
    (b) Fertility estimates in selected African countries; sources of data methods of estimates, fertility levels pattern and trends for government demographers and planners (fourth quarter 1991) and
    (c) Method of measurement and analysis of childlessness and infertility from survey data in selected African countries (fourth quarter 1991)

10. Technical publication: Guideline on evaluating the interrelationships among infant and child mortality, socio-economic factors and fertility in African countries (fourth quarter 1991)

11. Report to the sixth session of the Joint Conference of African Planners, Statisticians and Demographers on an evaluation of the age–sex data of recent African population censuses (first quarter 1990)

12. Support for the training seminar on strengthening capacities for women in the application of science and technology to reduce their drudgery in rural areas (third quarter 1991)

13. Technical publication on barriers to access of rural women to land, livestock, other productive assets, extension services and credit in selected African countries (fourth quarter 1991)

14. Report to directors of centres participating in the Statistical Training Programme for Africa (STPA) on the participation of women in statistical development in Africa (fourth quarter 1990)

15. Studies of the Tangier-based MULPOC on:

(a) Female illiteracy in North Africa
(b) Economic and social conditions of women in rural areas
(c) Women's economic and social challenges in the 1990s
(d) Training Centres for women to increase the integration of women in development.

Annexe 13 Africa-wide ECA, UN and AAWC (PAWO)
Conferences on Women

1960   Seminar on Participation of Women in Public Life, organized by the United Nations, Addis Ababa, 12–13 December 1960

1964   Urban Problems: The Role of Women in Urban Development, organized by the United Nations Economic Commission for Africa, Lagos, 19 February–3 March 1964

1964   Seminar on the Status of Women in Family Law, organized by the United Nations, Lomé, 18–31 August 1964

1968   Seminar on the Civic and Political Education of Women, organized by the United Nations, Accra, 19 November–2 December 1968

1969   Regional Meeting on the Role of Women in National Development, organized jointly by the United Nations Economic Commission for Africa and the German Foundation for Developing Countries, Addis Ababa, 7–26 March 1969

1971   Regional Conference on Education, Vocational Training and Work Opportunities for Girls and Women in African Countries, organized jointly by the United Nations Economic Commission for Africa and the German Foundation for Developing Countries, Rabat, 20–29 May 1971

1971   Seminar on the Preparation of the African Women for Professional Life, sponsored by the All-African Women's Conference (a pan-African women's organization), Brazzaville, 17–25 July 1971

1971   Seminar on the Participation of Women in Economic Life, with reference to the implementation of Article 10 of the Declaration on the Elimination of Discrimination against Women and of General Assembly resolution 2716 (XXV), organized by the United Nations Division of Human Rights, Libreville, 27 July–9 August 1971

1972   Seminar on the Role of Women in the Liberation of Africa, sponsored by the All-African Women's Conference, Dar es Salaam, 24–31 July 1972

1974   Regional Seminar for Africa on the Integration of Women in Development with Special Reference to Population Factors, organized by the United Nations Centre for Social Development and Humanitarian Affairs in co-operation with the Economic Commission for Africa, Addis Ababa, 3–7 June 1974

1977   Regional Conference on the Implementation of National, Regional and World Plans of Action for the Integration of Women in Development, Nouakchott, 27 September–2 October 1977

1979   Second Regional Conference on the Integration of Women in Development, Lusaka, 3–7 December 1979

1984   Regional Intergovernmental Preparatory Meeting for the World Conference to Review and Appraise the Achievements of the United Nations Decade for Women: Equality Development and Peace/Third Regional Conference on the Integration of Women in Development, Arusha, 8–12 October 1984

1989   Fourth Regional Conference on the Integration of Women in Development and on the Implementation of the Arusha Strategies for the Advancement of Women in Africa, Abuja, 6–10 November 1989

Annexe 14 List of publications/documents by subject area

Agriculture and food

'The Role of Women in Population Dynamics Related to Food and Agriculture and Rural Development in Africa.' ECA/FAO Women's Programme Unit (E, F). Regional, 1974.

'Women in Food Production and Development in Africa'. Regional, 1974.

'Africa's Food Producers: The Impact of Change on Rural Women'. Paper prepared by Women's Programme Unit, for American Geographical Society. Regional, 1974.

'The Role of Women in the Agricultural Sector'. Regional, 1975.

'Transformation et Commercialisation des Produits vivriers en Afrique' (F). Regional, 1981.

'The Role of Women in the Solution of the Food Crisis in Africa' (E). Regional, 1984.

'The Flow of Resources to Women in Africa in the Context of the Food and Debt Crisis' (E). Regional, 1989.

ECA/ATRCW/ARCC

Report of the Regional Conference on Education, Vocational Training and Work Opportunities for Girls and Women in African Countries, Rabat. Regional, 1971.

Report of the Regional Conference on the Implementation of National, Regional and World Plans of Action for the Integration of Women in Development. Nouakchott, 27 September–2 October, 1977. Regional, 1977.

Report of the Regional Intergovernmental Preparatory Meeting for the World Conference to Review and Appraise the Achievements of the United Nations Decade for Women: Equality Development and Peace/Third Regional Conference on the Integration of Women and Development. Arusha, 8–12 October 1984. Regional, 1984.

Report of the Fourth Regional Conference on the Integration of Women in Development and on the Implementation of the Arusha Strategies for the Advancement of Women in Africa. Abuja, 6–10 November 1989. Regional, 1989.

Recommendations of Regional meetings for Africa on the Role of Women in Development. 17 pp. Regional, 1977.

ATRCW Research Publications. 1983 25 pp.

'A Path to Progress for African Women'. 1975.

The Origin and Growth of the African Training and Research Center for Women of the Economic Commission for Africa. 20 pp. plus annexes. Regional, 1977.

'African Women' (Tri-annual newsletter). Regional, 1973–77.

'ATRCW' (Semi-annual Newsletter). Regional, 1978–93.

Plan of Action for the Integration of Women and Development in Africa. 14 pp. Regional, 1974.

'Report of the Review Mission – African Training and Research Centre for Women'. 77 pp. plus annexes. Regional, 1978.

Reports (Annual) of the meetings of the Africa Regional Coordinating Committee for the Integration of Women in Development (ARCC). Regional, 1979, 1981–93.

Progress Reports (Annual) on the Activities of the African Training and Research Centre for Women (ATRCW). Regional, 1979–93.

'Issues and Problems Involved in the Question of the Integration of Women in Development'. 43 pp. Regional, 1977.

The Abuja Declaration on Participatory Development: The Role of Women in Africa in the 1990s (E). Regional, 1989.

Bibliographies and country studies

Country Reports (information on population, migration, education, training, employment and status of women in forty countries) each 15 pp. average. Regional, 1971–74.

'A Preliminary Survey of Avenues for and Constraints on Women's Involvement in the Development Process in Kenya.' Pala-Okeyo, Achola. 26 pp. Kenya, 1975.

Women and Development in Africa: An Annotated Bibliography (E). Regional, 1977.

Women and Development in Tanzania (E). Tanzania, 1980.

Women and Development in Ethiopia (E). Ethiopia, 1981.

La Femme camerounaise et le developpment (F). Cameroun, 1981.

Women and Development in Nigeria (E). Nigeria, 1982.

Women and Development in Mali (E). Mali, 1982.

Women and Development in Zambia (E). Zambia, 1983.

Women and Development in Zimbabwe (E). Zimbabwe, 1984.

African Women in Development. Regional, 1990.

African Women in Development. Regional, 1991.

Culture

Teaching Trainers of Day Care Centre Personnel. Regional, 1977.

'The Role of Women in Alternative Patterns of Development and Life-Styles in the Africa Region' (E, F). Regional, 1978.

Female Circumcision in Africa (E, F). Regional, 1982.

African Women and Cultural Identity (E). Regional, 1984.

The Incidence of Sexual Slavery in Africa: Sexual Abuse of Women in Cameroon (E). Cameroun, 1988.

Development, general and technical co-operation

The Africa Women's Development Task Force: Some case histories, 20 pp. Regional, 1983.

African Women's Development Task Force, 15 pp. Regional, 1976.

The African Women's Task Force: an Innovative Programme of Technical Co-operation Among Developing Countries. Regional, 1983.

Guide for the Preparation and Implementation of Project Proposals on Women and Development, 21 pp. (F). Regional, 1983.

Women in Africa to the Year 2000 (E). Regional, 1984.

Women of Africa: Today and Tomorrow, 81 pp. Regional, 1975.

'Women and National Development in African Countries: Some Profound Contradictions', *African Studies Review,* XVIII, 3. Regional, 1975.

'The Role of Women in African Development', *Economic Bulletin for Africa,* XI, 1, pp. 57–8. Regional, 1975.

'Technical Cooperation among Developing Countries and Human Resources Development: the Experience of the African Training and Research Center for Women' (E). Regional, 1978.

African Women in Development. Selected statements by Prof Adebayo Adedeji. Regional, 1989.

Economics and finance

The New International Economic Order: What Roles for Women? (E, F). Regional, 1977.

A Socio-economic Overview: Zimbabwe Women (E). Zimbabwe, 1981.
Situation de la femme dans les mécanismes de crédit et création d'un système de Fonds de garantie pour les femmes: cas du Congo, du Gabon et de la République-Unie du Cameroun. Congo, Gabon, Cameroun, 1982.
'The Impact of the Economic Crisis on the Vulnerable Groups in African Societies: Women' (E). Regional, 1988.
'Changing Socio-Economic Condition of Women in Africa in the Context of the Nairobi Forward-looking Strategies for the Advancement of Women' (E). Regional, 1988.
Guide for the Promotion and Development of African Women Entrepreneurs and their Access to Credit (E). Regiona, 1990.
Increasing the Access of African Women to Credit: An Integrated Approach (E). Regional, 1990.

Education and training

Report of 5 Workshops for Trainers in Home-Economics and Other Family-Oriented Fields. Sub-regional, 1973.
Manuel à l'usage du Personnel de formation et de supervision chargé des programmes visant a améliorer la qualité de la vie en milieu rural, 5 volumes (F). Regional, 1975–76.
Manual on Child Development, Family Life, and Nutrition (E, F). Regional, 1977.
Day Care in Eastern Africa: A Survey of Botswana, Kenya, Seychelles and the United Republic of Tanzania (E). Botswana, Kenya, Tanzania, 1981.
'Out of School Programs for Women in Sierra Leone' (E). Sierra Leone, 1981.
'Technical Publication on: The Situation, Analysis and Strategies for the Promotion of Girls/Women to Scientific and Technical Training and Professions'. Regional, 1990.
Evaluation Series No.1. *Report of Missions to Review and Follow up the Results of Itinerant Training Workshops,* 43 pp. Zambia, Swaziland, Somalia, Lesotho, 1976.
Study Tours in Kenya. 1977.
Rapport, Seminaire sur l'Amélioration des conditions de vie en milieu rural.
Central African Empire. 37 pp. annexes. 1976.
Congo People's Republic. 55 pp. annexes. 1975.
Gabon. 48 pp. annexes. 1975.
Rwanda. 87 pp. 1976.
Benin. 58 pp. annexes. 1976.
Cameroun. 1977.
Report of a Workshop for Planners and Trainers in Programmes to Improve the Quality of Rural Life.
Ghana. 118 pp. 1975.
Liberia. 1977.
Portuguese-speaking Africa. 1981.
Gambia. 1977.
Report of a Workshop for Trainers of Rural Women Leaders. Khartoum, 1976.
Report of the ECA Training Workshop on Communication, Planning Techniques and Adult Education. Lusaka, 1977.
Workshop for Personnel in Programmes to Improve the Quality of Rural Life. Sierra Leone, 1977.
Workshop on Food Preservation and Storage. 102 pp. Tanzania, 1976.
Manuel de Petites Industries accessible aux femmes en particulier les industries agroalimentaires (F). Zaire, 1990.

Employment and industry

Report on ILO/ECA/YWCA/SIDA Workshop on Participation of Women in Selected Projects in Handicrafts and Small Industries. Kitwe, Zambia. Eastern Africa, 1974.

'Towards Full Employment of Women in Ethiopia', UNECA for ILO Mission to Ethiopia, 1974, 30 pp. (E). Ethiopia, 1974.

'Employment of Women in the Sudan', UNECA for ILO Comprehensive Employment Mission, 30 pp. (E) annex. Sudan, 1975.

'African Women Workers: Analysis of the Position and Factors Affecting Women in Employment' (E). Regional, 1976.

Women and the Fishing Industry in Liberia (E). Liberia, 1979.

Women Workers in Ghana, Kenya, Zambia: A Comparative Analysis of Women's Employment in the Modern Wage Sector (E). Ghana, Kenya, Zambia, 1979.

Women Textile Workers in Ethiopia (E). Ethiopia, 1979.

Potters: A Study of Two Villages in Ethiopia (E). Ethiopia, 1980.

L'effet de la modernisation sur le travail des femmes exércant une activité indépendante au Mali, en Côte d'Ivoire et au Sénégal (F). Mali, Côte d'Ivoire, Senegal, 1981.

Women and Agriculture in Nigeria (E). Nigeria, 1982.

Women and the Industrial Development Decade in Africa (E). Regional, 1984.

'Training and Employment Opportunities for Out-of-School Girls in Ethiopia' (E). Ethiopia, 1981.

Marketing in Ghana: an analysis of Operational and Environmental Conditions (E). Ghana, 1984.

Women in the Artisanal Fishing Industry in Senegal and Ghana (E). Senegal, Ghana, 1984.

'Training and Employment Opportunities for Out-of-School Girls in Dar Es Salaam' (E). Tanzania, 1984.

Survey in Zambia, Cameroun and Ghana on Women as Small-Scale Entrepreneurs (E). Zambia, Cameroun, Ghana, 1987.

'Study on the Status of Women Entrepreneurs in the Informal Sector and on Measures for Strengthening Their Participation' (E). Regional, 1988.

Improving the Role of African Women in the Informal Sector: Employment-Development: African Women and the Informal Sector (E). Regional, 1989.

'Report of the the Ad Hoc Expert Meeting to Consider Modalities for Establishing a Regional Association of Women Entrepreneurs', Nairobi, 22–25 October 1991, 12 pp. plus annexes. Regional, 1991.

Information and communications

'Broadcasting for the Integration of Women in Development: the ATRCW Perspective'. 17 pp. Regional, 1977.

Directory of African Women's Organizations. 119 pp. Regional, 1978.

Information Kit for Women in Africa. 192 pp. 1981.

Roster of African Women Experts. 87 pp. Regional, 1991.

Women and the Mass Media in Africa: Case Studies of Egypt, the Niger and Sierra Leone (E, F). Egypt.

'Summary of On-going and Planned Projects of United Nations Agencies and Regional Institutions for the Integration of Women in Development in the Africa Region' (E, F). Niger, 1979; Sierra Leone, 1981.

'Access of Women to Decision Making in the Media in Africa'. Regional, 1985.

'Média et femmes rurales en Afrique'. Dawit, Turuworq, *Assignment Children*, 38, pp. 64–70. Regional, 1977.

National machineries

National Commissions on Women and Development and Women's Bureaux. 18 pp. annexes. Regional, 1975.

National Machinery for the Integration of Women in Development in African Countries. Regional, 1977.

Directory of National, Sub-regional and Regional Machineries for the Integration of Women in Development. Regional, 1983.

National Machineries for the Integration of Women in Development (E). Ghana, Senegal, Cameroun, Kenya, Tanzania, 1982.

Report of the Regional Seminars on National Machineries for the Integration of Women in Development. Regional, 1983.

Law

Law and the Status of Women in Nigeria (E). Nigeria, 1979.

Law and the Status of Women in Ethiopia (E). Ethiopia, 1980.

Mozambique: Women, the Law and Agrarian Reform (E, P). Mozambique, 1980.

Le droit et la condition de la femme au Maroc (F). Morocco, 1981.

Law and the Status of Women in Tanzania (E). Tanzania, 1984.

Law and the Status of Women in Ghana (E). Ghana, 1984.

Implementation in Africa of the Convention on the Elimination of All Forms of Discrimination against Women (E, F). Regional, 1987.

Comparative Study of National Laws on the Rights and Status of Women in Africa (E). Regional, 1990.

Violence Against Women in Africa. Regional, 1991.

Science and technology

'Taches excessives des femmes et accès aux techniques' (F). *Assignment Children* (UNICEF), 36, pp. 38–52. Regional, 1976.

'The Role of Women in the Utilization of Science and Technology for Development' (E). Regional, 1978.

'The Role of African Women in the Utilization of Science and Technology' (E). Regional, 1978.

'Indigenous Technology in Sierra Leone' (E). Sierra Leone, 1978.

Appropriate Technology for African Women (E, F). Regional, 1978.

Improving Village Water Supplies in Ethiopia: A Case Study of Socio-economic Implications (E). Ethiopia, 1978.

'The Role of Women in Paddy Production' (E). Sierra Leone, 1980.

Workshop for Trainers and Planners on Appropriate Technology for the Rural Family. Sierra Leone, 1982.

Traditional Palm Oil Processing: Women's Role and the Application of Appropriate Technology (E). Ivory Coast, Sierra Leone, Cameroun, 1983.

Statistics

'The Data Base for Discussion of the Interrelations between the Integration of Women in Development, Their Situation and Population Factors' (E). Regional, 1974.

'Les indicateurs socio-économique de l'intégration des femmes au développement: le cas du Mali' (F). Mali, 1981.

Strategies and planning

'Programmes and Projects for the Involvement of Women in Rural Development: The Experience of ECA', Daria Tesha. Regional, 1974.

'The Changing Roles of Women in East Africa: Implications for Planning Family-oriented Programmes.' 24 pp. 1974.

Intégration des Femmes au processus de planification du développement: les cas du Cameroun et du Niger (F). Cameroun, Niger, 1979.

Women and Development Planning and Policy in Malawi (E). Malawi, 1983.

'Women and Develoment Planning – An Issue Paper'. Regional, 1988.

Guidelines for the Incorporation of Womens' Concerns in National Development Plans. Regional, 1989.

'The Critical Needs of African Women and Appropriate Strategies in the Framework of the Gisenyi and Lusaka MULPOCs' (E). Regional, 1981.

Forward-looking Strategies for the Advancement of Women in Africa Beyond the End of the United Nations Decade for Women (Arusha) (E, F). Regional, 1984.

'How to Increase Resources and Opportunities for African Women for Their Further and More Equitable Participation in Development' (E). Regional, 1989.

Programme and Strategies for 1980–85: Equality Development and Peace. 25 pp. Regional, 1980.

Advancement of African Women – Forging a Strategy for the 1990s. 94 pp. 1991.

Note: (E) written in English
    (F) written in French
    (P) written in Portuguese

Annexe 15 Women's Programme and ATRCW staff

Name	Nationality
Margaret Snyder	USA
Daria Tesha	Tanzania
Nelly Okello	Kenya
Danielle Bazin	Haiti
Agnes Diarra	Niger
Nancy Hafkin	USA
Jean Ritchie	Great Britain
Suzanne Prosper	Mauritius
Mary Tadesse	Ethiopia
Sori Bangura	Sierra Leone
Marilyn Carr	Great Britain
Tsehainesh Haregot	Ethiopia
Chris Kateregga	Uganda
Jasleen Dhamija	India
Nawal El Sadawi	Egypt
Joscelyn Mackomick	France
Agnes Aidoo	Ghana
Victoria Mwamamnja*	Tanzania
Farida Gamati*	Tunisia
Denise Gazania*	Congo
Marianne Aribot*	Mali
Claire Siraninzi*	Burundi
Fatmata El-Ghundi*	Egypt
Magdalena Kenig	Poland
Dorothy Iwuji	Nigeria
Mebo Mwaniki	Tanzania
Jennifer Kargbo	Sierra Leone
Françoise Wege	Burundi
Constantine Ivanov	Russia
Petrina Amono	Ghana
Fama Bangura	Sierra Leone
Thomas Paquete	Guinea-Bissau
Eugenia Bruce	Togo
Rose Dakowa	Sierra Leone
Margaret Hammer	Germany
Victor Kisob	Cameroun
Mesgena Imelda	Ethiopia

Research assistants	Senior secretaries
Mekdes Gebre-Medhin	Renate Eder
Tadesse Alemu	Dinkenesh Yohannes
Ferehewot Yeabwork	Amsale Retta
Turuwork Dawit	Awetash Makonnen
Teckie Gebre-Medhin	Haddis Negash
Isaac Gebre-Egziabeher	Azeb Kenfe
Elizabeth Woldmariam	Claudine Sako
Irene Nkembe	

*MULPOC Co-ordinators

Annexe 16 ARCC presidents, 1979–92

Mme Delphine Tsanga	Cameroun
Mme Mariama Sow	Guinea
Mme Marguerite-Marie Ntandikiye	Burundi
Ms Selina Taylor	Ghana
Dr Charlotte Abaka	Ghana
Ms S.D. Nyoni	Zimbabwe
Ms Aishatu I. Ismail	Nigeria

Annexe 17 ATRCW organization, 1975

Office of the Chief Technical Co-ordinator

Planning, evaluation, information	Administration	National machineries

Programme of work
Liaison with donor
  agencies
Evaluation
Public relations and
  information
	Office management
	Budgeting
	Travel
	Reports
		Liaison with governments
		Seminars and consultancies
		  on national machineries
		Research planning and
		  follow-up

Unit: Rural Development, Training and Education	Unit: African Women's Development Task Force	Unit: Handicrafts and other Small-Scale Industries

Itinerant training
  workshops
Study tours
Teaching/training
  materials
Rural day-care: pilot
  demonstration
  centres
Formal and non-formal
  education
Fellowships/internships
	Liaison with national
	  organizations
	Identification of
	  volunteers
	Identification of
	  placements
	Training/evaluation
	  of projects
		Workshops/seminars on
		  SSI and village
		  technologies
		Project inventories/research
		Pilot projects/
		  demonstration centres
		Teaching/training materials
		Study tours

Source: *Origin and Growth of the ATRCW*, ECA, 1977

Annexe 18 ATRCW Organization, 1986

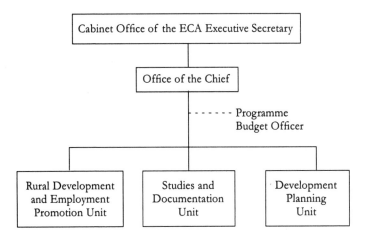

Annexe 19 The ECA's country-level activities concerning women, 1971–77

	UN status of country	ATRCW staff visit to country — Meeting	ATRCW staff visit to country — Activity plan	Itinerant training workshop	Follow-up training workshop or study tour	National seminar	Machineries follow-up	National ATRCW involved services	Research supported	Project planning or evaluation mission	Task Force Given vol	Task Force Received vol
Algeria	Oil producer	1976										
Angola	Not yet classified											
Benin	LDC MSA $-100		1974	1976		1975						
Botswana	LDC $100–200		1971 1972 1977	1973						1977		
Burundi	LDC MSA $-100		1976 •			1977						
Cape Verde	MSA $200–300											
Central African Emp	LDC MSA											
Chad	£100–200 LDC MSA $-100		1977	1976	1977							
Comoros	Not yet classified			2/RQ						1976		
Congo	$300–400	1971	1974 1977	1975								

Country	Classification						
Côte d'Ivoire	MSA	1974					
	$300–400						
Djibouti	Not yet classified						
Egypt	MSA	1972					
	$200–300	1974			1976		
Equatorial Guinea							
Ethiopia	$200–300				1973	1972	
	LDC	1974	1973			1976	
	MSA	1975			1976		
	$–100	1976					
Gabon	Oil producer	1971		1974			
				1975			
Gambia	LDC	1974	1974–75	1975		1976–77	
		1976					
	MSA	1977					
	$100–200						
Ghana	MSA	1976	1975				
			1976				
	$200–300						
Guinea	LDC	1977			1976	1976	
	MSA						
	$–100						
Guinea-Bisseau	MSA	1977					
	$200–300						
Kenya	MSA	1972, 74	1975–77	1974	1977	1976	
		1975, 76					
	$100–200	1977					
Lesotho	LDC	1971	1973	1974		1977	
	MSA	1972					
	$–100	1974					
		1977					
		1976					
Liberia	$200–300	1975	1975				1976
		1976	1976				

Annexe 19 (continued)

Country	UN status of country	ATRCW staff visit to country — Meeting	ATRCW staff visit to country — Activity plan	Itinerant training workshop	Follow-up training workshop or study tour	National seminar	Machineries follow-up services	National ATRCW involved	Research supported	Project planning or evaluation mission	Task Force Given vol	Task Force Received vol
Libya	Oil producer											
Madagascar	MSA					1976		1976				
	$100–200											
Malawi	LDC											
	$–100											
Mali	LDC		1974	RQ								
	MSA		1976			1977						
	$100–200											
Mauritania	MSA											
	$100–200											
Mauritius	$200–300	1977	1976	1977		1977			1978	1977		1977
Morocco	$200–300	1977	1976			RQ						
Mozambique	MSA	1971				1976		1976				
	$200–300											
Niger	LDC											
	MSA											
	$–100											
Nigeria	Oil producer		1974	1975		1976						
Rwanda	LDC		1974	1976	ST77				1977			
	MSA											
	$–100											
São Tomé and Príncipe	$300–400											
Senegal	MSA			1976								

Country	Classification									
Seychelles	$200–300 / Not yet classified	1974	1976	1977						
Sierra Leone	MSA	1976		1975, 1976, 1973		1976	1977	1976, 1974		
	$100–200									
Somalia	LDC / MSA / $–100	1974, 1976/77, 1972							1975	
Sudan	LDC / MSA / $100–200	1976	1976	1976		1974	1974	1975, 1977	1977	
Swaziland	$200–300			1973						RQ
Togo	$100–200	1971					1975	1975		
Tunisia	$300–400	1976				1976	1976	1977		
Uganda	LDC / MSA / $100–200	1971/77	1971		ST77	1976	RQ	1976, 1976		
United Rep. of Cameroun	MSA / $100–200	1976		1977	ST77					
United Rep. of Tanzania	LDC / MSA / $–100	1972, 1975, 1976	1971, 1975	1974, 1975	1975	1975	1975	1976, 1977		
Upper Volta	LDC / MSA / $–100		1975, 1976	1975, 1976		1975	1975	1976		1977
Zaire	$–100		1973	1973	1976					
Zambia	$300–400		1974, 1971, 1974			1975	1975	1975, 1976		

Source: Origins of Growth of the ATRCW of the ECA, ECA, 1977

**Annexe 20 Selected ATRCW activities related to women
entrepreneurs, 1980–92**

Workshop on Handicrafts and Small-Scale Industries Development for Women in
Francophone Countries. Addis Ababa, 27–30 November 1978. ATRCW/SDD/
ITW/80/02. 1980.

Workshop on the Participation of Women in Development through Co-operatives
with Special Emphasis on Handicrafts and Small-Scale Industries. ATRCW/
SDD/ITW/80/01. 1980.

Women and Co-operatives: Egypt, the Libyan Arab Jamahiriya and the Sudan. ECA/
ATRCW/RES/02/80, 1980.

Study Tour/Workshop for Project Managers and Trainers in Employment and
Income-Generating Activities for Women. Swaziland, October 1982.

Traditional Palm Oil Processing: Women's Role and the Application of Technology. ST/ECA/
ATRCW/82/02. 1983.

Training Seminar on Entrepreneurial Skill for French-speaking Women. ATRCW
and the Centre de Gestion Ivorien de Gestion des Entreprises (CIGE), Abijan,
25 February–3 May 1985.

Seminar on the Role of Women in the Marketing of Foodstuffs. Bangui, 27–31
October 1986.

Seminar on the Role of Cooperatives as a Means of Integrating Women in Development. Cotonou, Benin, December 1986.

Sub-regional Seminar on Measures to Improve Women's Management Skills.
Nairobi, Kenya, 19–22 January 1987.

Sub-regional Management Seminar. Gisenyi, Rwanda, May 1987.

Study Tour to Ghana for Business Women from Eastern and Southern Africa,
Accra. ECA/ATRCW/PWES/87/3, 1987.

Seminar on the Development of Cottage Industry. Kigali, Rwanda, December 1987.

Sub-regional Seminar on Measures to Improve Women's Management Skills. Douala,
Cameroun, November/December 1988.

Study on the Status of Women Entrepreneurs in the Informal Sector, Kenya, Mauritius, Zambia
and Swaziland, ECA/ATRCW/88, 1988.

*The Role of Women in Agro-industries in Four Eastern and Southern African Countries:
Botswana, Lesotho, Tanzania and Zimbabwe.* ECA/ATRCW/88/2, 1988.

Expert Group meeting to Review Documents for Publication on African Women's
Entrepreneurship, Development, and Access to Credit. Addis Ababa, Ethiopia,
2–5 April 1990.

Ad-hoc Expert Meeting on Modalities for the Creation of a Regional Association
of Women Entrepreneurs, Nairobi, Kenya, 8–10 April 1992.

Annexe 21 Abuja Declaration on participatory development: the role of women in the 1990s

In November 1989 African governments adopted the Abuja Declaration on Participatory Development: the Role of Women in the 1990s. Its message is the following:

Areas of substantial progress made by African women

— In education, enrolment of girls has increased at all levels.
— The surge of research has convincingly established the crucial role women play in African economies, especially in agriculture and food production.
— Most governments have established focal points for the advancement of women, often referred to as national machineries.
— Non-governmental organizations have proliferated in the region, especially since 1985, to cater to women's needs.
— Many governments have promulgated or improved national legislation on employment, maternity leave, marriage, inheritance and property, education and constitutional rights. 49% of African states have ratified the Convention on the Elimination of All Forms of Discrimination against Women.

Areas of slow progress

— Less progress has been made in increasing employment; fertility levels and maternal mortality rates remain high. Access to resources such as credit and technology need improvement.
— Greater efforts need to be made to increase enrolment of girls in science-based training programmes and professions.
— Women are still inadequately represented in the political process at national and international levels.
— For mainstreaming and bridging strategies to be effective, concrete actions need to be taken through well-designed implementation strategies supported at the highest levels of government and development assistance.
— Governmental strategies need to recognize and take into account the importance of women as primary natural resource managers.

Facing the 1990s

The socio-economic transformation and recovery of Africa require a major shift in policy towards this vast human capital (women). At the same time African governments are urged to put an end to internal strife, civil wars and abuses of human rights which are depleting the continent of its valuable human resources. Action at national, sub-regional, regional and international levels is spelled out to achieve the following:

Target 2000

— Parity in literacy, primary and secondary education and at least 40% of university enrolment.
— At least 20% of total enrolment at university level in the fields of science and technology.
— At least one out of five of all vacant government professional posts should be filled by a woman.
— Increased opportunities in the formal sector, support to the informal sector, ensuring access to credit, enhancing and facilitating entrepreneurial efforts are advocated.

— Measures to stimulate the economies of Africa should be undertaken while avoiding the adverse effect of restructuring them.

— At least one in eight top policy and decision makers in Africa (cabinet minister, high civil servant, top echelons of the armed forces, police and judiciary and top management in parastatal and private corporations) should be a woman.

— Government should promulgate laws to eradicate cultural practices that dehumanize and disinherit women especially in the areas of birth, education, marriage and widowhood. Religious leaders, traditional rulers, professional bodies and women's organizations should act as pressure groups in this effort.

— All African countries should sign and ratify the Convention on the Elimination of all Forms of Discrimination against Women and ensure its ratification or their accession to it.

— Greater effort should be made to forge links between NGOs and government-sponsored organizations for women.

— All women living in shanties and hamlets in the rural and poor urban areas should be provided with decent and durable shelters.

Progress made by governments and all relevant institutions in the implementation of the above targets is to be reviewed and assessed in 1994.

Annexe 22 Chronology: the evolution of ATRCW

pre–1960   Women's economic, social, political involvement and leadership. Societies largely gender-parallel. Experiences of colonialism and independence struggles.

1960–71   Independence movement sparks women to organize at regional, national levels; women join UN delegations and speak to ECA: regional conferences, the birth of ideas and creation of foundations and staffing for a regional programme based on the new women/development concepts; research on economic activities; African governments give ECA a mandate.

1972–74   Path-breaking years: the ECA 5–Year Programme for Women sets a strategy; initial national training of trainers in rural life; national machineries seminars encourage institutionalizing womens' concerns; group of documents including regional data base put Programme in a pioneering position in the UN; promotion of research; planning and financing the ATRCW.

1975   Setting institutional structures: ATRCW and the Volunteer Task Force; an African governmental mandate, a global mandate and global influence by/on African women and ECA at the Mexico IWY Conference.

1976–79   A mandate realized: the ARCC and its sub-regional committees provide political infrastructure; ARCC influences OAU to set up women's unit in its secretariat; a programme review completed and regional inter-agency committee formed; sub-regional outreach, and emphasis on influencing ECA substantive divisions at Addis headquarters and outreach at MULPOCs.

1980–85   New concerns at Copenhagen; co-operation with other regional commissions, with UNIFEM, INSTRAW and Vienna; new mandates: Lagos, Arusha and Nairobi.

1986–90   Decentralization: opportunities for closer influence on the government planning process. The Abuja Declaration sets first-ever targets in education, science/technology, health, etc.

INDEX

Abuja: conference at, 161, 173, 181–3;
  Declaration on Women, 127, 132,
  174; 'Scale', 173
accountability, 82
Accra, urban markets of, 31
active labour force, definitions of, 56
Adagala, Karetsa, 181, 184, 186
Addis Ababa, 16, 29–30, 79, 114, 126;
  conference at, 4, 37, 40, 55, 94;
  population seminar at, 63, 87;
  regional meeting at, 128; TEPCOW
  meeting at, 128
Adedeji, Adebayo, 114
Adjustment with a Human Face, 7
Adu, A.L., 29
advisers, expatriate, 68
Africa Priority Programme for
  Economic Recovery (APPER), 161,
  169–70
Africa Regional Co-ordinating Com-
  mittee, 3
Africa Regional Standing Committee,
  79
Africa: exports of, 5; indebtedness of,
  5, 28, 84; industrial sector of, 163;
  self-reliance, 122; total debt of, 168
African Federation of Women Entre-
  peneurs, 185
African National Congress (ANC), 131
African Plan of Action, 123
African Regional Co–ordinating
  Committee (ARCC), 37, 86, 116,
  118, 124–27, 130, 134, 144, 147–48,
  151–53,155, 166, 172, 180, 189;
  Yaounde meeting, 150; 169
African Regional Training Institute, 32
African Training and Research Centre
  for Women (ATRCW): African
  Regional Standing Committee of,
  111; budget, 114–15; employment
  policies of, 154; evaluation of, 129;
  First Draft Constitution, 110; its
  donors, 112; networking systems,
  120; nutritional workshop, 146;

Publications and Reference Unit,
  144; Review Mission of (1978), 147;
  studies on law and the status of
  women, 171
African Women's Development Task
  Force, 77, 90, 96
African Women's Volunteer Task Force,
  66
agri-business, 82
agriculture, 15; market-orientated, 28;
  mechanization of, 30; production,
  61; subsistence type, 39
Agroh, Rebecca, 96
Aidoo, Agnes, 97, 145
AIDS, 72; and women, 183
Aighebussi, J, 148
Alemu, Tadesse, 144
All Africa Women's Conference
  (AAWC), 28
anaemia, 162
Anglo-Ashanti war, 21
animal husbandry, 46
'anti-poverty' approach, 12, 15
apartheid, 5, 131–132, 145, 165, 181
Arab Women's Commission, 76
Arungu, Rose, 155
Arusha: conference at, 143, 161,
  163–67, 173; strategies of, 127, 153,
  172
Asantewa, Yaa, 21, 29
Asare, Janet, 64
Asiyo, Phoebe, 75, 77, 144, 182
Associated Countrywomen of the
  World, 29
Association of African Women for
  Research and Development, 132
Awori, Thelma, 99
Ayele, Etagengn, 108

Babangida, Ibrahim B., 172
Babangida, Maryam, 172
Baeta, Barbara, 97
Bamako, conference at, 26, 28
Bangura, Sori Bai, 100, 126